• • • • • **Grit, Guts, and Genius**

Also by John Hillkirk and Gary Jacobson

Xerox: American Samurai

Grit, Guts, and Genius

True Tales of MegaSuccess:

Who Made Them Happen and How They Did It

John Hillkirk and Gary Jacobson

Houghton Mifflin Company

Boston   1990

For information about permission to reproduce selections from this book, write to Permissions, Houghton Mifflin Company, 2 Park Street, Boston, Massachusetts 02108.

Library of Congress Cataloging-in-Publication Data

Hillkirk, John.

Grit, guts, and genius : true tales of megasuccess : who made them happen and how they did it / John Hillkirk and Gary Jacobson.

p.   cm.

ISBN 0-395-56189-2

1. Success in business — United States.   I. Jacobson, Gary. II. Title.

HF5386.H614   1990   90-39809

338.0973 — dc20   CIP

Printed in the United States of America

Book design by Jennie Bush, Designworks, Inc.

BAN 10 9 8 7 6 5 4 3 2 1

Contents

v

Contents

Introduction

There is a revolution brewing in the United States, and it's beginning to permeate every sector of American society. A new legion of superheroes with startling ideas and pathbreaking philosophies has begun to lead the country in a new direction.

Ford chairman Donald Petersen turned his company around and created a blueprint for management in the 1990s; ABC's Brandon Stoddard ("Roseanne," "thirtysomething," "The Wonder Years") put sizzle into network TV; Peter Guber and Jon Peters, the hottest producers in Hollywood, splashed *Rain Man* and *Batman* on the silver screen; and Notre Dame's Lou Holtz, Peter Lynch of the Magellan Fund, and two *Philadelphia Inquirer* reporters showed everyone how to reach the top, year after year.

That's a far cry from the dismal 1980s, when the United States seemed to be wobbling into mediocrity. Back then, American companies took the easy route and thrived on sequels: New Tide, New Coke, *Star Trek IV* . . . or was it *V?*

In this book, you'll discover new champions from widely different backgrounds. Some are highly educated (Petersen's a Mensa member), but others never went to college. Some are rich, others poor. But they are all curious kids at heart. They are constantly spouting out ideas — or asking you what you think. They'll consider an idea from anywhere: like Walt Disney, "Absolut genius" Michel Roux looks for ideas in employees' wastebaskets. But their work, like a Warhol painting or a Hitchcock film, has a unique flair to it that almost anyone would recognize.

Talking to any of these people is exhilarating because they use both sides of their brains. One minute, they're rational and logical. The next, they're laughing, or even crying.

They're also extremely patient people. The rest of society is obsessed with instant gratification. The successful recognize that the mastery of any skill takes time. They are willing to spend weeks, months, or even years in the trenches, seemingly getting nowhere. The successful tend to structure their lives around profound but simple philosophies. Everyone around them knows what they stand for. As Holtz likes to say, "If you preach too many things, you teach nothing."

And, perhaps above and beyond everything else, they don't take their work too seriously.

"We only live for seventy or eighty years and work for twenty-five to thirty years," says producer Guber. "So get your joy out of what you're doing. You can't believe you're making the cure for some disease."

In this book, you'll find twenty-seven chapters that explain why each of these people succeeded. The individual chapters are miniature case studies that underscore their methods, work habits, and philosophies. In addition, the success stories are grouped under eight common themes. These themes highlight the most compelling reason for the success of an individual, a team, or a company.

- *Trust your gut.* It's easy, and safe, to follow in someone else's footsteps. But pioneers prefer the path less traveled. And that is making all the difference. "Roseanne" and *Batman* succeeded, and the California Raisins danced their way into our hearts, because their creators ignored the experts and listened to a voice within.

- *Make the complex simple.* A philosopher once said that true genius is the ability to make the complex marvelously simple. Pulitzer Prize–winning reporters Donald Barlett and James Steele, and former Magellan Fund manager Peter Lynch, make a mighty successful living doing just that. They've learned how to turn an avalanche of information into everyday English and into investment decisions that anyone can understand.
- *Tap the power of every individual.* The top-down approach to managing people simply doesn't work anymore. Entering the 1990s, outstanding motivators such as Petersen, Holtz, and New York police chief Lee Brown are turning the pyramid upside down. They're fostering teamwork and tapping into a hotbed of ideas that nobody knew was there.
- *Sell fantasy and reassure people.* Ronald Reagan and Disney have more than California homes in common. They both sell us the illusion that everything is going to be okay. That has turned out to be a very powerful formula for success. People are looking for an escape from a dog-eat-dog world plagued by drugs, street crime, and hypercompetitive workplaces. They'll pay a hefty price if you sell them a comforting bill of goods.
- *Tap the power of information.* The clever marketers at Frito-Lay, Information Resources, Inc., and Nintendo know more about our buying habits than we do ourselves. They succeed by building huge data bases of information, then tearing it apart to determine what to sell, when to sell, and where to sell.
- *Master quality.* American companies have stuck by the notion that nobody can manufacture "perfect" products or provide flawless service 100 percent of the time. Try telling that to Motorola or Florida Power & Light. Those two giants have become world-class experts at quality. Nobody is better at it, including the Japanese.
- *Target, target, target.* If you get close enough to your target, the bull's-eye is awfully tough to miss. The producers of four "yup-

ix

pie" products — catfish, Absolut vodka, Corona beer, and Ektar film — discovered what it takes to zero in and attack a lucrative market with products designed to scratch a particular niche.

- *March at a slow and steady pace.* In a world of extremely rapid change, it's relatively easy to get in, make a quick killing, and then bail out. That doesn't always work. Three successes that seemed to come from nowhere — Hyundai cars, the Pro-Choice March, and a National Spelling Bee champ — have been at it for years. They all made long journeys, step by minuscule step.

Of course, the themes highlighted above aren't all-encompassing. In each chapter you'll find elements of two or more themes. For instance, Petersen revived Ford by tapping the power of individuals. But he also asked Ford's designers to trust their instincts when designing the company's cars. Guber and Peters trust their guts, but they're also obsessed with quality. Frequently, they shoot movie scenes over and over again until they're virtually perfect. As you'll discover, almost everyone featured in this book shares a steadfast determination not to produce something second rate. Their own high standards ensure that perfection will always be within their grasp.

"These are the people you look for when the engine fails," says Roger Ailes, the media consultant to Presidents Reagan and Bush. "These guys will land the plane in a storm, with no engine, by the seat of their pants. These are the kind of guys you don't want to screw around with when they're doing what they do well because they'll beat you. They'll beat you bad."

Grit, Guts, and Genius

Trust Your Gut

one

You've probably seen a dozen movies in which maverick heroes triumph because they defy conventional wisdom and go with what they feel inside. In *Star Wars,* Luke Skywalker shuts off his targeting computer and trusts "the Force" within him to guide his ship and destroy the Evil Empire.

In the real world, it seldom happens that way. People usually lack the courage to ignore a world full of naysayers and baskets of market research, and go with what they feel inside. That's a major reason so few people succeed.

It's very difficult to trust your gut. It takes a tremendous amount of self-confidence to bet your company, or everything you own, on some wild-ass idea that may never work. But to achieve big successes, you've got to take big risks.

The people in the following chapters did that. Peter Guber and Jon Peters, the hottest producers in Hollywood, bet their company on *Batman* even though Warner Brothers told them the idea was absurd. Will Vinton, the creator of the California Raisins characters, was fired from his job because he insisted on making creatures out of clay. Brandon Stoddard, the genius behind "Roseanne" and "thirtysomething," turned ABC television around by telling his writers to ignore everything else on TV and create shows that they themselves would want to

1

watch. And two little-known niche players, Sid Cato (the "Guru of Annual Reports") and Don Beaver, founder of New Pig Corporation, proved that you can make the seemingly dull spring to life — if you trust your gut instincts enough to make it work.

The world is full of great ideas. But ideas are only as good as someone who seizes them and acts. Anyone can sit back and argue, "I could have done that." But the key question is, Did you have what it takes to risk your neck on it? Did you have the self-confidence to move forward despite what anyone else said?

The methods these people employ aren't easily grasped. But what they basically do is pay close attention to an inner voice. The secret isn't in listening to everyone else. It's in listening to yourself.

"Go with what your heart tells you," says Seth Werner, who dreamed up the Raisins ad. "A lot of times your emotions are stronger than your rational thoughts."

Of course, the risks taken by the leaders featured here aren't based solely on emotions. Each of them has the experience and expertise to recognize what will work. They're willing to take a risk because they've been there before.

They also possess a rare ability to make everyone else share their vision — and to keep a project on track when a lot of key players start bailing out. In the Guber and Peters chapter, you'll see how the producers kept *Rain Man* alive even though three directors quit. Stoddard nurtured "Roseanne" through some well-publicized squabbles. And Vinton kept his team of animators together through the painstakingly slow process of filming a Claymation advertisement.

Their approaches differ, but not nearly as much as their rewards. Cato begins each month with no money in the till. Guber and Peters are the richest producers in Hollywood. But if you listen closely to any of them discuss his or her work, it's an obsession, not a job. Proving the world wrong is an extremely powerful motivator.

2

Batman and *Rain Man*

Flip Sides of the Same Hollywood Coin

June 26, 1989. The rest of Los Angeles was busy battling another crazy Monday morning rush hour. The country's hottest moviemakers, Peter Guber and Jon Peters, were sitting in their makeshift office at Warner Brothers' Burbank studios, relishing a morning they'll never forget.

That weekend, their latest masterpiece, *Batman*, had set an all-time record at the box office. Moviegoers nationwide had shelled out more than $42 million, easily smashing the $37 million record set just weeks before by *Indiana Jones and the Last Crusade*. Guber could barely contain himself. Peters couldn't sit still. The phone rang. Peters grabbed it. It was Steven Ross, Warner's chairman. Warner Brothers, as you might recall, was locked in a battle to take over Time Inc. "Thank you, thank you, thank you," Ross told him. Peters cupped his hand over the phone and whispered to Guber, "It's Steve. He loves ya, babe, loves ya. He says *Batman* coming in the midst of all this is like a mitzvah to him." The phone rang again. It was actress Kim Basinger congratulating Peters, her recent flame.

The scene that morning, with Guber and Peters for the better part of two hours, was tough to imagine. Here were two guys in their forties — one (Peters) a former hairdresser clad in sneakers and white tennis shorts; the other a pigtailed, hyperactive cinematic genius —

3

snickering "I told you so's" at a world full of naysayers who predicted *Batman* would never be made, let alone succeed.

"Eight years ago, we said 'Batman' and people said 'Yech!' " said Guber. "Four years ago: 'Batman.' 'Yech!' A year and a half ago, Warner Brothers said, 'Look at this research. It's the lowest possible. The only people who want to see a Batman movie are five-year-olds. No one's going to want to go to this film.' Then we cast Michael Keaton as Batman and they almost killed us! Bat-freaks all over the world started screaming at us. But we took the risk. And today, we're getting the reward."

Risk. Adventure. Passion. Teamwork. Listening to a voice within. That's what lies at the heart of Guber-Peters's unmatchable streak of successes. (Before *Batman* came *Rain Man, The Color Purple, Gorillas in the Mist, The Witches of Eastwick, Missing, Midnight Express, An American Werewolf in London, A Star Is Born.*) Guber and Peters's films have been nominated for fifty-two Academy Awards. Recognizing their talents, Sony in late 1989 paid $200 million for the Guber-Peters Entertainment Company. Sony put the two producers in charge of another acquisition, Columbia Pictures, Inc.

In 1989, this dynamic duo walked away with four Oscars, including Best Picture for *Rain Man*, another predicted flop that took four years and survived four directors before making the big screen. The reluctance and outright fear to risk filming *Rain Man* was understandable. As Guber concedes, "Imagine spending $22 million to make a movie about two guys sitting in a car, one of whom is autistic, riding across the country. No punching. No plane crashes. No sex. It's not Rocky or James Bond. The only action is when one guy yells for a second and the other says, 'You hurt me.' "

Throughout the 1980s, "the key word behind our success was risk," says Guber matter-of-factly. "No risk, no reward. And not just a creative risk but a measured, intelligent business risk."

To understand the risks that Guber and Peters take, and the way they make a film, you've got to understand a little about how they operate.

Guber and Peters met at a party in 1975. Guber, Boston-raised and with four academic degrees, including one in law, was running Columbia Pictures at the time. At age thirty-two, he was already a shining star in Hollywood.

Peters was Barbra Streisand's former hairdresser. As their relationship evolved into a romance, Peters began to work his way into moviemaking. With Streisand's help, Peters produced *A Star Is Born*.

Shortly after he met Guber, Peters approached him with a story idea. The two men teamed up to produce *The Eyes of Laura Mars*, starring Faye Dunaway. Guber and Peters have been working together ever since.

Like any great team, Guber and Peters share certain traits. Both are workaholics and perfectionists. They love wrapping themselves up in a project and scrutinizing every last detail. They like seeing the finished product — and enjoy basking in the spotlight when it's through. But what they truly love is the process of making a film. The carving, the whittling, the shaping of each and every scene.

"It's an obsession," says Jon Peters. "People ask me if I can have dinner with them. I can't. I'm obsessed. And Peter's the same way. You have to be committed to it every waking hour."

They've also mastered that all-too-rare ability to bring out the best in each other. "I bring out a certain side in him and he does the same for me," says Peters. "It's like a ball team. He'll do something and I'll say, 'Oh my God, that's unbelievable.' And then I'll feel something, and he'll jump in and act on the idea."

Once on the set, Guber and Peters try to watch the movie unfold like a "creative shepherd." Sometimes you have to stand back, Guber says. Other times you have to bite, sometimes you have to kiss. "So we're constantly weaving in and out, in and out."

In many ways, the stories behind their two recent megahits,

5

Batman and *Rain Man,* are a perfect metaphor for the two men's individual interests as well as strengths.

"Peter had the genesis of *Rain Man* and I had the genesis of *Batman,*" Peters explains. "Collectively, they represent us."

Peters tends to mastermind blockbuster pictures (*Batman, The Witches of Eastwick*) that literally lift you out of your seat. His special talent is his ability to attract top actors — and keep tight reins on projects that could easily race out of control. It was Peters who convinced Jack Nicholson to play the Joker in *Batman.* And it was Peters who oversaw the film's creation on a sprawling set at a London studio.

"With *Batman,* Jon wrote a new chapter in the book of great producers," says Warner Brothers president Mark Canton. "Jon brought out the best in everyone, and managed a delicate relationship with Jack [Nicholson]. He walked onto a set that filled five city blocks and managed it like a general."

Guber is more introspective. In deciding what films to make, he looks for scripts that feature quiet heroes fighting battles that average people confront in their daily lives. His pet projects have included *Rain Man, The Color Purple,* and *Gorillas in the Mist.* "Films about the human spirit just move me," he says. "I love a film that makes you laugh, makes you cry, and has unexpected heroes. People you find interesting. *Rain Man* was just a piece in a puzzle of who we are. The shut-down individual [Raymond] and the fast-talking, creative kid [Charlie] are alive in each of us. And they compete with each other all the time."

In their quest for blockbusters, many Hollywood producers tend to respond to what Guber calls the "lowest common denominator in themselves." Instead of listening to an inner voice and trusting their own judgment, they focus on what some invisible audience wants to see. "I have a child in me that's alive, that I nurture," says Guber. "And I let that child play. It gets excited and enthusiastic. As an adult, I just guide that child so he doesn't create havoc."

6

Batman *and*
Rain Man
producers
Jon Peters and
Peter Guber

Guber's special gift is his ability to see a script's potential where others might not. Says Canton, "That why I call them Mr. Inside and Mr. Outside. Peter is nonpareil in finding material. He's the best there is. Then Jon comes in with the passion to shoot the movie."

Guber discovered long ago that the core of many great movies has relatively little to do with the special effects, the casting, or the cinematography. It has much more to do with stories that speak to issues people want to hear about and experience emotionally. "When I was a young student in Italy, an instructor showed us where Michelangelo stood. Right here," Guber said, pointing downward. "And this fellow picked up a piece of marble and said, 'Michelangelo saw what was inside a stone. Then he would whittle away the pieces to expose it.' That's my philosophy. The material is the magnet. We shape it. We form it. But the material — a book, a play, a screenplay — is the magnet. The less seen we are, the less visible our handprint is on it, the better. It's not about us. It's about the product."

Guber and Peters can be "tough, even sharks" when they have to be, says Barry Morrow, who wrote the original *Rain Man* screenplay and the award-winning TV movie *Bill*, starring Mickey Rooney. "But Peter has a bigger heart than is well known. There's a side of him that wants to be remembered as a producer of films that make a difference."

Individually, and as a team, Guber and Peters possess a rare trait. They have the ability to look at a script and see the finished movie before a single scene has been filmed. They develop a vision that they're somehow able to convince everyone else to accept and work toward.

"Oftentimes, you hear an idea and you see an image," says Peters. "You see the image. You see the movie. You make the movie. The director, the writer, and all that get painted in over time. But basically, we *see* things finished."

In Guber's opinion, many Hollywood films, such as *Batman* and *Ghostbusters*, are big targets. They cost $30 million or more. Their sets and special effects tend to be as important as the characters. They work best on the big screen — with 70mm film and Dolby stereo sound. Such films are just as difficult to make as more cerebral pictures. You have to do them to stay in the game.

Films like *Rain Man* are almost the opposite. Says Guber, "*Rain Man* was really a very intimate, teeny, tiny picture. *Rain Man* was a very small target for us . . . far, far away." Early on, it was envisioned as a TV movie starring two real-life brothers, Dennis and Randy Quaid. Guber saw more than that. He believed that *Rain Man* contained universal messages about family, love, and loss. He believed that it would strike a chord about the bonds between two brothers — and the trauma of suddenly being reunited with a family member you never knew you had.

"Every family has secrets," says Guber. "Someone in my family went to a mental institution. Until I was thirty, I didn't know that person was there. Someone else in my family was adopted, and I didn't know that until I was driving down the road one day and he told me. That's what Charlie Babbitt [Tom Cruise's character] discovers: a secret. He gets freaked out by it. Then he has to deal with it. In the process, he discovers another whole side of himself. *Rain Man* worked because it appeals to something that's universal: loss and love. Everybody wants to be loved, especially by a family member. And each character in the film experiences a loss."

Pop psychologists say the movie worked primarily because it made viewers feel better about themselves. At the beginning of the movie, the viewer feels superior to both characters — the cocky, greedy Charlie and the mentally impaired Raymond. As the film moves along, both characters improve.

9

"By the end, we feel like they're more like us," says Roger Rollin, a Clemson University professor of literature. "The movie makes us feel comfortable about retarded people . . . confident, in a sense, that they can become more like us."

The movie also capitalizes on a gradual shift from the "me" decade of the 1980s to the "we" decade — George Bush's "kinder, gentler" nation that some see emerging as we enter the 1990s.

Morrow's original script for *Rain Man* was sheer Hollywood — and considerably more complicated than Guber thought it should be. In that version, two middle-aged brothers are taken prisoner by white-supremacist survivalists who imprison them in a barn. Charlie rescues his brother by assembling a motorcycle and hurtling the two through flames engulfing the barn.

Guber, along with Dustin Hoffman and director Barry Levinson, realized the strength of the story was in the characters, not the plot. As Levinson told *Rolling Stone* magazine, "Many audiences like gizmos, plot things, cops and all that kind of shit in which I'm not interested. If I can show the autism for what it is and understand it — show the frustration and the humor — if I can make the relationship work with these two guys on the road, then that's enough for me."

With that approach in mind, Hoffman spent months studying autistic savants — seemingly retarded adults who have superhuman abilities for such things as remembering dates, adding numbers, or replaying an entire musical composition after hearing it once. One of the people he studied was Morrow's friend Kim P., an autistic savant who can memorize entire phone books yet can't tell you where the kitchen forks are kept. Hoffman spent an entire afternoon just watching Kim, mimicking his every move. Hoffman and Cruise also shared meals and went bowling with two brothers (one autistic, one not) who became models for their characters. Still, Hoffman had a very difficult time developing his Raymond character. The challenge was that while

10

most actors feed off the other actors, Raymond could neither look at nor listen to anyone. Here was a character devoid of emotion who nobody could really touch. As Hoffman, who was paid a hefty $5 million for his work, told *USA Today*, "I couldn't do it. I could not do the character. I just couldn't find him. It was the scariest moment of my life."

At one point, Hoffman told Levinson he wanted out. But then, while filming the scene in which Raymond realizes he's not wearing his own underwear, Hoffman finally discovered an inner sense of what he needed to make Raymond's character come to life. "It hit me . . . like an explosion."

Perhaps Guber's greatest feat was keeping *Rain Man* alive despite the fact that three directors (Marty Brest, Steven Spielberg, and Sydney Pollack) were invited to make the film but, one by one, decided to abandon it. (The film also passed through the hands of five writers before completion. It also was filmed as MGM/United Artists, the production house, was on the verge of becoming extinct.)

"Marty was six weeks away from principal photography and we're all sitting in New York with Dustin and Tom Cruise, and Marty says, 'I can't do this picture . . . I don't see it,'" Guber recalls.

Then Spielberg joined the set for five months, Pollack for nine months, before walking away. "Each time a filmmaker passed, Jon and I would say, 'Okay, let's get the material back. We'll find a way to do it,'" Guber says.

The other directors simply didn't buy into Guber's vision of *Rain Man*. He kept telling them, "The story's there. Turn on the lights and the cameras. Let's just do it." But they weren't persuaded. Pollack, for instance, sat down with Guber at one point and shared his own vision of the film. "I just can't lick this," Pollack told Guber. Not until Levinson came on board did the Oscar-winning *Rain Man* begin to appear.

"The trick is to recognize it when you've got it," says Guber.

11

"The first three directors got scared because they were frightened by *Rain Man*'s simplicity. What we recognized was, 'It's there. It's in the marble.' "

The Making of Batman

Batman was anything but a teeny, tiny picture.

It evolved into a $40 million blockbuster, chock-full of special effects, including the Joker's maniacal antics, twenty-eight Batsuits (cost: $250,000), and two $125,000 Batmobiles. Instead of paring down the script, a group of seven — Peters, Nicholson, Keaton, Canton, actor Robert Wuhl, director Tim Burton, and screenwriter Warren Skaaren — rewrote the script six times, consistently adding more to the Joker's role.

Skaaren says the team would sit down at nine or ten A.M. and spend all day tossing ideas out, rewriting Sam Hamm's original script over and over. Then Skaaren would go back to his hotel and stay up almost all night carefully reworking the next day's action. Some of the new lines were Nicholson's: "I'm of a mind to make some mookie" . . . "She's the kind of girl who puts steam in a man's stride." Others were Skaaren's: "I am the world's first fully functioning homicidal artist."

Closely monitoring every script change — and supervising shooting on the set — was Peters, the ultimate hands-on producer. "Jon made everyone very comfortable," says Skaaren. In fact, several of the scenes, especially the ending, were Peters's idea. "Sometimes he even stood up and acted out a scene for us."

Peters had a deep-rooted reason for paying such close attention. He grew up reading Batman comics, even dressing up as Batman at parties as a kid. He hated the way Batman was portrayed in the campy 1960s TV series starring Adam West. Peters and Guber obtained the movie rights to Batman in 1979, but patiently waited for the proper time and script to resurrect the legendary character.

12

"We wanted Batman to be kind of an inventive guy . . . funny, outrageous, with an aggressive side to him," says Peters. "We wanted him to be kind of a dark character who's a bit schizophrenic — a modern-day street hero, not like Superman in little leotards."

Peters had observed what had been happening in the world around him. He saw society's disgust with the decline of our inner cities, particularly New York. He studied the frustration of people who had been helplessly victimized by crime. Bruce Wayne, as you may recall, decided to become Batman after his parents were murdered before his eyes. This Batman, Peters decided, should exemplify a "usually normal man who puts on a cape and goes out and beats the shit out of everybody."

This Batman movie wouldn't be just for kids. It would "take you to a completely different world for two hours, wrap you up in it, then spit you out," says Peters.

In Hamm's screenplay, Peters saw the emergence of the dark, aggressive character he was looking for. This Batman was much like the original hero conceived by Bob Kane at DC Comics in 1939. (Kane created Batman after thinking about a Leonardo da Vinci drawing of a man wearing batlike wings. His secret identity was akin to Zorro's.) Peters carefully began to assemble his Bat-team. Early on, the producers considered casting Bill Murray or another comic actor as Batman.

Then Peters, Canton, and Guber saw *Beetlejuice,* an offbeat film directed by thirty-year-old Tim Burton and starring Michael Keaton. They loved the film, and Peters saw a dangerous, insane side to Keaton that he'd never seen before. He decided to hire Burton as director and to cast Keaton as Batman.

The prize catch was Nicholson — the perfect choice to play Batman's insane archenemy, the Joker. That happened when Peters and Nicholson were filming *The Witches of Eastwick*. Peters brought the idea up one day at about four A.M. At first, Nicholson laughed it off.

13

But Peters convinced him. Then he flew Nicholson to London, where he saw *Beetlejuice* and met Burton.

Hiring the relatively inexperienced Burton, and tabbing Keaton as Batman, was a huge risk. Batman fans worldwide screamed foul at the choice of Keaton. To counteract that perception, Warner Brothers sent Kane on the road to comic-book conventions. He persuaded fans to give this "serious Batman" a chance.

Also fueling interest in the movie was perhaps the most extensive publicity campaign ever dreamed up. Everything was built around the famous "Bat" logo — a black bat set against a gold background. The design, by consultant Anton Furst, was created in London. It was intentionally sketched to create a sense of danger, an edginess. It also bears a feature perceptual psychologists call "figure ground ambiguity" — meaning that you can look at it and see a Bat logo or the black tonsils inside a gold mouth. At first, the studio wasn't buying it. As Peters recalls, "We brought the logo back to Warner and they said, 'You can't use that as a campaign. You can't have a movie logo without Nicholson, Keaton, and Batman on it.' "

The creators persisted. Says Peters, "We believed that because there's so much curiosity about this character, the less we do, the more it will bring audiences in. And it would be cool — it would have an attitude to it like, 'How dare they just market this thing.' "

As Warner quickly discovered, this odd Bat logo had a life of its own. "The more we tried to beat it, the more we realized it was just unbeatable," says Rob Friedman, Warner's publicity director. "The logo was so striking, almost bigger than life."

In many ways, the prerelease Batmania had relatively little to do with the movie itself. The logo became the latest fad — like the "smiley face" or the Pet Rock. Says pop psychologist Deena Weinstein of DePaul University, "It's just people being in on the latest hype. They don't want to be behind the new trend."

Friedman's knockout punch: a superb ninety-second trailer,

shown as a preview at thousands of U.S. movie theaters, that convinced eager moviegoers to line up for tickets weeks before *Batman* debuted.

In shooting the film, Peters and Burton scrutinized every psychological detail. For instance, they didn't want this Batman to appear invincible. Hence, they outfitted Keaton with a bulletproof vest.

"If you notice, we purposely had Batman falling flat on his back in the first scene," says Skaaren. "We wanted to convey his vulnerability. The big problem with Batman in the comics is that he wasn't real. We had to make him real to a modern audience."

This Batman was emotionally vulnerable, too. He falls for Vicky Vale (Kim Basinger) and is continually obsessed with grief about his parents' death. As a result, this Batman is a hero viewers can easily identify with — a real human with deep-rooted psychological hang-ups who is ever aware of his own mortality.

"This Batman is not a full hero," says Weinstein. "People want Batman to be neurotic and have real problems. He's a very vulnerable, troubled human that we can identify with."

Clemson's Roger Rollin has spent a great deal of time studying heroes throughout history. He says there are basically three types of fictional heroes: (1) divine beings, like the gods in Greek mythology or today's Superman, that have supernatural powers; (2) mortal beings, like Batman, who are overwhelmingly cunning and powerful and who move in a world in which the laws of nature are slightly suspended; and (3) earthly heroes, such as Matt Dillon of "Gunsmoke" or the comics' Steve Canyon.

These days we have a very real emotional investment in real-life heroes — Oliver North, Ronald Reagan, Gary Hart. But they often wind up disappointing us. Says Rollin, "They have a very short shelf life because people or the media immediately point out their weak spots. That's why people turn to fictional heroes. Since they're a fantasy, their lives can be controlled. Writers can even rewrite their

15

past. You'll never hear that Batman abused Robin or beat his mother. If Batman ever killed a baby, we'd lose interest."

As Rollin points out, TV and the movie screen play a big role in diminishing the stature of would-be heroes. He asks, "What percentage of the population, after all, can identify Captain Kirk and Mr. Spock, and what percentage the first two astronauts to walk on the moon?"

People are always looking for a messiah, someone who shares our cultural values and can magically make everything right. "That's a very powerful desire — it's kept Christianity going for two thousand years," says Rollin. "We hope the president will do it but he can't. So we look to stranger-savior heroes like Batman and the Lone Ranger to be our fictional messiahs. In the sixties, Batman might not have worked. We had no faith in any heroes back then."

Though it may seem that this Batman movie is entirely new, it's really an assemblage of several age-old formulas. In both epics and pop romance, the normal forces of law and order are unable to deal with the danger at hand. Batman, like Beowulf of the Old English epic, must be called out to deal with the city's dragons. There's usually a beautiful lady — in this case, Kim Basinger, as Vicki Vale in *Batman* — at his side as he faces death and overcomes it, providing us with our own sense of victory, even immortality. It conveys, in psychological fashion, the message that "nothing can happen to me."

Though not a hero in the ordinary sense, the Joker — like Darth Vader in *Star Wars* — appeals to us, too. He represents the dark side (Batman's alter ego) trying to steal the city — and the girl — from that goody-two-shoes, Batman. Of course, in keeping with our cultural bent, in the end evil always succumbs to good.

Even more striking than Batman's character was the set itself. Furst's version of Gotham City was envisioned as "hell erupting through the earth." Actually, hell erupting through New York City would be more appropriate.

16

"Batman fits in because Gotham City really is America," Peters says. "We are living in a decaying world and people identify with that."

The menacing city in *Batman* is diametrically opposite the squeaky-clean midwestern Metropolis seen in all the Superman movies. Gotham City's buildings purposefully dwarf the street below, ensuring little perceptible difference between night and day. The set itself was labeled "retro-40s." In keeping with Batman's fifty-year history, it mixed past and present — reporters using modern-day tape recorders but outdated flashbulb cameras, no videocams — in a surrealistic time warp. Designer Bob Ringwood said he styled the costumes and other objects the way they would have looked if someone in 1945 envisioned life in 1989.

The cinematographer, Roger Pratt, used "tonal separation" — lighting the movie as if it were black-and-white but filming it in color. Pratt used similar techniques to film *Brazil*. This kind of lighting made the key character — the green-haired, white-faced, red-lipped Joker — stand out even more.

Nicholson, of course, was allowed to be Nicholson. As he told *Newsweek*, "Most actors are afraid to go as dark as they might, but I always say, 'Let's really get black.'"

No detail was overlooked. The Batmobiles were built from the ground up, from the shells of two 1968 Chevy Impalas. They were outfitted — one actually ran up to 93 mph — with turbine blades from a Harrier fighter jet, deadly machine guns, and a body with the features of a Stealth bomber. The car's biggest problem was the sliding roof, which kept jamming on Batman's five-inch-high pointed ears. For Keaton, Batman's costumes were a perspiratory nightmare. He'd sweat through two a day. In keeping with current style, his Batsuit was black, not blue and gray as in the comics. It was created by casting a soft rubber mold over Keaton's body. Some of the twenty-eight suits have a seam up the back for front shots, others up the front

17

for rear shots. The cowl and the Bat-ears were purposely designed to be sexy. One woman viewer said she never liked Keaton, but Batman was the sexiest character she'd ever seen.

"In the end, the truth is that we succeeded because we questioned everything," says Canton. "And we created a hero that is parallel to our times. We tapped into the energy, the feel of the world we live in. It's a dangerous world that we can't get through without a sense of humor."

The producers certainly will be laughing — all the way to the bank. Peters estimates that, everything included, *Batman* will soar past $1 billion in revenues: $300 million in the United States, $300 million overseas (*Batman* was the first film to gross £2 million in Britain on its opening weekend), more than $100 million on videotape, plus TV, records (the soundtrack was the number-one album in the summer of 1989), and merchandise.

Lighting Up a Dark Theater

Regardless of who's carrying the cinematic ball, Peters and Guber agree on two premises: Don't take life — or films — too seriously, and don't ever look back.

"We're basically in the business of new businesses," says Guber. "We're starting over every time — new anxieties, new stress, new fears. But fear doesn't paralyze us. It catalyzes us. If we're a little anxious, a little nervous, it tells us we're on the right trail."

After ten years together, does it ever wear thin? Sure. Sometimes Guber feels like he wants to pop Peters "right in the kisser, and he wants to — *Pow!* — pop me, too. But we're always focused: 'How do we make it better? How do we make it great?' "

Making it "great" hinges on one fundamental challenge: How do you tap people's emotions?

"It's only about tapping the human spirit," says Guber. "There's nothing else you can do. Films have to hit you here or here" — he

18

points to his heart and then his crotch — "before they make you think. People have either got to laugh or cry or clap or cheer. Basically, people are closed, insecure, frightened. In this dark theater, they laugh with everyone, cry with everybody. It's okay. It's a safe space. It's just images flickering on a screen that tap into their souls. And when they come out, they pass on, not what the story is really about, but their enthusiasm about a film that makes you feel something great. So they think, 'Yeah, I'll pay $5 or $6 to go out and laugh and cry and cheer a little. Why not?' "

New Pig

The "Oink" Factor of Success

The challenge for Don Beaver, founder of New Pig Corporation, was to take a dull, low-tech enterprise like industrial cleaning and make it fun. "I can't imagine someone being in business just to make money," he says.

In that effort, Beaver, not yet forty, succeeded beyond his highest expectations, creating a business-media phenomenon that even he has difficulty understanding.

New Pig, which makes absorbent materials that soak up leaking oil and grease from factory machines, is the darling of the entrepreneurial magazines. *Inc.*, *Venture*, and *Success* have all featured New Pig — *Inc.*, in fact, several times. Even *Industry Week*, *Across the Board*, *Forbes*, and *Fortune*, magazines usually aimed at executives of much larger companies, have noticed the little Tipton, Pennsylvania, firm, founded in 1985.

Why has an outfit with fewer than two hundred employees and about $15 million in sales in 1989 been more successful in attracting attention than companies several hundred times its size — in a decidedly unglamorous industry at that?

Start with the company name, a hook that snags attention. Beaver ignored the advice of his marketing and public relations firm when he selected New Pig. (The absorbent socklike products New Pig makes are called PIGs, for Partners in Grime. Another way to think

20

of the product is as a diaper that goes around the base of a machine.) The experts thought such a name would attract ridicule. Beaver thought a little ridicule, aimed in the right direction, could be a tremendous benefit. And besides, what other name could more simply and effectively tell the company's story? Real pigs grovel in the mud and muck. That's New Pig's business. The first PIGs were even stuffed with ground-up corncobs.

To complement the name, and have more fun, Beaver continued the theme. The company's address is Pig Place, One Pork Avenue. Its toll-free order line: 800-Hot-Hogs. OINK, in big pink letters, is written on company folders. Inside, a pink pipe cleaner, twirled in the shape of a pig's tail, is stuck in a rounded pocket that looks like the back end of a pig. New Pig's product catalog is called the Pigalog. Notes are taken on company-issued "Oink" pads. Beaver is often seen wearing a hat with a pig snout and posing with live hogs in promotional materials.

"I get a lot of people asking me what I attribute all the attention to," says Beaver, who describes himself as a "hopeless entrepreneur." "We do work at it."

If forced to select a single factor for all the media attention and New Pig's business success — revenues increased 50 percent in 1989 — Beaver points back to the company's name and says "simplicity." By that he means the ability to communicate to many different audiences, without confusion, what his company is all about. Many business leaders, Beaver says, mistakenly think only in terms of public relations. But in addition to the media, a company must also communicate to customers, employees, potential investors, potential business partners, and government regulators. Employees who truly understand their company's business, Beaver says, are more focused on what really counts and do a better job.

"We found out early on that if we couldn't be succinct, if we couldn't quickly tell someone what we do, then we were not going to get them interested in buying our products and we were not going to

Don Beaver, founder and president of New Pig Corporation

get them interested in lending us money or investing in us," Beaver says. "If the guy on the loading dock doesn't understand what you're trying to do, then you're in trouble." He tested many of the company's early marketing materials by taking them home to his second-grade son. Beaver knew that if his son could understand the material, then most people could.

That lesson about simplicity was reinforced in the spring of 1989 when Beaver wanted to expand New Pig's business by offering a consumer product. In March, while on vacation in Naples, Florida, he was in a shopping mall studying the behavior of shoppers. He was trying to figure out a way — maybe a kiosk — to sell consumers a $7 dust rag. The rag was chemical-free and made out of a Du Pont material that attracts dust and dirt. But $7 for something that consumers usually get for free with every discarded T-shirt?

Beaver knew it would be a hard sell, but he was ready to spend a year and up to $750,000 trying to find the right way to peddle the rag to housewives and other consumers. In April, he changed his mind. "I came back to our board of directors and told them if we spent another cent on selling to consumers it would be a mistake," Beaver said. Instead, New Pig went back to what it knows best, its industrial customers. The rag material, now also configured in mitts and something called a Dust Bunny for heavy-duty use, is popular in the prepress areas of printing plants and the finishing areas of auto plants.

"When we were trying to crack the consumer market, it took me twenty minutes to explain to someone what we were trying to do," Beaver says. "That's one reason we didn't make it." Now he's thoroughly committed to what New Pig knows best. "There are more than a hundred thousand factories in this country that have so many weird cleaning problems that we know how to solve," Beaver says. "We're already involved with twenty-five percent of them, so why not stay focused on that market?"

23

California Raisins

"Oh, I Heard It Through the Grapevine"

O ne night not so long ago, in a college dormitory not too far away, a brash young fellow named Will Vinton sat down with some friends to drink a few cold beers. The group began to play around with some clay that Will had lugged home from one of his art classes. First the "sculptor" of the group would carve a face. Then Will would snap a photograph. Then the sculptor would pick up his clay creation and drop a lip, raise an eyebrow, or crack a smile. Click. Another photograph. Lo and behold, the funny-looking creatures they carved began to take on a character all their own. Pretty soon the table was filled with clay figures, scattered among a growing pile of empty beer cans. After a while, Will's friends gave it up and went to bed. But young Will sat there with his camera. He began to imagine what it would be like to bring these characters to life. He thought, if you photographed the characters after each minor change, and then converted the still photos into film, you could create an illusion of motion. His characters would appear to walk and talk, maybe even sing or dance. He marveled at the thought of what such simple figures, made of nothing but ordinary clay, would appear to do. But he decided his ideas were nothing more than the stuff of fanciful, youthful dreams.

"There I was, at U-Cal Berkeley among thousands of incredibly bright people," says Vinton, now in his early forties. "I was just overwhelmed. I thought, How could there possibly be anything new under the sun?"

What he didn't know was that he was on to something so incredibly new and so phenomenally appealing that it would one day lead to the most successful and popular television commercials in recent history. The Vinton-created California Raisins, those ridiculous-looking clumps of clay, would sing "Oh, I Heard It Through the Grapevine" and dance their way into our hearts — and rescue the raisin-growing industry from virtual stagnation.

In 1989, close to three years after the Raisins debuted, the campaign still ranked third in the annual Video Storyboard survey of 24,000 adults. The ad's sponsor, the California Raisin Advisory Board, spent a mere $6.8 million running the ads in 1988. Yet the Raisins ranked number one on Storyboard's survey and easily outscored number-two Pepsi, which spent $106.4 million, and number-three McDonald's, which coughed up a staggering $386 million on TV advertising. As Vinton had imagined, the Raisins took on an aura all their own. In a 1988 Q-Score study, the Raisins ranked second only to Bill Cosby in popularity. The ads captured three Clios, the top award for TV commercials. Perhaps most amazing of all was the reward. In 1987 and 1988, raisin sales jumped 20 percent, to 400,000 tons a year.

Before the ads appeared on September 14, 1986, raisin sales were dropping at the rate of 1 percent a year. Directors of the Raisin Board and their members, five thousand California raisin growers and packers, were beginning to panic. They had a huge harvest coming on and no one to sell the raisins to. So they asked their San Francisco–based advertising agency, Foote, Cone and Belding, to find out why raisin sales were shriveling up like a grape in the hot sun. The agency discovered that consumers were well aware that raisins were healthy food and a perfect snack for kids. No surprise. All the advertising up until that time was geared toward feeding that perception. The old

25

ads, showing raisins dropping onto other foods, won Clio awards but nobody bought more raisins. As Foote, Cone dug deeper, they learned that raisins simply had no emotional appeal. "People thought raisins were wimpy, lonely, dull," says Robert Phinney, former director of the Raisin Board.

At first, the strategists had no idea what to do. How do you breathe life and personality into a dried-up grape? How do you convince adults who had quit eating raisins to pick them up again? Foote, Cone's group creative director, Tim Price, decided to turn the project over to two creative young copywriters, Seth Werner and Dextor Fedor. Werner had a hot track record: in 1982, he won the first of five Clios for a Sohio gasoline spot about antiknock fuels. In 1984, he won a second Clio for the Stroh's beer campaign featuring Alex the beer-drinking dog. (That campaign, as seemingly absurd and offbeat as the Raisins, hasn't died either. It ranked number eight in Storyboard's 1988 survey of most-popular TV ads.)

Werner and Fedor began brainstorming and got nowhere. Then the two of them went over to a friend's house one evening and talked about it there. Werner muttered, "We'll probably do something stupid like have raisins sing 'Oh, I Heard It Through the Grapevine.' " Everybody laughed.

The next day at work, the two of them had second thoughts. Well, why not, Werner thought. Maybe the song would help raisins look hip and cool. The idea to mold raisins out of Vinton's "Claymation" figures didn't occur right away. Werner knew he didn't want to use people dressed in raisin costumes. Then he toyed with the notion of using cell animation, the process that creates the figures you see in regular animated cartoons. In fact, Foote, Cone did a test spot using cell animation. A day later, Werner was struck with the idea of using Claymation.

"It was a way to make it almost seem real," says Werner, now president of the Dallas-based Bloom Agency.

As always, creating a TV ad is one thing; convincing the sponsors and your boss to back it is something else entirely. It had taken Werner fifty proposed scripts to get the two "Alex the Dog" spots on the air. When Werner approached Price with his dancing raisins idea, he almost turned him down.

"We were walking out of the garage when he told me about it," Price recalls. Price told him he'd seen clay figures resembling chickens dancing around in commercials for Kentucky Fried Chicken and they looked disgusting. Werner screamed back, "Don't worry! It won't be like that."

Price agreed to go along with it, but concedes, "It was hell for a while. Everyone wondered what a personified raisin would look like."

The next step was, of course, the toughest: selling the concept to the raisin growers. Foote, Cone arranged a meeting with Phinney and about forty packers and growers. Werner and Fedor didn't have anything on tape to show them yet. So they both put on white gloves, cranked up the "Grapevine" song and lip-synched it themselves as they danced around like supercool raisins. Not exactly Broadway, but it worked.

"We don't take ourselves too seriously," says Phinney. "So we thought, Maybe people will get a kick out of seeing these little shriveled-up things singing and dancing around. In a way, it was faintly ridiculous."

In retrospect, the fact that Phinney and the raisin industry "had the guts to go with it is simply amazing," says Price.

"Basically, clients get the kind of work that they deserve," says Werner. "And the raisin growers got what they deserved. They left us alone. They let us do it. And they benefited because of that."

Vinton didn't realize it, but he was about to get the biggest break of his twelve-year-old Claymation career. Like Werner, he too had struggled long and hard to establish his reputation in a world full of conservative naysayers. In a college architecture class, he was assigned

27

Will Vinton with his California Raisins and other creations

a paper on the history of the Acropolis. Instead of a paper, he turned in a film treatise using his clay models. After graduating from Berkeley, Vinton settled on a filmmaking career. He worked as a photo director, editor, and production assistant on low-budget commercials. But the longer he worked, the more he realized that nothing seemed to be as alive or as magical as those primitive clay figures he'd built back in his college dorm. Like many pioneers, Vinton was an odd sort. In high school he was one of the few who played both football and rock-and-roll, and also marched in the high school band. He read Newton's *Principia* and became convinced that he was destined to do something radically different — to become a master at something that no one else did. So in the dark confines of his Portland, Oregon, basement, he and an old college friend, Bob Gardiner, began to create a cast of characters from clay.

At the time, Vinton was working for a firm called Odyssey Productions. He approached Odyssey's partners with a proposal to merge his Claymation process into the company. They turned him down flat and subsequently fired him. Vinton didn't give up. He and Gardiner developed a Claymation film, called *Closed Mondays*, about a drunk who wanders into an art museum and watches the characters come to life. The film was an immediate hit and, in 1975, captured an Oscar as the Best Animated Short Subject. Still, Vinton was struggling. He drove around Portland in a beat-up Volkswagen. His annual earnings barely exceeded $5,000 a year. Even after he won the Oscar, his father called him and demanded, "When are you going to get a real job?"

But Vinton had a vision that he, like Walt Disney, would slowly and steadily pioneer a new production medium. For financial support, he did Claymation commercials for Rainier beer and the local pear growers. He teamed up with Disney on a feature film, *Return to Oz*. But he resisted offers to make "quick and dirty money" and risk spoiling Claymation with inferior work. "That would have caused us to create a 'system' to get the work out fast," says Vinton. "I'm glad we went so slow."

29

When Foote, Cone called, Vinton was raring to go. He loved the idea and immediately assembled a research team to develop the spot. Vinton and his seventy-five employees at Will Vinton Productions don't simply sit down and start to mold clay. First they spend several weeks studying humans who serve as models for the clay characters they hope to create. For instance, a thirty-seven-year-old actor named Pons Maar became the basis for the Domino's Pizza "Noid." The animators make videotapes of Maar bouncing around the studio. "I get to jump up and down and act like crazy for half an hour," says Maar. The animators run their cameras at half speed so that when they play the film back, Maar appears to be moving twice as fast. Then they use the films, and Maar's voice, to create the Noid out of clay.

For the original California Raisins ad, Vinton's animators purchased videotapes of Motown anniversary concerts and other performances. Then they hired dancers to perform to the "Grapevine" music. For a 1989 Raisins ad, featuring Michael Jackson as "Michael Raisin," the animators filmed Jackson strutting and twirling around on a Hollywood stage. Jackson also acted out the parts of six back-up singers. The "Michael Raisin" ad debuted on July 28 at 5,700 movie theaters nationwide.

Next comes the hard part. The animators study the films and begin to mold Claymation characters out of Plasticine clay and metal armatures that they hope will resemble what they see on the screen.

"We look for expressions or some unique thing an actor does that we can incorporate into each of the characters," says Vinton. "It's a terrific process that lets us score the music, set the timing, before we even begin the animation process. It works much better than trying to edit everything afterward."

For the first Raisins ad, Vinton and his co-workers created twenty-five to thirty clay raisins, each about seven to eight inches tall and weighing one and a half pounds. Aside from their white gloves, no two of the raisins are alike. Some wear sunglasses, others sneakers. A few are fat while others are thin. The animators also created a huge assortment of snack foods (boxes of popcorn, rippled potato chips, chocolate chip cookies, and so on) to sit in the audience.

Shooting each commercial, in one of eleven miniature studios, is an excruciatingly laborious process that lasts anywhere from a month to three months. Using a computer-driven 35mm Mitchell camera, the animators snap a photograph of the motionless clay figures. Then they make up to sixty very tiny adjustments — raise an eyebrow, tilt an arm — on every one of the clay characters. Ultimately, they snap twenty-four photos for each second of film that you see on TV. So a sixty-second commercial actually consists of 1,440 still photographs. (The original thirty-second Raisins ad contained 720 different scenes and took five weeks to shoot.) Explains David Altschul, Vinton's production director, "We create an illusion of motion in three dimensions." The effort tries every animator's patience; it often takes an entire day in the studio to create a single second of film.

Matching the moves of Motown was a nightmare. A raisin is one of the most difficult objects in the world to bring to life. "If I were ever to describe the essence of Claymation, I'd never describe something round, brown, and plump as a raisin," Vinton says. "They have no arms, no legs, no hips, and they're not exactly full of life."

In some inexplicable way, though, the Raisins seemed to grasp the essence of the hip and cool Motown style. "Grapevine" was already an all-time classic that had just been featured in the smash movie hit *The Big Chill*. Somehow it appeared to bring the Raisins to life.

"One of the fabulous things about the Raisins is that no one can really explain the idea," says Werner. "In fact, the more people try to put their finger on it, the stupider it sounds."

Aside from the music and Vinton's painstaking handiwork, the sponsors and the creators did several things right. For one, they were extremely careful to cast the raisins as entertainers, not salesmen.

TV ads often depict someone making a conscious choice of a product, then turning to the camera and smiling. Price says, "People are totally turned off by that. The magic of the spot just flies away. The only selling we do with the Raisins is when we have the other snack foods in the audience look on frightened, then back away."

Price says the Raisins were purposely cast as fun-loving, crazy California guys, just like the Beach Boys having fun in the summer sun. The idea was to "make people see raisins as funny little hip things. Then people will think if they eat raisins, they'll be hip, too."

The Raisins embodied what people everywhere — from Topeka, Kansas, to Paris, France — think of California's life-style. As Bruce Grieve, product manager for Post Raisin Bran, told the *Arizona Republic:* "If they'd been Nebraska Raisins, it wouldn't have worked."

Vinton believes the ads caught on because they touched the innocent little kid in every one of us. The music — rerecorded with a 1980s-style heavy dreambeat and CD-quality sound — took many thirty-to-forty-year-olds back to their carefree teens or college days. The ads, in a sense, were targeted at the "Big Chill" generation. But they were also designed to be hip and contemporary enough (one struts the Michael Jackson moonwalk) for everybody.

"We all need stuff like this to keep the world light," Vinton says. "That's what's most exciting and fun about Claymation. It sort of tickles everyone in a kidlike way, and you let down your guard for a minute. Even as jaded as I ought to be by now, when a good scene comes to life, it's absolutely mesmerizing."

Sid Cato

The Guru of Annual Reports

S ometimes the best way to be successful is to do something no one else is doing. And do it with passion. Consider Sid Cato. It's hard to imagine a business-news desk at a major newspaper or magazine in the United States that doesn't have Cato's telephone number on file somewhere. He is interviewed by the media about a hundred times a year and has been quoted in virtually all of the important business publications. Many have written profiles about him.

Why?

He has made himself the top authority — making him an eagerly sought news source — on annual reports, those glossy corporate accounts of performance that flood the mails to shareholders every March and April. Personally reading about a thousand annual reports a year, Cato charts their trends and unsparingly critiques their preparers in a monthly mailing, *Sid Cato's Newsletter on Annual Reports*. Because of his biting style, Cato has been called eveything from the Ralph Nader of annual reports to Sid Vicious. "I insult my subscribers," Cato says. "We do not pander. We do not give you what you want. After the first year in the business I decided I was going to be partisan. I was going to go up or down in flames."

Institutional Investor magazine, in a 1988 profile, called Cato the "self-appointed watchdog" of the annual report industry. "Cato wages a one-man war against corporate obfuscation, chief executive vanity and numbingly boring writing," the magazine said. "Any company that fails to measure up to his strict report-writing criteria is publicly raked over the coals."

Cato never holds back an opinion, even on himself. "I'm the nation's foremost annual report expert," Cato quickly tells callers to his rural Waukesha, Wisconsin, home, which also serves as his office. "Nobody else is doing what I'm doing." In business, Cato says, the secrets of success are not always what they seem. In his own case, he says many people think he is successful because he speaks well. He thinks it is because he is so outrageous. He isn't afraid to tell anybody anything if he believes it.

One issue of his newsletter, for example, began with this headline: "Get a Haircut and a Job, Hippie!" It featured two photographs of Kenneth Yarnell, Jr., president and chief operating officer of Primerica Corporation. One showed Yarnell as he was pictured in the company's annual report, long hair over his ears and shirt collar. The other photograph was enhanced, at Cato's instruction, to show Yarnell with a neat, short haircut. Cato called Primerica "a company dedicated — if you'll pardon the long-since-hackneyed phrase — to maximizing shareholder value. If not to visiting the barber."

About the only questions Cato won't discuss are the number of subscribers to his newsletter (he calls it a break-even proposition) and how much money he makes. "More than half my adult life I have spent working for myself," he says. "At the beginning of every month there is no money in the till."

Along with the newsletter, Cato offers seminars on the annual report business, speaks to executive and investor groups about what makes a good annual report, and consults with companies seeking help with their annual reports. His best advice is simple: "Tell the truth." Every September, his lists of the 10 best and 10 worst annual reports of the year appear in *Chief Executive*, a high-priced, glossy magazine for CEOs. The issue, which also includes an annual ranking of executive compensation, is always one of the magazine's most popular. It also gives Cato high credibility and visibility within the industry.

"Sid's the only guy I know of who sits back and judges annual reports on a regular basis," says J. P. Donlon, the editor of *Chief Executive*. "What intrigues me about him is that he is an independent. He is a specialist with a background in annual reports. He is not a frustrated analyst."

When Cato first approached Donlon in 1984 about running a ranking of the best annual reports, Donlon liked the idea, but only if it was accompanied by a list of the worst annual reports. "People learn from failure more than they do success," Donlon

Cato never holds back an opinion . . . He isn't afraid to tell anybody anything if he believes it.

says. Over the years Donlon has become convinced that when Cato speaks, people in the annual report business and chief executives listen. "A lot of people are wary of that list, and when it comes out," the editor says, "they don't want to be among the worst." Adds Dale Cooper, in charge of a General Motors annual report that once made Cato's 10 worst list: "You don't like it, but you can't help but notice."

Cato, born in 1933, has always been in the communications business. While in high school he worked at a small daily newspaper in Marshall, Michigan. "Everything we do prepares us for something else," Cato says. "The headline writing and page makeup skills I learned when I was sixteen are what I'm still using now." While in the military, he worked at *Stars and Stripes*. Then it was a series of public relations jobs for the National Safety Council, Greyhound Corporation (where he worked on his first annual report in 1962), his own and other PR firms, and Bunker Ramo Corporation. He has also

35

worked as a professional photographer and actor, and has done voice-overs for commercials.

A personal tragedy in 1975 almost ruined his life. His second wife and two of his children were killed in a car accident. Cato, who was driving, was seriously injured but recovered physically. The psychological recovery took years. "I was running day and night, doing anything to buy time, anything to keep alive," he says. He eventually wrote a book about the experience, *Healing Life's Great Hurts*, that he says helped him cope. It was written feverishly, in a period of twenty-eight days in mid-1983. That's also when he decided to start his newsletter and devote full time to his passion, annual reports.

Cato, who estimates he has personally helped produce more than fifty annual reports in his career, calls them a corporate Rorschach test. "They're a road map to the business world," he says. "While their overall quality is improving, he says that seven of eight he receives still reflect poorly on the companies that issue them. "Americans are constantly becoming more sophisticated," Cato says, pointing in particular to such technological innovations as satellite communications. "This is evolving in the corporate suite into an understanding that they've got to do a better job communicating. The annual report can be one of a company's best communications tools."

Cato, working alone with a computer that compiles his statistics, rates annual reports on a 135-point scale, scoring everything from the cover design to the chief executive's letter, the writing style, and the financial disclosures. He regularly surveys his subscribers to compile special reports on such subjects as preparation costs (the average exceeds $3 per copy) and the health of annual report preparers. Most preparers, for example, said they did experience some trauma during annual report season. Almost 14 percent said they broke out in a rash or hives. "Heaven will not have annual reports, but Hell will," one preparer wrote Cato.

That affinity for statistics also shows up in Cato's dealings with

36

the media. Every call is logged on a computer. He knows the largest number of calls he has ever received from a single reporter working on a single story (thirteen, from the *Wall Street Journal*), and the longest telephone interview (three hours, by the *Boston Globe*). "I'm a precise guy," laughs Cato.

Cato carefully guards his credibility by declining payment for consulting work with companies whose reports make his 10 best or 10 worst lists. If he advises a company and its report subsequently makes his 10 best list, he refunds the fee (usually about $1,000 to critique a report). Above all, Cato believes he is on a mission to improve annual reports. His published policy statement probably says it best: "Should any subscriber to Sid Cato's Newsletter on Annual Reports be relegated to our list of 10 worst ARs, we will provide a free year's add-on to the existing subscription. We will have failed miserably, and this will be our way of trying to make up for it."

37

Brandon Stoddard

The Thin Man Behind "Roseanne"

It was January 8, 1986, and Brandon Stoddard, the newly appointed president of ABC Entertainment, was disgusted with what he saw on American television. "I was angry about what ABC was," says Stoddard. "I was ashamed. Annoyed. But mostly I was angry about the bullshit that was on the screen. I knew what we had on the air was junk beyond belief."

That day, Stoddard shocked a bevy of pencil-wielding Hollywood reporters with his prescription to wrestle ABC back from the dead. He said that TV viewers "are tired of the predictable, the superficial and the cartoon on network prime time. I believe that the audience is not being treated with an essential attitude: respect."

Of course, everybody loves to criticize network TV. But Stoddard, now president of ABC's in-house production unit, wielded both the track record and the clout finally to do something about it. He is widely considered the father of the TV miniseries for developing "Roots," "The Winds of War," "The Thorn Birds," and "War and Remembrance." As president of ABC Motion Pictures, he was the genius behind phenomenally popular films such as *Silkwood*, *The Flamingo Kid*, and *Prizzi's Honor*. He came to ABC-TV in late 1985 on a rescue mission: to resuscitate ABC from its comatose state and revolutionize network television. "Before Brandon got here, we were floundering," admits ABC's Bob Wright. "Whole nights of the week were lost. We had started producing TV programs for some unknown audience in Peoria. It turned out nobody was watching them."

ABC wouldn't be broadcasting to empty living rooms for long. In less than two years, Stoddard would engineer perhaps the most profound turnabout in network television history. In 1988, ABC won a total of twenty-one Emmy awards, more than any other network. His first show, "thirtysomething," captured an Emmy as TV's best drama — the first time in eighteen years that ABC had won in that category. Another Stoddard masterpiece, "The Wonder Years," captured an Emmy for the best comedy. That was the first time in network history that two first-year shows won such prizes. Largely thanks to Stoddard, ABC leaped past CBS to number two in the ratings wars. But Stoddard's crowning achievement was undoubtedly "Roseanne," a situation comedy that zoomed past "The Cosby Show" to number one in the Nielsen ratings and became the biggest hit of 1989. In September 1989, ABC won five Emmy awards. Stoddard's shows won four of them. In 1990, "Twin Peaks," a series Stoddard helped nurture, caught the country by storm.

It's relatively easy to look at Stoddard's shows and spot the similarities: they're well written, they're extremely well cast and directed, but above all, they're about people and situations that are very real.

"When 'thirtysomething' hit the air, everybody said, 'What is this? Oh, my God, I don't believe this,' " Stoddard recalls. "There're no cops or chase scenes. . . . It's just a bunch of people, and kind of weird, not universal people. And they said, 'Gee, this is about character and relationships and about how human beings behave.' "

It's so real, in fact, that some viewers apparently don't realize where the show ends and reality begins. Tim Busfield, the red-bearded star of "thirtysomething," was walking down a grocery store aisle when a fan came up, chastised him for leaving his TV wife and

39

kids, and slapped him across the face. Busfield told her, "Lady, this isn't real," but his pleading obviously didn't do much good.

Stoddard didn't create "Roseanne." He doesn't write the scripts for "thirtysomething" or "The Wonder Years." But he put in place a philosophy, and an environment for change, that invited others to begin approaching network TV in a totally different way. Until Stoddard arrived, ABC's eggheads and its independent programmers tended to think in terms of Them (the audience) and Us (the broadcasters). In Stoddard's opinion, they were convinced that it was okay if they thought their programs were dumb and boring because the little old lady in Peoria would love it. They thought, We'll go home and watch PBS, and she'll sit home and watch "The Love Boat."

In his 1986 attack on network television, Stoddard tried to wreck that notion, arguing, "I'm going to bet my job that the little old lady in Peoria thinks it's dumb and boring, too."

If you've ever watched network TV, you know exactly what Stoddard is talking about. All too often, the programs slip into a formula. "Get in doubt?" Stoddard says. "Throw in a car chase. Get in doubt? Throw in a sex scene. Viewers will like that. And it was awful. It had absolutely no connection to how people feel."

What Stoddard brought to the table was, in retrospect, a wondrously simple approach — write and produce TV shows that *you* and your friends would want to go home and watch. Get rid of this notion of Us and Them. He told his troops, "If we aren't excited about it, if we don't think our shows are entertaining and involving, why the hell should they?"

Within ABC, Stoddard's crusade became a beacon of hope for his entire staff of programmers. The shackles on creativity and risk-taking disappeared. Power was shifted to thirteen divisional managers (in charge of children's programming, drama development, comedy development, and so on), who were given the autonomy to succeed or fail with programs the network never would have considered before.

40

Timothy Busfield, Patricia Wettig, Ken Olin, and Mel Harris of ABC's "thirtysomething"

"Under Brandon, they've allowed me to do my job without having to explain why or worry about them looking over my shoulder," said Stu Bloomberg, ABC's vice president of comedy and variety series development. "There's been such great freedom. We don't have all this second-guessing."

For nearly two decades, Stoddard had sat in on meetings where the producer and director told the writers to do such and such in act 2, or move this or that to act 3. When that happens, "You can just watch the writer's mind start to float away. Inside, he's getting angry and thinking, 'What's this little shit telling me this for?' As a result, the script winds up stinking beyond belief."

In that situation, instead of writing for himself, the writer structures the story to please his boss, mainly because he's scared. The result, says Stoddard, usually is programming that is flat, boring, and passionless. People writing for ABC were encouraged to go down a different path. He says, "Editors never pay the bills. Writers do. You only have a chance if there's excitement, enthusiasm among the writers."

Given the responsibility, the writers will do their work knowing it's up to them to succeed or fail. If the show flies, that's great. If it bombs, it's their fault. Stoddard's hands-off approach and his programming philosophy enabled his managerial team to talk to independent producers in a language ABC had never used before. That relationship is critical, since the independent houses create most of the smash hits on network TV. Before ABC's philosophy changed, "we couldn't get anybody good to return our phone calls," Stoddard says. "They didn't want to be at ABC. Hell, *I* didn't want to be at ABC."

Programming actions, of course, spoke louder than words. When ABC first test-marketed "thirtysomething," half the people who saw it hated it. The casting was too narrow. The yuppie-angst plots and scenes, such as one in which a character graphically discusses a birth

42

control device, seemed too extreme for network TV. But Stoddard plunged ahead — and surrounded himself with people who felt the same way. Outside producers saw that and the floodgates opened.

In early 1988, Bloomberg got a call from the hottest TV producers in Hollywood, Marcy Carsey and Tom Werner, the creative geniuses behind "A Different World" and the number-one-rated "Cosby Show." Carsey and Werner had a loosely formed idea for a comedy show about a working mother starring Roseanne Barr, a stand-up comedian they'd watched perform on HBO and the "Tonight" show. Ironically, the dynamic duo had approached NBC with their plan but NBC turned them down flat, just as ABC had refused to air "The Cosby Show" several years before. Carsey says, "We knew that we could have pushed NBC with our clout from 'Cosby.' "

But she and Werner were too excited about working with Stoddard. She says, "We really believed in the people at ABC. Just like Brandon, we thought the single biggest mistake is to do something for an audience out there that's different from yourselves."

At a breakfast meeting with Bloomberg, Carsey and Werner talked about the amazing fact that there wasn't one real blue-collar working woman on TV. Some shows featured working mothers, but they weren't realistically portrayed. They mentioned that 65 percent of mothers work, and most of them have a tough time just making it through the day.

"Lots of us in this company are working moms," says Carsey, a mother of two. "We know how funny it is, how hard it is, how awful it is. There are millions of moms out there who are tired and mad about how all this came to be."

The series they were envisioning would be almost anti-"Cosby." It would show what it's like to come home, after eight hours on the job, to a cranky husband, wailing kids, a kitchen littered with dirty dishes, and piles of laundry. It would show how hard it is for one family just to get along without killing each other.

43

"There just wasn't that kind of combustive family anywhere on TV," says Bloomberg. "We really felt the time was right for it."

They were once again violating all the TV rules: You should never put someone unattractive in a comedy. You don't show dirty kitchens. You idealize the American family.

Much has been made of the fact that "Roseanne" succeeded because the character proves that it's okay to be fat, it's okay to yell at your husband, it's okay for a working mom to scream at her kids. Perhaps. But the show began to click for two main reasons: the sheer strength of the scripts and the talents of Roseanne Barr and her TV husband, John Goodman. The scripts took a relatively simple subject — a wife wanting to quit her job, a daughter experiencing her first menstrual period, Mom being called in to see her child's teacher — and built a powerful story line and wisecracking script around it.

"We basically sat back and asked, What's going on in our own lives?" Carsey says. "We work, we go home, we raise kids. We're not so different from anyone else."

The producers brought in Matt Williams, a "Cosby Show" veteran, to write scripts and another working mom, Ellen Falcon, as director. (Both would later leave the show after widely publicized personality clashes with Barr.) But Barr and Goodman were the key. Just as they had done with Cosby, the producers gave Barr free rein to establish her own character.

"We'd seen Barr's monologues and we thought, If we can take that anger, that point of view, and give it to a working wife, we'll be in business," said Carsey.

Barr, in her monologues, ridiculed the old-style TV housewife. "I never could take that Lucy had to beg her husband for five dollars and then he spanks her," Roseanne told *USA Today*. "I've always hated 'I Love Lucy.'" Roseanne, a mother of two, has tried to show that women, as comedians or as family members, should be able to do exactly what men do.

The creators of "Roseanne" also realized that Barr's husband, who would bear the brunt of her verbal abuse, had to be a strong, lovable character, too. Goodman, a star in *Raising Arizona* (with Holly Hunter and Nicholas Cage), was the only actor they considered. In fact, the producers blew a premium time-slot on ABC because they had to wait four months for Goodman to finish making another movie, *Everybody's All-American,* co-starring Dennis Quaid.

"We watched the two of them, Roseanne and John, sitting on a couch and we could see the chemistry," Stoddard recalls. "From day one, we knew this show was going to be very, very special."

Special, perhaps, but why did it become such a megahit?

It certainly wasn't the result of some grand plan to tap into some predetermined audience. As Stoddard says, "I don't think any of us sit down and say, 'Gee, what is the collective unconscious of the American psyche today?' For example, the word 'yuppie' never crosses my lips." Adds Carsey, "Tom and I don't believe in trends. We don't watch for them at all." Stoddard, Carsey, and Werner don't believe in focus groups either; focus groups make too many mistakes. For instance, these groups concluded that "All in the Family" and "thirtysomething" wouldn't succeed. They said "Studio 5B" would be a superhit and it was a disaster. "If you've got a radically new idea, it's really hard to research it," Stoddard says. "The research relates to what people saw in the past. We didn't do 'thirtysomething' to tap into the baby boomers. We did it because we liked it."

Intentionally or not, "Roseanne" popped onto our TV screens at a perfect time for millions of working moms and husbands. In the past, TV tended to patronize working-class people, not identify with them. Says Stoddard, "Roseanne reflects the way women feel and their position in today's family. She's not perfect and svelte with gorgeous blond hair, and she says outrageous things. She picks up the kid and throws him off the couch and says 'I'm going to kill you.' And viewers look at that and say, 'That's me!' "

45

The comedy, much of it written or ad-libbed by Barr, takes the edge off the hard-hitting reality. As Barr told *Time* magazine, "I call my stuff three-day comedy. First they laugh, and three days later they go, 'Oh, God, this is what she was talking about.' Once the brain is stretched, though, they can't go back. It's too late." In one memorable scene, Barr and Goodman lie down in bed and agree that both will call in sick the next day. They boldly agree to sleep in for a change because both are tired of their stupid jobs. But just as they begin to drift off, Roseanne whispers, "Honey, is the alarm set?" and Goodman, muttering matter-of-factly through his pillow, says, "Yeah."

Ultimately, what Stoddard and company managed to do was to reach out from the TV and tug at people's emotions in a way they'd never been tugged at before. You laugh. You cry. You sympathize. But it's not because you're caught up in some sort of fantasyland that doesn't exist.

"That's why reality programming is working now," Stoddard says. "Most of TV when we started was full of bullshit. We realized that television, even more so than movies, can convey emotion. There's a deep intensity between the viewer and what's going on on that screen because it's real. And it's not being written by some guy up in Malibu with a silk shirt and chains."

Stoddard isn't sure why, but people are tired of being hyped, manipulated, maneuvered, and lowballed on TV. Perhaps they're reacting to the feel-good fantasy of the Reagan years. Or they're wising up to the fact that they can demand better. He says a new generation of viewers, largely the baby boomers, won't sit still for "Matlock" every Tuesday night like their parents will. Often, they'll watch only one or two shows a week. TV networks that don't cater to them will see their fortunes disappear.

"We have to develop shows with new rules, new approaches for them," Stoddard says. " 'Hill Street Blues' started all this. You have to teach people how to watch these shows. Older viewers say forget it:

they want this to happen in act one, this in act two, et cetera. Now there are no rules. The audience is so smart. They know a cheap joke. They know when they've seen something a hundred thousand times. So you have to involve them, give them something they can get a hold of and care about and connect to. You have to build programs around all those tiny little moments in people's lives."

Make the Complex Simple

two

There's a marvelous story, probably embellished by memory as are most sports legends, about University of Southern California football coach John McKay. This was when O. J. Simpson was rushing toward the Trojans' record book. At a clinic for high school coaches, McKay diagrammed a running play with a complicated blocking scheme that worked particularly well for his team. After he finished drawing the pulling guards, the sealing tackles and ends, and the leading backs, *X*'s and *O*'s covered the chalkboard. One coach, anxious to learn something he could use with his own team, asked for the real reason the play was so successful. McKay calmly turned to the board and wrote

"9.4." That, of course, was O.J.'s time (in seconds) for the hundred-yard dash. McKay was telling the high school coaches that O.J. was a superb athlete. No question. But more important, he was giving them a simple glimpse of athletic truth: Speed wins. Find your fastest players and make sure they get the ball. Because no matter how sophisticated the blocking pattern or how brilliant the strategy, if the runner is too slow, the play, and eventually the coach, are doomed.

One route to success, as the people in the following two chapters have learned, is to make the complex simple. With simplicity comes understanding. With understanding comes bet-

49

ter performance. The focus is on what really counts, and muddling distractions are ignored.

As reporters for the *Philadelphia Inquirer*, Donald Barlett and James Steele have won two Pulitzer Prizes and numerous other journalism awards. They take a mountain of information gathered through months of research, then they refine and focus it into easily understood stories for millions of readers. And because the stories are understood, they get results, such as indictments for criminals and changes in federal tax laws. Likewise, Peter Lynch, the recently retired master of mutual funds, relied as much on what he called the power of common knowledge as he did on stacks of company reports, brokerage summaries, and other elaborate investment research when he decided what stocks to buy for his huge Fidelity Magellan Fund. His wife, for example, pointed him toward one of his best investments (Hanes) because she liked the company's L'eggs panty hose. The best test of a company's products is the simplest: Do the people who use them like them? Lynch developed what he called a short, two-minute story explaining the essential reasons he owned a stock. When the story changed, he changed his strategy, by selling or buying more.

Making the complex simple is not easy. The key word is "simplicity," not "simplemindedness." The goal is to help people understand so they can do their jobs better or make better decisions. Even for Barlett and Steele, who have worked together for twenty years, it takes weeks of writing and rewriting to find the simple phrases that best convey their complex messages. The same challenge faces anyone who seeks to make the complex simple.

Barlett and Steele

The Pulitzer Touch

The final days of every project are always the same for investigative reporters Donald Barlett and James Steele. They usually work sixteen to eighteen hours, seven days a week, and grab quick meals at the Roy Rogers restaurant across Broad Street from the *Philadelphia Inquirer* building. Sometimes they are still tinkering with their copy at ten P.M. on the composing room floor, minutes before the pages close and the presses roll.

So it was in the spring of 1988 as they feverishly finished writing, rewriting, and polishing their series called "The Great Tax Giveaway." The seven-day, 40,000-word package of stories about special tax favors for the rich and powerful would eventually win a 1989 Pulitzer Prize, the second for Barlett and Steele, and become one of the most decorated pieces of journalism ever, winning ten major national awards.

But those would come later. Now, after fifteen months of research and preliminary drafts, they are hunkered down in their small, fourth-floor office just off the business-news department. It's crunch time, strictly do not disturb, when in walks Gene Roberts, *Inquirer* executive editor and president. In what has become a ritual visit near the end of each project. Roberts sits down, puts his feet up on a desk, and asks Barlett and Steele, "Well, what are you guys going to do next?"

51

"Our response almost each time is, 'Huh?' " says Barlett.

With deadline near, the last thing they want to think about is what's next. And that's exactly Roberts's motivation. "People doing long projects usually don't have any idea what they're going to do next," explains Roberts, who is credited with making the *Inquirer* one of the best newspapers in America. "There could be a lot of slippage if you don't get them thinking in that direction."

During a two-decade period of working together, an unusually long partnership in such an ego-filled field as writing, Barlett and Steele have written some of the most influential and acclaimed newspaper journalism in the country. Their work on the Federal Housing Administration (FHA), criminal justice in Philadelphia, foreign aid, Howard Hughes, the oil crisis, and nuclear waste has been widely copied by other papers. (The Hughes and nuclear projects also evolved into books, published by W. W. Norton.) Their work also gets results: criminal indictments, government reforms, and important policy shifts.

Known for their meticulous searches of public records, Barlett and Steele say one of the main reasons they have been so successful is the *Inquirer* system. They have found the perfect place in which to practice their style of reporting. In fact, they doubt if they could do the same level of work anyplace else. Under Roberts, the newspaper's editors encourage project reporting and good writing. Editors monitor projects closely and regularly make critiques and suggestions, but they also try to leave room for the reporter's autonomy. "I've never heard anyone around here say, 'Do it this way because I'm the editor,' " Barlett says. The newspaper, Barlett and Steele say, gives them the flexibility to do whatever needs to be done to complete a project. Barlett, for example, spent two weeks checking unalphabetized business-partnership ledgers in Chicago to find the names of the people involved in just one of the more than one hundred special breaks they investigated for the "Tax Giveaway" series.

Altogether, they interviewed people living in more than two dozen states.

For these reporters, along with flexibility comes the freedom to plunge into some topics without knowing exactly what they'll find. "We never assume what we're going to get and we never assume limitations on what we're going to get," Barlett says.

That kind of commitment costs money. Roberts says the *Inquirer* has no specific budget for investigative reporting; it's just part of the normal operating process. He wouldn't even guess how much "The Great Tax Giveaway" cost, saying it would imply that kind of reporting was a luxury when it should be a necessity at every newspaper. Counting reporters' time, travel, lodging, and other expenses, however, the tab for the series could easily have run into several hundred thousand dollars. Barlett and Steele say some of their biggest bills, sometimes even more than for travel, are for copying documents and searching electronic data bases.

Two principles guide their work. One is the essence of news and the admonition of newspaper editors everywhere: Tell me something I didn't know. The other is the product of curiosity and instinct: There is nothing you can't know. "There are only two constraints on learning anything," Barlett says. "Time and money. And one is the function of the other." One of the special tax provisions, for example, involved a foreign trust. Barlett was confident he could track the item, though it would probably mean checking records in several European countries. "I could have found out who was behind it," Barlett says. "But Roberts wanted the series published sometime during the decade."

Because of the nature of their work, Barlett and Steele are regularly threatened with lawsuits. As in the "Tax Giveaway" series, their stories can cost certain individuals millions of dollars. But, and they are reluctant to admit it, they have never been sued. Just by saying that, they fear they'll hang a giant target around their necks on future stories. "I'm trying to get through my career without being sued," Barlett says. "I think the main reason we haven't is because of the documentation we compile on a story. It's hard to argue with a piece of paper."

Barlett and Steele both joined the *Inquirer* in 1970, the same year the paper was bought by Knight Newspapers. Barlett, then thirty-four, was an investigative reporter and Steele was a twenty-seven-year-old urban-affairs reporter. Barlett previously worked at the *Chicago Daily News*, the *Cleveland Plain Dealer*, the *Akron Beacon Journal*, and the *Reading* (Pa.) *Times*. He also served as a special agent with the U.S. Army Counter Intelligence Corps. Steele previously worked at the *Kansas City Times*.

Their first collaboration came in 1971. It was a project about widespread FHA fraud in Philadelphia. Real estate speculators had been buying substandard houses, making minimal repairs, and then selling the houses at inflated prices to poor families who couldn't afford the upkeep. When the new owners defaulted, mortgage companies — who made the loans through the speculators — collected the government mortgage insurance. Like the great savings-and-loan fiasco of the 1980s, a government program had literally taken the risk out of speculation and guaranteed huge profits. The byline on the finished articles read: By Donald L. Barlett and James B. Steele. Although they split the writing duties evenly, the byline has remained the same ever since.

"What was supposed to be a three-month project just evolved and went on for a year, resulting in federal grand jury indictments," Steele says. "When it was over, everyone assumed we would go our separate ways."

They didn't. Instead, they proposed a series of articles on the Philadelphia criminal court system. Their findings, after a seven-month investigation, were summarized near the top of their first story: "All too often, the innocent go to jail, the guilty go free or receive

Donald L. Barlett and
James B. Steele,
Pulitzer Prize–winning
reporters at the
Philadelphia Inquirer

light sentences. It is a system that really is no system at all and it has very little to do with justice."

Neither knows exactly when they became an inseparable team. They simply continued working together. "The irony of it all," says Steele, "is that nobody ever said, 'You guys are a team.' " Now they wouldn't work any other way. "One of the most powerful things is bouncing ideas off each other, using each other as a sounding board," Steele says. "Especially on some of the real complicated things like taxes."

At some of the other papers where he worked, Barlett says editors teamed him with younger reporters who could learn from his experience. He didn't want that at the *Inquirer*. What first impressed him about Steele was his accuracy and thoroughness. "Neither of us has an overwhelming ego when it comes to writing," Barlett says. "When you're dealing with complex stories, there are a million and one ways to write them anyway. Whether you're getting to the people, the readers, is what's important, not who writes it."

Their first Pulitzer Prize, journalism's highest award, came in 1975, for a series that ran in 1974 entitled "Auditing the IRS." It was also the first Pulitzer for the *Inquirer*. From then through 1990, under Roberts's direction, the *Inquirer* won 17 Pulitzers, second only to the *New York Times*, with 21 Pulitzers during the same span.

"Most people who undertake investigative reporting go out hoping to catch a crook or free someone from jail," Roberts says, explaining the appeal of Barlett and Steele. "It may be important, but even if their hunch is right they may never be able to prove it. Barlett and Steele's method is to take something intrinsically interesting and examine it. The subjects they choose are good stories no matter how they turn out."

Burl Osborne, editor and president of the *Dallas Morning News* and a member of the board that selects the Pulitzer Prize winners, says Barlett and Steele are particularly good at getting "right to the bone" of an issue. "And they frequently choose hot-button subjects," says Osborne, emphasizing the importance of a strong story idea.

One of Roberts's favorite Barlett and Steele projects is "Oil: The Created Crisis," completed in 1973 soon after he became editor of the *Inquirer*. The first gas lines of the decade were shocking American consumers. Prolonged problems were forecast. Instead of repeating the conventional explanation of too much demand and too little supply, Barlett and Steele wrote that the shortages resulted from the oil industry's emphasis on overseas production, a lack of refining capacity in the United States, and bad government policy, especially President Nixon's failure to lift oil import restrictions when he took office. For example, at the same time American multinational oil companies were urging their customers in the United States to conserve and cut oil consumption, they were urging European and Asian customers to buy more oil.

The stories outraged the major oil companies, who disputed some of the findings and implications. (In 1980, another Barlett and Steele series, "Energy Anarchy," also brought protests from the oil companies, especially Exxon.) But despite the pressure, Roberts has never wavered. "I think the finest reporting they've done has not won awards because it was too far ahead of its time," Roberts says. "There was no way of testing the accuracy of it. The first oil series was read a lot and caused a lot of commentary but it didn't win a Pulitzer. By the next year, however, events had caught up and it was a big story."

That first series on oil, Roberts admits, may have set the stage for the Pulitzer-winning series on the IRS, which revealed how the agency failed to collect billions in taxes that were due, and how enforcement policies favored the wealthy. "What I always figured is that by the time another year rolled around, they had appeared so right and prophetic that people felt they should get the Pulitzer," Roberts says. "But of the two stories, oil was better."

Likewise, Roberts thinks timing helped "The Great Tax Give-

57

away." Barlett and Steele had done a number of stories over several months in 1986 about the Tax Reform Act, analyzing its effect. But even though they revealed many of the same special-interest loopholes they would again address two years later, the 1986 stories didn't get much reaction. "Another year went by," Roberts says. "People thought their taxes were going down, but they went up instead. They started thinking they had been had. If they didn't gain, who did? Barlett and Steele come along and tell them."

The reaction was overwhelming. Forty thousand requests for reprints of the articles came to the *Inquirer*, more than for any other Barlett and Steele series or *Inquirer* special project. The two reporters received hundreds of letters from readers, many of whom also sent letters to Congress. "I used to believe that the 'American Dream' could be attained through education and hard work," Elizabeth Ehrhorn of Mount Gretna, Pennsylvania, wrote after reading the series, "but now I know that it comes through influence peddling and knowing people in high places." The public outcry forced Congress to yank many of the newest special-interest breaks from pending legislation.

In addition to the Pulitzer for national reporting, "The Great Tax Giveaway" won the Associated Press Managing Editors Public Service Award, the George Polk Award for Economic Reporting, the Scripps-Howard Foundation's Roy W. Howard Award, the Sigma Delta Chi Distinguished Service Award in Public Service, the Investigative Reporters and Editors Gold Medal, the Gerald Loeb Award for Distinguished Business and Financial Journalism, the American Bar Association Silver Gavel Award, the National Headliner Award Special Citation, and the George Orwell Award for Distinguished Contribution to Honesty and Clarity in Public Language. Barlett and Steele are especially fond of the last award because it was given by the National Council of Teachers of English.

"There are not too many other awards to win," Roberts says.

Normally, Barlett and Steele begin a project with a general idea and spend the first few weeks reading everything available on the subject. "I think that's one way we're different," Barlett says. "Most newspaper people tend to focus on specifics at the start. We tend to vacuum everything we can at the start and narrow the focus as we go along."

On "The Great Tax Giveaway," however, they had a running start because of their earlier work. "Once the Tax Reform Act passed, we thought the transitional rules alone were worth looking at," Steele says. "The series was a rifle shot."

In 1986, congressional tax writers added at least 650 transitional rules to the tax code. These tax concessions, which were intended to cushion the impact of the shift from the old law to the new, cost at least $10.6 billion, according to government estimates. Probably several times more, Barlett and Steele wrote. In 1988, when the Barlett and Steele series ran, Congress was ready to do it again, adding private provisions to a bill designed to remedy some of the defects in the 1986 act.

The most insidious thing about the special-interest provisions, which tended to benefit the rich and influential, was that they were written in obscure language that hid the identities of the beneficiaries. The tax-writing committees refused to reveal their names. That's one reason the reporters' project took fifteen months. (Another result of the series was that it helped start a movement in Congress to make public the names of the intended beneficiaries of special tax breaks.)

When the series finally ran, it displayed many of the trademarks of Barlett and Steele: clear, concise writing; nothing fancy or slick; an ability to translate complicated subjects and concepts into easily understood terms; and, as Steve Lovelady, the *Inquirer*'s associate executive editor, says, "an overwhelming avalanche of evidence."

Here's how Barlett and Steele began their report:

59

Imagine, if you will, that you are a tall, bald father of three living in a Northeast Philadelphia rowhouse and selling aluminum siding door-to-door for a living.

Imagine that you go to your congressman and ask him to insert a provision in the federal tax code that exempts tall, bald fathers of three living in Northeast Philadelphia and selling aluminum siding for a living from paying taxes on income from door-to-door sales.

Imagine further that your congressman cooperates, writes that exemption and inserts it into pending legislation. And that Congress then actually passes it into law.

Lots of luck.

The story of how those opening paragraphs came about gives some insights into how the *Inquirer* system works and why the newspaper, and Barlett and Steele, have been so successful. The worst sin a newspaper can commit, Lovelady says, is to waste superb reporting on a story that is poorly written and organized. The *Inquirer* tries to deliver the total package.

"That series went through several revisions," says Lovelady, who oversees project reporting. "Nothing seemed to get to the heart of it. Nothing seemed to grab the reader by the throat. They had given me rough drafts of the first three parts and I didn't like how any of them began. But I was daydreaming in my office one day and scribbled that hypothetical on a piece of scrap paper. Just about that time, Barlett walked in. I showed him the opening, which I thought would work with part three of the series. He said, 'Forget part three. This is the opening for part one,' and he walked away."

The opening, which took all the secret machinations in Washington and dropped them on the reader's doorstep, was quickly followed by specific examples: a Fort Worth widow who could escape $4 million in estate taxes; a Dallas company that could avoid nearly $6 million in taxes and penalties; a Long Beach, California, pipeline company that could eventually avoid a half billion in taxes; and many more.

"The lead wouldn't have worked without the specifics that followed," Steele says. Together, they made the point much more powerfully than either the hypothetical by itself or the examples by themselves.

Editing Barlett and Steele, Roberts says, is not like "editing everyday human beings. They hatch all these schemes to get more space in the paper. When you ask them a question, they say, 'That's a very good question, we'll report back to you.' When they do, it means another ten pages of copy."

In this age of bite-size, *USA Today*–influenced journalism, Roberts defends the length of *Inquirer* projects. "Some stories have to be long because they deal with complicated subjects," he says. "If you tried to do it short, you wouldn't really prove your case." With length, however, comes the obligation to make it readable. Even Roberts tinkers with the wording on some *Inquirer* projects, including Barlett and Steele's.

While the finished result of their months of research makes for fascinating reading, Barlett and Steele say their methods are "often not very exciting." When they examined American foreign aid, for example, some State Department officials, after much reluctance, finally put them in a room with a table that was piled high with documents. Thinking Barlett and Steele would be discouraged by the mound of material, the officials were surprised when the reporters returned day after day to methodically read it all. They review all documents themselves rather than use assistants. "You can't predict in advance when you might see something that leads you in another direction," Steele says. That tenacious approach caused *Newsweek* to headline a story about Barlett and Steele "Two Reporters You Don't Want on Your Tail."

In the early years of working together, they waited until they finished all their research before writing. Now they write sections of articles as they are researching. They say it helps them organize their material, focus it, and determine what else is needed.

61

A great danger in project reporting is losing focus. Reporters become overwhelmed by the amount of material they have or they get sidetracked. "Every paper is littered with the bodies of guys who have gone off on tangents," Steele says. Barlett says he and his partner have been able to avoid this pitfall by relying on their instincts about what's important. "I don't think we've ever thought about going down the wrong track," he says.

Lovelady employs an effective technique to avoid what he calls journalistic dry holes. At any one time, the *Inquirer* may have a half-dozen teams, each with two reporters, working on projects. If Love-lady senses a reporter is getting lost in his or her material, he makes the reporter stand, not sit, in front of his desk and explain in twenty-five words or less what he or she is trying to do. He borrowed the idea from old-time Broadway producer David Belasco. "Belasco said if you can't write your idea on the back of my calling card, then you don't have an idea," Lovelady explains.

Because of the *Inquirer*'s consistent success in winning awards in recent years, the paper has been accused by some of writing for prizes, not for readers. Roberts disputes the charge. "The truth is, we have no idea what's going to win a Pulitzer, and the best stuff almost always doesn't," he says. There also has been some feeling that the Pulitzer board acts like a club, passing out prizes to its members. Roberts is on the board, which selects the ultimate winner from a list of three finalists submitted by a jury. "The fact is, whenever an *Inquirer* or any Knight-Ridder story is on the table, Gene Roberts is out of the room," the *Morning News*'s Osborne says. "People aren't allowed to judge work from their own organizations. In reality, I've seen good friends argue with good friends about what should win."

For their part, Barlett and Steele say they don't think about prizes while they work on their projects. They judge the success of a story by reader response, phone calls, and letters. They acknowledge internal pressure to continue to do good work, but no pressure to win prizes. "What drives us is whatever we're doing," Steele says. "We like the subject, we enjoy the work." Besides, they admit, after "The Great Tax Giveaway," a lot of pressure is gone because they know nothing else will ever quite measure up. "There's no way in the world another series is going to win as many awards as the tax series," Barlett says.

That leaves them only to ponder Roberts's eternal question: "What are you guys going to do next?"

Make the Complex Simple

Peter Lynch and the Magellan Fund

Zen and the Art of Investing

I f Hollywood ever makes a movie about Peter Lynch, the stock-picking wizard who compiled the most envied mutual fund record on Wall Street before retiring at age forty-six in early 1990, here's the opening sequence:

Lynch, dressed in a nice but anonymous dark suit and overcoat, emerges from his suburban Boston home. It's 6:15 on a cold November morning and still dark. A light breeze blows Lynch's white hair as the camera follows him to a waiting car. The Andy Warhol look-alike gets in next to the driver, says hello to his car-pooling neighbors, quickly wipes the fog from his metal-frame glasses, and plugs a small reading lamp into the cigarette lighter. As the opening credits roll, this modern-day Goldfinger flips through annual reports and studies investment research during the forty-five-minute commute to his downtown Boston office. There, as he settles behind his cluttered desk, with more research reports piled high on tables and the floor around him, Lynch can be heard explaining to his first business contact of the day, a European money manager calling from London, "I never drive to work. It's a waste of time."

When you ask Peter Lynch how he was able to compile the most successful mutual fund investment record of the 1980s, he is quick with answers. Among the primary factors he looked for before investing in a company was an industry he could understand. If the company had a mundane name and little or no competition, if it made an

64

everyday product that people had to keep using, if its own executives were buying shares, and if it wasn't followed by many Wall Street analysts, all the better. And there had to be some evidence of continued earnings growth.

Above all, Lynch says about investing, keep it simple. Develop a succinct story — two minutes or less — telling why you own a particular stock. If the story improves, buy more. If it deteriorates, sell. "Go for a business that any idiot can run, because sooner or later any idiot probably is going to be running it," he says.

Lynch also worked harder than just about anyone else in the business. One of the reasons he retired so young was so that he could spend more time with his family. His job had become an all-consuming passion. Example: a 1989 interview in Dallas. "Are we almost finished?" he asked his interviewer as the time approached half past noon. "I've got to call my companies." Even though Lynch was in the middle of an eleven-day nationwide tour promoting his best-selling stock market book, *One Up on Wall Street,* on radio, television, and in newspapers, he couldn't miss this daily regimen. For the next hour, he called executives of firms his huge Fidelity Magellan Fund has invested in or might be investing in, asking them how, if at all, the company's story had changed. He continually took notes. Lynch called about two thousand different companies a year on the telephone and personally visited with executives of another five hundred. His first question: When was the last time a Wall Street analyst visited the company?

That was just part of his normal research routine during a seventy-hour work week. He regularly called Wall Street analysts and other fund managers, asking them what they had learned recently. His reading list consisted of annual and quarterly reports, brokerage summaries, and financial-news publications. His stack of daily mail was three to four feet high. It accumulated on side tables in his office all week until Saturday, when he decided which 5 percent he wanted

65

to read. "If you want to call me Saturday morning at seven A.M., I'll be at the office," Lynch said then. One week a month he was on the road visiting companies. He rarely took vacations, and when he did, he usually combined the trip with visits to companies.

Lynch then blended all the serious research with what he calls "the power of common knowledge." By that he means taking what you know from everyday living and putting it to investment use. This ability to think and act like an individual investor is what separated him from other large institutional investors, Lynch says. His wife, for example, once liked a new kind of panty hose (L'eggs), so he bought stock in the company (Hanes). It turned out to be one of his best investments. Another big winner was La Quinta Motor Inns. He was talking with one of the largest franchisees of Holiday Inns when the person praised La Quinta. "If a company ever says something positive about a competitor, it's true," Lynch says.

Out of this approach filtered an investment style that was more of an art form than a science. Syndicated financial columnist Scott Burns calls it "informed innocence."

"What is most striking about Lynch is his total lack of hubris," Burns wrote in 1989. "He does not manage by modern portfolio theory, there are no computers grinding and screening away, and there is no single compelling idea that informs the Lynch view of the world. His name and Boston College education notwithstanding, Lynch views the world with a Zen-like clarity, uncluttered by preconceptions, ready to accept the positive where it is found — and invest in it."

There is no arguing with Lynch's results. *Institutional Investor*, the bible of money managers, says, "No one in the history of money management has ever performed so well with such a big mutual fund." The *Wall Street Journal*, in its 1989 centennial issue, called Lynch one of the ten most influential business people of his time. "Peter Lynch didn't invent mutual funds," the *Journal* said. "He didn't create an organization to sell, nor did he introduce a wildly innovative investment product. The Newton, Mass., native simply set a string of performance records that, like Babe Ruth's or John Wooden's, may be broken but should never be forgotten."

The best testament to Lynch's ability is the performance of Magellan itself. It is the largest stock mutual fund in existence, with about one million shareholders. Lynch joined Fidelity in 1969 after earning an M.B.A. at the Wharton School of Finance and Commerce and spending two years in the army. When he took over the fund in May 1977, it had assets of about $20 million invested in 40 stocks. When he retired, it had assets of more than $13 billion invested in about 1,400 stocks. If you had entrusted Lynch with $10,000 when he took over Magellan, your investment would have been worth more than $250,000 when he retired. Lynch's fund never

Above all, Lynch says, keep it simple. Develop a succinct story — two minutes or less — telling why you own a particular stock.

had a down year, not even when the market plummeted in 1987. Magellan, clobbered like everyone else by the crash, started buying again a couple days after October 19 and finished the year up 1 percent. If you're in the stock market, Lynch says, you have to expect big declines as well as big gains and look at the long term. His great stocks, he says, were strong performers in the second, third, and fourth years he owned them.

Helped by that record and reputation, Lynch's book remained on the best-seller lists for months in 1989 and was uniformly reviewed as one of the best stock market investment guides of recent memory. Lynch won't say what he earned at Fidelity, but several publications estimate his income at more than $3 million a year. More important to his personal finances is his 5 percent stake in Fidelity, the privately

67

held financial services firm that runs Magellan and many other funds. His share could be worth $100 million, by some estimates.

While information was the cornerstone of Lynch's system, his actual purchases of stock were guided by two other closely related principles. First, companies, like people, have life cycles. Simply put, if a company has a fifteen-year glory period, Lynch says, an investor should avoid the first five years, when things may still be shaky, and the last five years, when competition swarms the industry. Concentrate on the middle. "It's not the nature of the capitalist system for companies to continue to do well," he says.

The second principle could be called nibbling. When Lynch thought he had found a good stock, rather than jump in all at once he would buy just a little. That forced him to keep watching. If the company's story continued to improve, he'd buy more. Lynch compares this process with stud poker. As his hand improved, he raised his bet. Then, when he thought he had a big winner, he'd make a huge commitment, buying a million shares or more.

At one point during 1989, for example, Magellan held a $400 million stake in the Federal National Mortgage Association, and $100 million–plus stakes in Ford Motor Company, General Electric, American Express, IBM, and General Motors. Of the sometimes more than 1,400 stocks the Magellan Fund owned at any one time during Lynch's tenure, about 200 accounted for more than half the fund's money. When he liked one stock in a particular category, he often bought many companies in the same category. Once, Lynch laughs, he owned stock in practically every auto company in the world.

The most significant stock Magellan ever owned was an auto company, Chrysler Corporation. At one point, when the existence of the company was in doubt, the stock bottomed at $1.50 a share. Lynch thought he had enough information about Chrysler's turnaround prospects to buy when the stock was $4, but he held back. He started buying at $6, unadjusted for later splits, in early 1982. The price increased fivefold in two years, and fifteenfold in five years. At one point, Lynch had committed 5 percent of Magellan's assets to Chrysler stock.

Even then, one of the main reasons Chrysler improved so much came as a surprise to Lynch. He thought the company's Laser and Daytona models would be hugely successful. Instead, the Voyager and Caravan minivans, which he hadn't attached much importance to, created a whole new market segment. Chrysler minivans account for 3 percent of all the cars and trucks sold in the United States.

"That's what really made the company go," Lynch says. "And that's why you can't put this investment stuff in a computer."

Tap the Power
of Every Individual

three

As kids, we learn through fairy tales that every creature has something to contribute, if given the chance. Rudolph the red-nosed reindeer is the laughing-stock of the herd until Santa Claus, the insightful leader, asks him to guide the sleigh.

Recently, a new breed of leaders has begun to apply that philosophy. They are reaching down into their organizations to tap the unique knowledge and insights of every individual. They have discovered a wealth of energy and expertise that almost nobody knew was there.

This new breed ranges from Notre Dame coach Lou Holtz and New York police chief Lee Brown to Donald Petersen, the CEO who revived Ford Motor Company. It includes little-known leaders such as the educator Peter Kline and the coaches of the Little League world champions from Trumbull, Connecticut.

New-breed leaders return power to people on the front lines and give every person a sense of responsibility. They ask people what they think instead of just telling them what to do. At Ford, Petersen gave workers the power to shut down the assembly lines and to design cars they'd love to drive. Brown takes power from City Hall and gives it to cops walking the beat. In Kline's classrooms, students, not teachers, are in charge. Holtz and the Little League coaches show deep respect and

71

admiration for every person on their teams.

Some of their methods are surprisingly similar. To build self-esteem, Kline's teachers conduct "birthday circles," in which students form a circle around a fellow student and take turns completing the sentence "I'm glad you were born because . . ." And Holtz sometimes tells his players to go around the locker room, one by one, and say what they admire in one another.

These leaders also set lofty goals that everyone involved can take pride in. That's nothing revolutionary. But the people you'll read about here take that idea one step further: they show each and every person how they can help the organization achieve that goal, from building the perfect widget to blocking and tackling on the football team.

In some areas, their approaches differ. Holtz often talks about his number-one goal: winning the national championship. The Little League coaches keep their aspirations to themselves. Petersen and Kline are quiet leaders who shun the spotlight and credit their teams or students for their achievements. When he was Houston's chief of police, Brown had his own monthly television show.

But the common ground, "people power," enabled all five to accomplish what many considered impossible.

Grit, Guts, and Genius

Ford's Donald Petersen

CEO of the Decade

L egend has it that sometime around 1980 an unusual "visitor" dropped into Ford Motor Company's automotive design center. This creature of a new habit tapped design chief Jack Telnack on the shoulder and pointed to photographs of the Thunderbirds that Ford was currently developing.

"You're a professional designer. You're far and away the most knowledgeable person there is about what we ought to do," the visitor said. "Do you like these cars? Do you feel proud of them? Would you park one of these cars in your driveway?"

Telnack wasn't quite sure what to make of it. You see, the visitor was a total surprise but not a total stranger. It was Donald Petersen, the company's president and chief operating officer. At first, Telnack was tempted to stand by the company's plan. But he saw an honesty in Petersen's inquisitive face that he couldn't ignore.

"Actually, no, I don't like these designs," Telnack told him.

Petersen granted Telnack a few weeks to come up with a new model. Telnack sketched the kind of car he'd personally love to own — a sleek, aerodynamic model with features similar to the European styling found in Mercedes-Benzes and BMWs. Telnack didn't realize it at the time, but the sketch he had just made would dramatically affect the design of Ford's 1983 Thunderbird and the wildly successful

73

Ford Taurus, destined to become the best-selling midsize car in the United States.

"That one conversation turned everything around," says Telnack.

Much has been made of Ford's phenomenal comeback in the 1980s. With Petersen at the helm, the company surged past General Motors in profitability in 1987. In 1988, Ford celebrated its third straight year of record profits. Petersen, who became CEO in 1985, was honored as the nation's top CEO by virtually everyone who was asked. *Chief Executive* magazine named Petersen "CEO of the Year" in 1989. *Fortune* asked 206 CEOs to name America's most effective leader: 25 percent chose Petersen; 23 percent picked Chrysler's Lee Iacocca. In early 1990, Petersen opted for early retirement, leaving behind a blueprint for managerial success in the 1990s.

Petersen, like any great team player, prefers to share the credit. He likes to say, "If you see a turtle on top of a fence post, you know it didn't get there by itself."

But it's fair to say that Ford would not be where it is today without Don Petersen. "He's one of the best I've ever seen," said Bill Marriott, CEO of Marriott Corporation. "He's taken autocracy and turned it into teamwork." Nancy Badore, Ford's director of executive development, says, "It used to be that work got dictated down the pyramid at Ford. Thanks to Don, we've started to send work up the pyramid."

In the late 1970s, Ford Motor Company had lost contact with customer reality. Telnack and his team of three hundred designers hadn't forgotten how to design good cars. In fact, the walls were plastered with sexy sketches that turned yellow and wound up in the garbage can. But Ford's top managers were conditioned to do everything the way they always had. Often that meant boxy, me-too cars that nobody — not even Ford — could get the least bit excited about. Very few executives had international experience. They weren't will-

74

ing to risk their necks. Says Telnack, "Management told me that they wanted something unique, but they looked at everything we did with 'Detroit eyes.' "

Petersen knew he had to shake everybody up as quickly as possible. And he knew that taking a trip "downstairs" would help to obliterate the old way of doing things. "Our people were so consumed by all the rules and regulations that they mentally just threw up their hands," Petersen says. "They were so constricted that there wasn't much they could do."

Something began to dawn on Petersen. He realized that the "enemy" wasn't really the Japanese. It wasn't the hourly workers manning Ford's assembly lines. It was Ford's bureaucracy, a management style that snuffed out creativity and smothered teamwork, making it impossible for Ford's people to show what they could really accomplish.

"American workers were mad," Petersen concedes. "They're not as mad now but they were really mad. And I don't blame them, because they were being blamed for things over which they had no control at all."

Petersen's plan: Turn the pyramid upside down. Leave the ivory tower. Walk down into the trenches and ask the welders, the engineers, the guys sweeping the floor: What do you think? What should we do? How can your job be improved?

"Until you start asking people what they think, and getting them into a teamwork mode, you have no idea what they're going to come forth with," says Petersen. "You may think you know, but you don't."

Between 1980 and 1982, Ford lost more than $3 billion. The company teetered on the edge of extinction. Smack in the middle of that period Petersen, along with then-CEO Phillip Caldwell, committed the funds for more than eighty "Employee Involvement" programs. Petersen led by example, walking into factories where a Ford

75

executive had never been seen before and asking his trademark questions. Even Petersen didn't realize what he was about to unleash. In prying into about 350,000 minds, Ford discovered a gold mine of ideas and suggestions that nobody knew were there.

As Alton Doody and Ron Bingaman noted in their 1988 book, *Reinventing the Wheels,* many workers' suggestions were marvelously simple: A body-shop supervisor said it was stupid to use three cumbersome welding guns to attach the fire wall to the Taurus. Why not just one?

Ford employees involved in manufacturing the 1984 Ford Tempo and Mercury Topaz made 666 suggestions. Three fourths of their suggestions were adopted.

Four years before Ford began manufacturing the Taurus, Petersen sent executives to the Atlanta assembly plant to ask how Ford could build a better car. Workers there made 1,400 suggestions; half were adopted.

In Atlanta, workers said it was silly to use several different-size screws to affix interior moldings. Ford began to use universal screws. Simple, yes. But a typical employee suggestion saves Ford anywhere from $300,000 to $700,000. And it's still going on. In July 1989, Petersen talked about a glass plant that was having trouble with windshields damaged during shipping. Apparently, wooden bumpers designed to hold the glass in place were either breaking or scratching the glass. Employees meeting on weekends in a garage designed a plastic-covered bumper. The idea shaved costs by $20,000 a year at that plant alone.

Offering up these ideas and seeing them implemented caused Ford's employees to undergo a sea change in attitude. As Petersen tells it, "I don't know how many times I've had an hourly employee say, 'You know, that's the first time I can recall being asked what I think. It makes me feel as though what I do is important.' "

Communication was the key — and not just in asking the right questions, but in answering them. Some Ford employees, as well as

Donald E. Petersen, former CEO of Ford Motor Company

Ford suppliers, used to have no conception of the role they played in the company. In other words, a line worker might be packing a widget or welding a frame without any idea where it ended up — or what nightmares he might create if he did his work improperly.

To remedy that, prototypes of every new Ford car are shipped to every assembly plant in the country. Even suppliers get to see what role they're playing. When one thirty-five-year-old veteran saw the Taurus prototype, she said she had often wondered, "what in the world they do with all the carpet we make."

"For most employees, the most helpful thing you can do is get everyone moving toward a common goal," says Petersen. "If they get to see what they're participating in, that helps enormously."

Organizing the "Team"

Of course, Petersen's handiwork didn't begin or end with an employee-involvement program. To instill a sense of teamwork, he somehow had to destroy the internal rivalries and competitive backbiting that existed throughout the company.

That effort began at the highest possible level: at the policy and strategy committee meetings attended by every Ford executive. Petersen started to go to these meetings in 1975 when he became the head of Ford's diversified products operations. He was shocked to discover that nobody really talked to one another. Each executive would speak about his own issue, but there were no comments about what anyone else had to say.

"I was not expected to speak unless it was in *my* area," Petersen recalls.

Petersen had spent four years, from 1971 to 1975, managing Ford's truck business. There he had discovered a deep sense of camaraderie that would guide his managerial efforts for the remainder of his career. He had seen, in the truck operation, "an island of employees who worked closely together . . . There was a calmness to the place, people confident in their ability but not trying to outshine everyone else." The benefits showed: Ford's truck business was soaring by the time Petersen left. Yet he was barred from commenting on truck matters at the company's highest-level meetings. It was exactly the opposite of what he'd just experienced.

So in 1980, when Petersen became president and chief operating officer, the old way of running many Ford meetings melted away. He suggested, in effect, that the committee organize itself as a team and take full part in every discussion. "It was important to get that group to start being what they are: the most broadly knowledgeable senior executives in the company," Petersen says. "Now it's a good free flow."

Petersen's message — meet in teams, bounce ideas around, knock down communication barriers — began to make its way down through the company. "It had to start at the top," Petersen says. "Then you expected that they'd go back and conduct their meetings in a similar manner."

Petersen led by example. In August 1989, he visited Ford's Norfolk plant. As is customary now, everybody met as a team: the plant managers, union officials, and so forth. But then they walked outside for photographs — presumably one featuring Petersen with the managers, another with the union guys.

"Why don't we take just one picture with everyone together?" Petersen said, adding with a chuckle, "That was a little bit of a holdover from the old days."

Quality Really Is "Job One"

In 1980, Petersen sat down and watched an NBC documentary entitled "If Japan Can, Why Can't We?" The show featured a seventy-nine-year-old statistician named W. Edwards Deming. Deming isn't well known in the United States (although he's getting to be), but in Japan he's known as the messiah of Japanese industry. Deming had gone to Japan in the 1950s and showed them, in meticulous statistical detail, how to manufacture virtually perfect products. To honor him, the Japanese created the prestigious Deming Prize for quality control. It remains the highest honor any Japanese company can receive.

After watching the documentary, Petersen grabbed the phone and told assistants to invite Deming in for a three-day meeting.

"It took a few months to convince him to visit," recalls Ed Baker, Ford's director of quality planning.

Deming wouldn't come until Petersen got on the phone and assured him that he personally would listen to what Deming had to say. When Deming arrived in January 1981, he went straight to Petersen's office. What he offered was a statistical system that ensured that products would be built right the first time — without defects that would have to be repaired afterward. In effect, defect "detection" would be replaced with defect "prevention." What he preached was "continuous improvement."

"Do you want each of your employees to be better each year?" he asked Petersen.

"Of course," Petersen responded.

"Then you must want a structure to push continuous improvement, and then you'll accomplish remarkable things."

Deming's idea was so simple. But Petersen says it was one of the most powerful ideas he'd ever heard. American automakers, Ford included, had always been inclined to set goals. Production goals. Quality goals. Employee goals. Deming hates goals. Often they force workers to work too fast. And often, by the time you reach a goal, your competitor (the Japanese) will have swept right past you.

"Quality, in his mind, was very different from what we had always thought," says Baker. "He drove us to redefine what our culture was — to drive fear out, to retrain everyone . . . He is a genius who had the right answer for Ford."

Deming was hired on as a monthly consultant. But his teachings would never have hit home if it weren't for Petersen. After being

80

ignored for forty years in his own country, Deming is understandably cynical and critical of American managers.

"There's a lot to do but nobody's doing enough," Deming says in a terse, gruff tone. "I'm doing my best . . . but we're still slipping, aren't we?"

In meetings at Ford he came on strong, ridiculing management for what they'd done to Ford employees. Deming says that 80 percent of quality problems are caused not by hourly workers but by poor management.

"He defiantly flung it at us using an almost abusive approach," recalls Badore. At first, Ford's managers were tempted to brush it off, even ignore him. But Petersen had become Deming's personal sponsor. "Everyone realized Petersen was behind this man. Everyone knew something *really* different was going on at Ford."

Driving (Literally) the Message Home

Petersen, who started out as a mechanical engineer, has always been known as a "product" guy. He and Caldwell determined early on that the next hero at Ford would not be a person or a group but a car — the 1986 Taurus — built by a worldwide team.

Ironically, what Petersen and hundreds of other executives didn't know was how to perform a uniform test drive of the company's cars.

"The engineers would think they'd made some new improvement, in suspension or something, so they'd invite me over to the track to drive one of the prototypes," Petersen says. "I had the feeling I wasn't a good enough driver to tell them anything useful."

Instead of passing the buck, Petersen decided to take driving lessons. He hired Bob Bondurant, a former professional racer, to teach him the tricks of running a new car through its paces.

He's no A. J. Foyt. But Petersen became quite renowned as a test driver.

"Don has the special ability to ask the right questions when it

81

comes to engineering the car . . . and he really wants the answers," says Telnack, who became Ford's worldwide design chief.

The Japanese leapfrogged U.S. automakers, not only with their painstaking attention to every detail, but also with their ability to deliver a unique driving experience. You can't define it, but their cars often feel sturdier, more precise. Ford hasn't reached that point yet, but Petersen tried to lead his company there.

"I sat down and tried to write a description of a driver's car — the relationship between man and machine," Petersen says. "We want to surprise and delight the customer so he feels just right . . . the tactile sense, the wonderful positioning of everything."

Petersen has talked to engineers about the fact that a Ford car is an *automobile*, meaning it must be evaluated in motion, not sitting in some showroom. The driver must like the feel of the steering, the way the clutch works, and so forth. And not just in a performance car — in any car.

By getting behind the wheel, Petersen was driving home yet another quality credo: Quality is defined by the customer. Everything Ford does must be guided by customers' wants and needs.

Ford has always had test drives. But now "customers" like Petersen — and hundreds of other Ford managers trained by Bondurant — have their say about every car.

Japanese, But Not Too Japanese

A CEO who preaches teamwork, lives it, and abides by it might run the risk of crushing the one advantage Americans have always had over the Japanese: the power and creativity of the individual. One of Japan's favorite sayings is, "The nail that sticks up gets hammered down."

Petersen invokes a basketball analogy to explain his philosophy: that you can nurture both teamwork and creativity throughout the company. "Think about Isiah Thomas of the Detroit Pistons or Magic

Johnson of the Los Angeles Lakers," he says. "Both are great team players but they're also known for their individual skills. Other players are known for their particular areas of brilliance. But Magic and Isiah are the stars. There has to be a leader somewhere, some kind of focus."

And there's one thing Petersen knows he can always count on: if an American autoworker has an opinion, he'll tell you about it. Especially if you ask.

"Our hourly guys now have a freedom of expression that I doubt I'd ever hear in an Asian plant," Petersen concludes. "I view that as that special plus this country has. We have the freedom to say or do whatever we want."

Peter Kline

A Miracle Cure for the Nation's Schools

Five years ago, Michael Alexander was just another frustrated inner-city school principal. The soft-spoken head of Chicago's Guggenheim School looked out his office window and saw nothing but despair. Teachers with no hope. Classrooms clogged with four hundred kindergarten through eighth-grade students — all black — doing just enough to get by. Apathy. Boredom. Drugs. Nobody seemed to care.

Then Alexander spotted a way out. He knew the school's twenty-one teachers had the basic skills to do their jobs. But archaic teaching methods were so ingrained in them that it was impossible for any real learning to take place in their classrooms.

Alexander took a gamble — and some Title I funds — and hired Peter Kline, the guru of a startling new educational philosophy. Kline's approach, called integrative learning, draws from recent brain research that shows we each possess seven types of intelligence. He and his colleagues have developed ways to involve all seven types of intelligence in the learning process. Their methods make use of everything from rap music and dance to games and athletic contests to help stimulate creative thinking as well as embed facts in the brain's long-term memory. The result: miraculous improvements in student performance, as well as in teachers' attitudes.

84

As you may know, American public schools are in horrible shape. One third of the country's eighteen-year-olds are educational failures: 300,000 dropped out of school and another 300,000 can't even read the diplomas they graduated with. Illiteracy is crushing the nation's ability to compete with Japan, West Germany, and other countries. In 1990 alone, U.S. firms will spend $25 billion teaching workers skills that they should have learned in school. Motorola, for example, has to teach 50 percent of its factory workers how to read and write.

"My objective is to help you, the student, become independent of me, the teacher."

There's a social cost to consider, too. Every undereducated child is apt to wind up on the welfare rolls — or even worse, turn to a life revolving around drugs and crime. President Bush and drug czar William Bennett are trying to attack the drug problem primarily by choking off the supply and offering treatment to addicts. Educators know that will never work. They say the problem starts with kids who don't know enough — or value their self-worth enough — to "just say no."

The Guggenheim School is living proof that radical improvements can be attained in the worst situations imaginable. It shows that schools can be rescued with very little extra training or public funds. Using current methods, educating a child from kindergarten through twelfth grade costs society about $40,000. Training each teacher in integrative learning techniques would cost just $1,000 per child.

Consider Guggenheim's story. In February 1985, Kline and a few colleagues spent thirty hours training Guggenheim's faculty. Over the next twelve months, the school was transformed. Before Kline arrived, Guggenheim ranked last among eighteen Chicago schools in reading and eighth in math. In 1986, the year after Kline's visit,

85

Guggenheim ranked second in both reading and math. The percentage of students achieving one year's progress (in reading) in a single school year soared, from 27.5 percent in 1985 to 55.7 percent in 1986.

The results have rocked the education establishment. In 1989, educators from Australia to Brooklyn flocked to Guggenheim to see what Kline had done. New York City sent twenty school principals; twelve more came during their personal vacation time to learn about it. Even multinational corporations began to get involved.

"I was not a strong believer at first," says Frank Vullo, director of academic affairs at Eastman Kodak in Rochester, New York. "I thought, if all this is true, why aren't all educators using this?"

But Vullo quickly discovered that Kline's methods were the key to solving Kodak's training problems — and shaving training costs by up to $20 million a year. Kodak has trained fifty instructors — and fifty Rochester School District teachers — in integrative learning techniques. He says the results have been "fantastic . . . this really could be the solution for the nation's public schools."

Like Kodak, the education establishment is deeply conservative. It's difficult for many educators, particularly administrators, to embrace a new way of doing things.

But school districts throughout New York State — Rochester, Oswego, Brooklyn, Syracuse — are starting to employ Kline's methods. Says Jeanne Slattery, an assistant to the superintendent in Rochester, "School people are conservative and it's tough for them to think in such different terms. But I'll tell you something. Our teachers love it. It's a much more powerful way to teach because it really engages kids' minds."

Integrative learning begins with the notion that learning should be fun. Think back to those times in your life when you really learned something — how to ride a bicycle or how to play a musical instrument.

In many cases, you learned because your entire body was involved in the experience. At schools today, you're expected to learn in one of two ways: reading from a book or listening to the teacher lecture. Kline says that's ridiculous.

"You were not born to sit in a chair eight hours a day and listen to someone talk, or to pore over books year in and year out," he writes in his 1988 book, *The Everyday Genius*.

He says such methods address only two of our seven intelligences — our linguistic skills and our logical/mathematical skills. They ignore the other five types of intelligence:

- Musical: the sensitivity to rhythm, pitch, and organization of sound found in composers, conductors, and other musicians.
- Spatial: the visual ability found in architects and painters to create a mental image or sense of gestalt.
- Kinesthetic: the control of one's body and of objects, a common talent among athletes, street-smart kids, dancers, and actors.
- Interpersonal: the sensitivity to others found in politicians, teachers, and salespeople, which allows them to relate to and influence others.
- Intrapersonal: the self-awareness of novelists, philosophers, and others, which allows them to develop a deep sense of self.

Every person possesses all seven intelligences, but some areas are more highly developed than others. Teachers familiar with integrative learning look for ways to tap all seven, simultaneously allowing students to exercise their strengths and strengthen their weaknesses in each area. For instance, an inner-city black grows up in a culture that emphasizes kinesthetic intelligence. Teachers in all-black classrooms might ask students to learn by making up words for a rap song, or create a skit with each student playing a part in a musical play.

87

Guggenheim teacher Nancy Ellis used integrative learning techniques in a history lesson. She gave each student a sign to wear that identified him or her as a great scientist, such as Galileo, Kepler, or

Einstein. Then she tossed out a ball. Whoever caught the ball had to say something about that scientist. Kline says students must be given a sense that they, not the teacher, are in control of what's happening. The use of the ball gets the entire body into the act.

Joan Pilot, a teacher at Chicago's Hinton Elementary School, tried a similar technique in her class. One child named John was her slowest learner. He wouldn't normally participate in classroom activities. But when the children began tossing the ball, they discovered that John was the best at throwing and catching. He rapidly gained status among the kids — and his schoolwork started to soar.

To build up spatial intelligence, Kline and his colleagues encourage mind-mapping — representing each idea not just with a word but also with a visual image. He has found that the mind can store pictures and retain them in memory many times better than words. Also helpful is guided imagery — remembering facts, such as the order of the nine planets, with the help of an imaginary tale.

Integrative learning even works with adults. In the past, Kodak workers enrolled in an electronics class would spend months learning the color codes for various types of resistors. One of Kline's instructors made up a song, to the tune of "The Twelve Days of Christmas," that contains the same material. Says Vullo, "They learned in five minutes what used to take nine months."

Integrative learning isn't just fun and games. Much of what Kline teaches draws from recent research on the brain.

For instance, scientists at the National Institute of Mental Health have determined that the brain is made up of several distinct parts. At the base of the brain is the oldest, or reptilian, portion. This portion takes care of our most basic needs and survival instincts. When our lives are threatened, we tend to downshift into this area. Unfortunately, Kline says, most classrooms cause kids to downshift into this area, too. Although their lives aren't in danger, many young students are terrified about being called on or humiliated. Their automatic

88

responses replace thoughtful ones. To avoid this, Kline emphasizes that teachers must totally eliminate fear from every classroom and replace it with a sense of progress and self-worth. Always accentuate the positive. Kline even uses a game, called the birthday circle, to help build self-esteem. In this game, one child sits in the center of the circle while each person takes turns completing the sentence "I'm glad you were born because . . ."

The next highest part of the brain, the limbic system, is the seat of all emotions. In the 1950s, a Bulgarian psychotherapist named Georgi Lozanov did extensive studies on the relationship between the limbic system and our long-term memories. He was intrigued by the fact that geniuses so often possess childlike qualities. Picasso once said that when he was a child, he could paint like an adult, and when he was an adult, he had to learn to paint like a child. Lozanov decided that the secret to accelerated learning is to re-create the natural learning environment of the infant. He suggested that teachers conduct a classroom as if it were a living room or even a child's playroom. Instead of drilling them with lectures, he suggested that students study while listening to classical music or involving themselves with the material through songs, dances, and physical activity.

For reasons scientists don't quite understand, music helps teachers tap directly into a child's long-term memory. Remember in school when you crammed for a test, then forgot the material entirely? When music accompanies the process, you don't forget. No one forgets the words to "Mary Had a Little Lamb" or "Rudolph the Red-Nosed Reindeer." Another classic, "Peter and the Wolf," is an example of a childhood yarn set to music that many adults never forget.

"With these methods, we're talking directly to the child's nervous system," Kline says. "Imagine the power in that."

Another brain researcher, Nobel Prize winner Roger Sperry, did extensive studies on the brain's left and right hemispheres.

89

Sperry cut the corpus callosum, the connecting link between the two hemispheres, as a means of treating epilepsy. He was able to study the hemispheres separately, and discovered that the left hemisphere is the logical side. It deals with language, math, and sequential learning.

The right side of the brain is the creative, intuitive, imaginative, and musical side. It relates more easily to emotions. Kline is convinced that when the two sides of a person's brain are separately engaged, the person experiences conflict. But when both are tapped simultaneously — by a teacher who makes learning fun — much more learning takes place. "When you play music or a game, a whole lot more of your brain is active," Kline says. "You're not feeling stress, so your barriers disappear."

All of Kline's methods revolve around a profoundly simple philosophy: "The key to education is adapting teaching to the way we naturally learn." Everybody learns differently and has different interests, but every child — in fact, every adult — wants to learn. If you doubt that, consider that America is a nation of insatiable test takers. The number-one selling game is Trivial Pursuit; "Jeopardy" is one of the top-rated game shows. From an early age, kids are persistently bugging adults with questions about things that fascinate them. Sometimes their speculations are bizarre — that "our universe is a tiny atom in some giant's thumb." They become obsessed with everything from stargazing to skateboarding.

Kline says we usually ignore these distractions and direct kids' attention to things like multiplication tables. He says that squanders our most precious natural resource: the enormous potential of the human mind. Instead of squelching kids' interest in such things, we should channel it into ways that help them learn. He says the skateboarder might be fascinated by the physics of skateboarding or the way that balance relates to human anatomy. The stargazer might study math by counting the stars. The important thing, Kline says, is that you shouldn't dampen a child's curiosity. "We need to help kids mix their creative interests with knowledge and discipline, so they can keep alive the magic of their vision while acquiring the tools for mastering the adult world . . . The most valuable gift you can offer is to help them become aware of their opportunity to offer their uniqueness to the world."

Much of this may seem like common sense, but schools have, for several decades, gone down a different path. U.S. schools — like U.S. factories — have been designed to keep people in line and to "carry out orders," not to encourage independent thinking. Recently, Ford Motor Company and other corporations have begun to tap into their workers' minds, empowering them to make decisions and offer suggestions that would improve the company. They've also organized workers into highly effective teams. But schools, Kline says, discourage kids from charting their own course or trusting their own sense of self-worth. Schools thrive on competition — an environment that often turns kids into stressed and irritating overachievers or self-doubters who feel they can't compete. Like his counterparts at Ford, Kline is fighting to reverse the traditional top-down approach and hand power back to the students themselves. He assumes they have as much to learn from one another as they do from their teachers.

"My objective is to help you, the student, become independent of me, the teacher," says Kline. "If I am skillful enough, you will eventually get the impression you are doing everything yourself."

A funny thing happens when kids go through school believing that. They really begin to sense that their own thoughts, beliefs, and actions really count for something. After graduating, they're apt to be more flexible in their thinking, better able to confront new and unexpected challenges, and more willing to question the way things have always been done. And that, Kline argues, will make them much better citizens.

91

"We've created a nation of non–risk takers because everyone's afraid to trust their instincts," he says. Integrative learning "reactivates the individual's natural desire to be in charge, think clearly, and act decisively. Thus it provides the education that a strong-minded and competent citizen needs."

Lou Holtz

The Fighting Irish and the Japanese

L ou Holtz is a scrawny little West Virginia native who makes a habit of telling everyone how stupid he is. "Look at me," he says matter-of-factly in a punchy drawl. "I stand five ten, a hundred and fifty-two pounds, talk with a lisp, wear glasses, and look like I've been afflicted with beriberi and scurvy most of my life."

Before you begin to sympathize, remember that this jug-eared king of humility, who finished 234th in a class of 278, also happens to be the most successful college football coach in the United States today. In early 1989, his Fighting Irish at Notre Dame captured the national championship by pummeling West Virginia, 34–21. That was no fluke. Before coming to Notre Dame, Holtz coached four other college teams: William and Mary, North Carolina State, the University of Arkansas, and the University of Minnesota. In each case, he inherited a losing team and wound up taking the team to a bowl game in his second year at the school. In fact, fourteen of the nineteen teams he's coached have gone to bowl games.

Lou Holtz the football coach is living proof of what happens when you listen to Lou Holtz the motivator. By following his own simple guiding principles, he has become the type of person that Lou Holtz admires: the overachiever. His incredible ability to get the most out of people has been the driving force behind everything he has

93

accomplished. It's the reason that companies such as IBM and 3M shell out up to $15,000 a pop to have Holtz give pep talks to their top managers. And it's the reason that the nation's most outstanding high school football stars, given the opportunity to attend any university they want, often wind up at Notre Dame.

"To me, overachievers are an absolute necessity," says Holtz, leaning back in a blue leather chair in an office that so many other coaching legends (Knute Rockne, Ara Parseghian, Dan Devine) have occupied. "We are constantly looking for people who come closer to realizing the true potential that they have. You might say Notre Dame has success because it has so many overachievers."

As Holtz sees it, there isn't much difference among the nation's best college football teams. On any given Saturday, Notre Dame could get knocked off by Penn State, USC, West Virginia, or any other perennial college football power. The athletes are similar in size, speed, and intelligence. More often than not, they're well coached while they're on the playing field. What separates Notre Dame men from the boys is attitude.

"Ability is what you're capable of doing," says Holtz. "Motivation determines what you do. Attitude determines how well you do it."

Look at what Holtz accomplished when he became head coach at the University of Minnesota. The season before Holtz arrived, Minnesota had lost every game and had been defeated in seventeen straight games, by an average score of 47–13, dating back two years. Eighteen months later, Minnesota went to a bowl game. The program had gone downhill because of the team's poor attitude: everyone expected to lose, so they did. Holtz came in and turned things around entirely. He says, "It wasn't because of the coach. It was because of the attitude."

Every athlete that Notre Dame recruits has ability. Otherwise, he wouldn't be among the two thousand high school stars that Holtz and his assistants scrutinize each year. Usually, the athletes are motivated by their desire to excel and win a national championship. The tough job is to inspire people with the right attitude and provide them with the skills to be the best they can possibly be.

"Last year [when Notre Dame won the championship], to be honest, I didn't think our team was that good," admits George Kelly, Notre Dame's assistant athletic director. "But they just continued to believe that they couldn't lose. He made them believe that."

Among his players, Holtz has taken on an almost Napoleonic stature. Says Pat Eilers, a star on the championship team, "It's incredible to have someone like him leading you onto the battlefield."

Holtz is no miracle maker. What you see happen on the playing field is the result of months and years of careful recruiting, grueling practices, and meticulously targeted speech making.

"We have instant coffee, instant tea, and instant restaurants," says Holtz. "Everybody looks for a quick fix. There isn't any. You build it day by day. You don't panic. You don't overreact. You don't change your principles. If you preach the same thing over a period of time, and it doesn't change, one of two things is going to happen: they're going to believe in you or they're going to leave."

It begins in the recruiting process. Holtz knows he has a good shot at landing one of every two athletes he talks to. Notre Dame's winning tradition and its academic excellence account for that. So he looks for those recruits who have put football in proper perspective.

He begins by asking each recruit, "Why do you want to come to our school? Do you want to come to Notre Dame because it's prestigious? Because it has a reputation? Or because you want to be prepared for life and compete against the very best, week in and week out?"

What he's searching for, again, is the proper attitude. "You can afford to be wrong on talent. If a player comes here and he's not as

95

talented as you thought, he can still help us on the football field. But if he has the wrong attitude, he not only won't succeed, but he'll ruin a lot of other people, too. It's like a cancer."

To weed players out, Holtz looks for recruits that are good students and willing to make sacrifices. "If a player wants a big-city life, or if he wants to lift weights all the time, he won't be successful here," Holtz says.

He also rejects those who are primarily interested in playing professional football. He tells potential players, "The average pro career is three point nine years. Even if you're lucky enough to make the pros, your career is over at age twenty-six. The average life span is seventy-five years. So what are you going to do after that?"

What he looks for, perhaps above and beyond everything else, are athletes who have serious goals in life. "You can't motivate a group of people or a team," he says. "You have to motivate people individually. And that motivation has to be in an environment in which the person has a goal — something they really want to accomplish in their lives."

Holtz's obsession with goal setting dates back to the lowest period in his life. The year was 1966. Holtz, twenty-eight, had just been hired as an assistant coach to Marvin Bass at the University of South Carolina. Holtz's wife, Beth, was eight months pregnant at the time, and Holtz had spent virtually every penny he had to make a down payment on a house. One month later, Bass quit his job to go to the Canadian League. Holtz was unemployed and struggling.

Then his wife bought him a book, *The Magic of Thinking Big*, by David Schwartz. Holtz had never read much before that. In fact, he wasn't very motivated to do much of anything. "There are so many people, and I was one of them, who won't do anything special with their lives," he says now.

But he was desperate. The book said you should write down all the goals you want to achieve before you die. Holtz gave it a try. He

Lou Holtz, Notre Dame's football coach

came up with 107 goals, including: have dinner at the White House; be on the Johnny Carson show; see the pope; win a national championship; be coach of the year; jump out of an airplane; go down in a submarine. The more he wrote, the more excited he got. "My whole life changed."

What Holtz discovered in his own simple way was the power of positive thinking. He tapped into his dreams, figured out exactly what he wanted to strive for, and wrote his ideas down. They would become a guide and a yardstick of his success for the remainder of his adult life.

Armed with his own new attitude, Holtz began to study both the Bible and the great coaches. He read, over and over, *You Win with People,* by former Ohio State coach Woody Hayes, and John Wooden's *They Call Me Coach.* Gradually, he began to form a core philosophy that he would teach to every team he eventually coached. That philosophy begins with the notion that you must believe in yourself. As Holtz says, "If you get people to believe in themselves, they'll set bigger goals."

To make his players believe in themselves, he tells them to follow three basic rules: Do what's right. Do your very best. Treat others as you'd like to be treated.

Sound simple? They are. But Holtz argues that those rules will answer the three basic questions that he asks of every player, and every player asks of him. The questions: Can I trust you? Are you committed? Do you care about me?

"People might think this is corny, but I don't care," Holtz says. "This is what I believe. And this is what we try to operate on."

He looks at it this way. If you don't do "what's right" in a given situation, you'll have a poor image of yourself in your subconscious mind. And, if you have a poor self-image, you'll want others (coaches, fellow players, and so on) to praise you and approve of you. Often, when a football program breaks down, as it did at Minnesota, it's because the players and coaches don't trust each other or don't care about each other.

Once the philosophy is understood, Holtz sits down with the team to talk about goals. He asks: "What do you want to accomplish? What can you do as a team? Here's what I think we can accomplish."

In January 1988, after Notre Dame lost the Cotton Bowl to Texas A&M, Holtz called a team meeting. He presented what the players call the "perfection speech." He explained how each player would be perfect in the classroom, practice the best, and be a perfect person overall. Then he asked whoever wanted to win the national championship in the season ahead to stand up. Everybody stood up.

"That kind of set the tone," Eilers recalls.

A few months later, as the team began to get bogged down in twice-daily practices, Holtz would remind the team, "You know, you're the guys who stood up and said you wanted to be great."

"He made it sound as if it was our decision to be number one," says Eilers. "I'm amazed at how he got everybody to be so self-motivated."

Of course, you don't win national championships just with lofty ambitions and fancy philosophies tossed around in a preseason speech. Holtz has the football savvy to design and call great plays on game day. In fact, he's widely regarded as one of the best game-day coaches in the country. He's also fanatical about fundamentals and conditioning — words that many Notre Dame players learn to hate.

Fundamentals (blocking and tackling) and discipline underlie Holtz's entire program. On his first day at Notre Dame, Holtz walked into a team meeting and immediately kicked a player's feet off the stage and told everyone to sit up straight. "You literally could hear everybody's spine crack," defensive end Frank Stams told *USA Today*.

That winter, he initiated his new team with six A.M. workouts. He joked about it, saying it was "already eleven A.M. in London," or

99

"We'll practice half a day today, eight to eight." The players got the message.

"Starting at six A.M. was hell," says Ned Bolcar, a Notre Dame tri-captain. "But it brought us all together. When you're suffering that early in the morning, who do you look to for camaraderie? The guy next to you."

At practices, Holtz works the team like a drill sergeant with a Ph.D. in psychology. Sometimes he doesn't say a word. But if he spots something he doesn't like, watch out. Once, when quarterback Tony Rice blew a play, Holtz ran from the sideline onto the field and tackled him. Then he sat on him and yelled about what Rice had done wrong. On another occasion, Holtz grabbed Chris Zorich, the six-two, 270-pound nose tackle, by the face mask and screamed at him for fighting — a big no-no on an Irish practice field. After he grabbed six-three Tim Grunhard in a similar hold, Grunhard told the *Wall Street Journal*, "I kept thinking, Why am I letting this little guy do this? But it's not his physical size, it's his emotional and spiritual size."

Holtz has occasionally gone too far. Once he shattered a finger in eight places while trying to catch a punt. But his on-field antics are neither mindless nor misguided. Eilers, for instance, remembers when he transferred from Yale to Notre Dame in 1986. That spring, the smallish (five-eleven, 195-pound) Eilers was trying out at defensive safety, a position he'd never played before. After the third play, Holtz trotted out, grabbed him by the face mask, and said, "You know, Eilers, I've been trying to find a place for you to play on the field, and I don't know, son, I don't know if you can play here or not."

Eilers thought, Oh no, after all this transferring, now this. So he dug in and thought, Hell, I'm going to prove him wrong. Within a few plays, he was catching on.

"I responded well to that," says Eilers. "It's as if Coach knows what to say. He says it's up to you, that you're competing not against another team but against yourself."

100

Once a team is assembled, and the season is under way, Holtz excels at two things: keeping each game in perspective and knowing when to talk and what to say. Before each practice, Holtz calls the team together and talks to them for three to five minutes about anything that's been on his mind. Holtz is a great spontaneous speaker, but these sessions are carefully crafted and prepared.

Once he told the team about IBM. He explained what a great company it is, how IBM people strive to be the best, and how they're always prepared to win. "You know football's no different from that," he said.

He always has something new to talk about. On another afternoon, he told the players that he had gone to visit St. Mary's School for Girls and talked to the nuns. The nuns told him how much they enjoyed the games and how they prayed for the team every Saturday. He told the team, almost in tears, "You know, if you guys can't come out here and give a hundred ten percent for these nuns, I don't know what else will motivate you." He also told the team about a lady in a wheelchair who had an incredibly peaceful look on her face. He had asked her how she could be so peaceful, and she said she had put her faith in Mary on the Dome, a famous symbol at Notre Dame, and did the Rosary every night. Holtz told the team to put its faith in Mary, too.

To determine when he should talk, Holtz sits in the back of the room and observes the players and tries to figure out the team's mood. "You get a feeling from their body language," he says. "Are they positive? Negative? Are they interested? You can tell by the way they interact with one another. You walk into the locker room: Are they joking, down, depressed? You can't be encouraging one another, joking around, if you don't think you're going to be successful. But if they get on one another in a sarcastic way, that's not good."

While at Arkansas, for example, he noticed that his team lacked confidence for its upcoming battle against Oklahoma in the 1978 Orange Bowl. That wasn't surprising. Oklahoma was favored by 23 points. The media had drubbed Arkansas's chances. Holtz recalls, "The paper said we didn't have a chance in the world, and the team believed it."

Holtz called a team meeting at the Four Seasons Hotel. As the athletes walked in, they were quieter than Holtz had ever heard a team. It was time for the Holtz magic. The coach grabbed that day's newspaper and began to leaf through it. He said, "In any paper, you have a front page for those who want to read the news, comics for those who can't read, editorial page for those who can't think . . ."

He began to carefully fold the paper up into smaller and smaller squares. Then, as he continued talking, he seemed to be ripping the paper apart. ". . . and, you know, it's really amazing that you're going to roll over and die 'cause you read your obituary in the newspaper."

He warned them point-blank: "Don't let people tear you down. Don't let people cause you to lose faith and confidence in yourself and what you're doing."

Then he said, as he unfolded the paper, which was magically all pieced back together with no rips in sight, "If you believe in yourself, it's so easy to lift other people up. You know, you can win this football game if you really have a strong faith and you have a belief. If you believe someone's going to tear you up and you can't put yourself back together" — he showed them the fully reconstructed paper — "you're in real trouble."

His magic act finished, Holtz asked each athlete to stand up and say why he thought Arkansas *could* win the game. They got up, one by one, and pointed out they had the number-one defense and other pluses. As they talked, "you could see the whole attitude change," Holtz says. They trusted one another. They made a commitment to one another to be the best they could be. Says Holtz, "You could feel the love, trust, and commitment come together. You could tell they cared about one another when they started praising one another, and I'll tell you, it's amazing what happens when you look for something sincerely positive to say about somebody."

The next day, the Arkansas football team had an unbelievable practice. People would later tell Holtz that they knew Arkansas would win just by the look on their faces when they ran out of the locker room. They destroyed Oklahoma, 31–6. But it wasn't the coaching, Holtz says. "It was a prime example of trust, commitment, and love."

Holtz doesn't keep a lock on the speech-making chores. He says anybody who has ever "achieved anything" is free to speak to Notre Dame's football team. Among those who've spoken at a practice are President Bush, former President Reagan, broadcaster Merlin Olsen, and leading businessmen.

To focus the team's energy, Holtz is particularly fond of mottoes, which he readily taps from anyone he happens to meet. One of his favorites is Count on Me. It means: "I'll be there at game time. I'll be ready. I'll be healthy. Trust me." That builds into teamwork, which Holtz says is nothing more than "just getting people to care."

The motto that exemplifies Holtz's approach to every game is WIN, or What's Important Now. In a grueling, twenty-five-week season, full of injuries and repetitive drills, it's easy for a football team to look past potentially easy opponents and become obsessed with upcoming *big* games against a nationally ranked powerhouse. That happened during the 1988–89 season when the Irish took on undefeated Miami and West Virginia. Holtz tries to overcome that with WIN. "If some other team has the ball on your four-yard line with two minutes left, it's so simple: What's Important Now?" If Notre Dame loses just one game, any game, the championship is history.

Holtz downplays every big game. The week before the Miami game at midseason, the coaches were careful never to mention the opponent's name. They referred to Miami as "the team we play on Saturday." Holtz did remind the players that Notre Dame had interrupted Oklahoma's 63-game winning streak in the 1950s and that the Irish had snapped UCLA's basketball winning streak in the 1970s.

"He made us think we didn't have to play above our heads," says Eilers. "He told us to go out and put our faith in the Lady on the Dome, him and his assistants, and everything will take care of itself. Miami was supposed to be unconquerable, but he said, 'To hell with that. We can beat these guys.' "

And they did. Notre Dame squeezed by Miami to seize possession of number one.

When the Fiesta Bowl approached, Holtz knew he had to guard against all the national-championship hype. So again he approached it like just another game. Nobody wore Fiesta Bowl slogans or badges. The team practiced in regular jerseys. They did fundamental drills, including a dreaded series of five drills Holtz calls "Buy your tickets for the county fair." A few people, including Devine and Mel Blount, the former Pittsburgh Steeler who'd played in four Super Bowls, spoke to the team. Other than that, it was business as usual.

"Coach kept us from getting caught up in all the hype," Eilers says. "He taught us you should eliminate all the peaks and valleys in life . . . to maintain an even keel."

Oddly enough, Holtz's seeming calm was the eye of his personal storm, according to his friend George Kelly. "Lou is a peak-and-valley guy around us, but he's not that way around the players. He managed to create for them a lighter atmosphere, convinced them to just enjoy the game."

In winning the championship, Holtz realized another of his 107 goals. He has about 20 left to accomplish, most of which he doubts he'll ever achieve.

That 1989 championship team convinced Holtz that the real strength of any team lies in its ability to abandon individual needs and band together for the greater good. It reminded him of a trip to Japan in 1974. He woke up very early, about five-thirty A.M., unable to sleep because of the twelve-hour time difference. He heard a strange cadence echoing around the buildings outside his hotel. He looked out and saw a team of Japanese construction workers doing calisthenics before they began their workday. Holtz was amazed.

"I thought, Wow, so that's the key to their success," he says. "They get with an organization. They have discipline and they have a strong feeling about that organization. Everybody is committed, all along the line . . . and the organization is more important than the individual."

Fine for the Japanese. But what about the ruggedly individualistic Americans? "The individual is ultra-important," Holtz says. "But there comes a time when you're on the field and you represent Notre Dame and you have no individual rights. Team rights supersede individual rights. When you walk off that field, you're an individual and you have individual rights. But while you're on the field, you don't."

Trumbull's Little League Champs

The True Boys of Summer

Tom Galla remembers his first practice at Williamsport, Pennsylvania, the mecca of Little League baseball. His Trumbull, Connecticut, All Stars were at one end of the field and the Taiwanese, who have dominated the Little League World Series for the past two decades, were at the other end. Trumbull players, already awed by the huge stadium, kept turning around and sneaking looks at the Taiwanese players.

Galla, the Trumbull manager, got mad. It's tough yelling at kids, he says, but sometimes it's necessary. He scolded his young players, telling them they weren't that great and that they would have to work hard if they wanted to win. Taiwan wasn't even in the same tournament bracket. Trumbull would have to beat two strong American teams before getting a shot at the Far Eastern champs. "I was such a miserable s.o.b. at that practice," Galla says. "I had never been that tough with them before."

His message got through. "That kind of woke us up from dreaming," says Andy Paul, a pitcher and outfielder. "When we first saw the stadium, we couldn't really believe we were there." Afterward, no one sneaked a look at Taiwan again.

If the Trumbull team were a business, experts would credit their surprise 1989 Little League World Series championship to strong leadership and innovative R and D. In baseball terms, that translates into Galla's Patton-like approach, and the creation of a new pitch — the Dart pitch.

The eventual result was a Cinderella sports story that reminded many people of the United States' hockey victory over the Soviet Union in the 1980 Winter Olympics. By all accounts it shouldn't have happened. But it did.

Trumbull, relying on just two starting pitchers for its sixteen tournament games leading up to and including the World Series, won its first two games at Williamsport and then faced Taiwan for the title. Going into the championship game, Taiwan had walloped its previous eight tournament opponents, 74–5. Teams from Taiwan had won thirteen of the previous twenty-two World Series championships, including the last three in a row, blasting the American finalists by a combined score of 43–1. It's supposed to be a game for kids, but in the past, with Taiwan, it often looked like men against boys.

Trumbull, however, with pitcher Chris Drury confusing the heavily favored Taiwanese with the Dart, won 5–2 before a crowd estimated at more than forty thousand at Lamade Stadium and a national television audience. It was the first championship by an American team in six years.

"That new pitch is why we won the tournament," Galla says. "Chris's fastball was moving sixty-three miles an hour and the Dart pitch, forty-eight miles an hour. When it got to the plate, it just died."

Little League baseball was born in Williamsport in 1939. The first World Series was played in 1947. Since then, the goal of every Little Leaguer who steps on the field in April is to play in Williamsport in late August. More than 2.5 million boys and girls in the United States and thirty-three other countries play Little League. When their regular seasons are completed, they form community all-star teams and begin the district, state, and regional playoffs that eventually lead to Williamsport.

That's where Galla, an insurance agent in his early forties, found himself at the beginning of July 1989. He and two assistants, Bob Zullo and Eddie Wheeler, brought together the fourteen best players from Trumbull's National League. Since Trumbull has two Little League charters and fields two tournament teams, Galla's squad was picked from a total of about sixty players on just five teams, an unusually small number. Compensating for the lack of numbers is a strong baseball program. Players in Trumbull, a town of about thirty-five thousand near Bridgeport, begin with tee ball at age six. The town also offers a winter baseball program at a recreation center for practice in hitting, throwing, and fielding. And the team had good athletes. Chris Drury, for instance, played on a Pee Wee national championship hockey team.

Going into the tournament, Galla and his assistants each had several years of Little League coaching experience. Galla had coached five years, winning a league championship each year; Zullo, in his early fifties, had coached ten years, including seven all-star teams; and Wheeler, in his early forties, five years. All three had played Little League baseball themselves, and all three had been catchers for their high school teams. Galla had also caught and played second base at Marietta College in Ohio. In 1988, Galla and Zullo had coached Trumbull's all-star team, which was eliminated in the district tournament, winning three games and losing two.

"I don't think a first-year coach could win the World Series," Galla says. "The coaches need to get comfortable with each other so they can get the players comfortable with each other." There were, obviously, disagreements among the coaches about the players and where they should play. Galla and his assistants were careful to discuss those differences in private, away from the players.

Zullo, whose job is supervising a roofing crew, compares coaching kids to managing a group of older workers: if they get along, everything seems to work more smoothly. "Once the team was picked, our basic theme was to try to get these kids to like each

Trumbull National Little League All Stars, 1989 World Champions, with Coach Tom Galla on the far left

other," Zullo says. "We didn't want any dissension or players screaming at other players when someone made an error. Face it, every one of these kids was likely to make an error. We didn't want them to compound the error."

Another big advantage for Trumbull was the experience of the players. Eight of the fourteen had competed on the 1988 all-star team as eleven-year-olds. Only one of the players on the 1989 team was eleven. In that age group, one year can make a huge difference because the players are much bigger and stronger. The two pitchers, Paul and Drury, also have August birthdays, the perfect month for Little Leaguers, who can't be thirteen before August 1. Both turned thirteen before the end of the World Series.

Trumbull selects its all-star team a little differently than most leagues. Normal procedure is for the coaches in the league to get together and pick the teams. At Trumbull, the players vote for their peers. Ten of the players on the 1989 team were selected by players and four were picked by the coaches. Before accepting each player on the team, Galla demanded total commitment from them and their parents. No vacation interruptions. No kids splitting their time between soccer and baseball. "I thought in the past there had been some preferential treatment," Galla explains. "I wasn't willing to be placed in the position of being accused of giving preferential treatment."

Galla is the first to admit, however, that it's nearly impossible to keep all of the players and their parents happy. There are always some who think they should be playing more. He tried to compensate by keeping competition open for several positions, depending on players' performances in games and practices, and their attitudes. For example, in the sixteen tournament games he used at least three different players at four different positions: catcher, third base, left field, and right field. "When the coach has confidence in you, you seem to play better," Galla says. "That same idea carries over into business, school, everywhere." The most at bats for any one player was 55. Galla's son, David, a second baseman, got 30 at bats.

"Having a son on the team was a problem," Galla says. Neither Zullo nor Wheeler had a son on the team. "I told Bob, 'You're going to have to take care of coaching David. You can be more objective.'" David Galla hit .365 during the sixteen games and .600 in the World Series. "The thing that made me proudest of my son was that he was able to play under all that pressure," Galla says.

Along with commitment from the players, the tournament also demanded commitment from the coaches. "If you've taken on an all-star team, you don't worry about your job," Zullo says. "The guy I work for is good about it. For the past ten years, he knows that from July to the end of August is my time."

After the end of the regular season, there is just a short period to prepare for the tournament. Trumbull began its practices on July 5. Its first game was ten days later. In that period, Galla held workouts every day — twice a day on weekends. He also scheduled mandatory pool parties and picnics. One night, when practice was rained out, Galla took all the players to see the movie *Batman*.

"I changed my philosophy," Galla says. "In 1988, I worked them to death. In 1989, I threw in all that fun, which was important. The comradeship of doing other things together united the kids a little closer." Chris Drury, who caught when he wasn't pitching and also played on the 1988 All Stars, agrees. "This year we really got to know each other and became great friends," he says.

Each coach had his specialty and tried to avoid meddling in the specialties of the others. Galla was the defensive coach, Zullo the batting instructor, Wheeler the pitching coach and team psychologist. "If I got too tough on them, or a kid didn't understand why he wasn't playing, or someone had tears in his eyes when he struck out, Eddie was always able to get them to talk to him," Galla says. "Tom's approach is kind of like a general," Wheeler explains. "Mine is to try to get them to do it for me."

Steve Kerr, a professor in the business school at the University of Southern California, has studied successful professional, college,

III

and high school teams, looking for leadership styles that can also be effective in business. In golf and tennis, where winning depends on independent, individual performances, Kerr says the most successful coaches are supportive and relatively easygoing. In football and basketball, where success depends more on the interdependence of team members, autocrats are more effective. " 'Autocrat' has gotten to be a bad word, but it's not," Kerr says. "It simply means a strict disciplinarian who knows what he wants."

Baseball is a much more difficult game to categorize because it combines both independence and interdependence, Kerr says. "The good-guy, bad-guy approach, with the stern disciplinarian at the top and the easygoing coach underneath, is not a bad model," he says. "The other way around wouldn't work. In the end, there are only a handful of ways of doing business, whether that business is putting out a product or winning games."

Daniel Schrein, a medical doctor who founded the Gladiators sports program for talented young athletes in Omaha, Nebraska, twenty years ago, says the most successful youth coaches are those who are both respected and truly liked by their players. These coaches create teams that resemble extended families. They have a personal charisma and the ability to communicate with their players without talking down to them. They create an atmosphere where the players are relaxed and confident on the field, because that's when they perform best.

"Another important characteristic," Schrein says, "is the ability to pretend you're angry when you're not, and pretend you're not angry when you are. We tend to treat kids like adults, but they're not. For example, you know kids are sometimes going to get distracted during a practice and start screwing around. You're not really angry at them but you have to pretend you are, to get them concentrating again. At other times, a kid may make a stupid error. You really are angry but you've got to keep cool, because if you get him upset he won't perform."

112

Galla, Zullo, and Wheeler understood that psychology and used it well. They also had a secret weapon, the Dart. The pitch was actually developed by Wheeler, who throws batting practice, two seasons earlier. A carpenter by trade, Wheeler was looking for something that was easy on his aging arm. "We needed a pitch that could give some movement without throwing curveballs," Wheeler says. "The curves hurt me more than the kids."

The Dart is basically a change-up, gripped between the thumb and index finger (or the thumb and two fingers, index and middle) in the nine o'clock and three o'clock positions. No seams are used. Instead, the ball is held on its skin. What makes the pitch so deceiving is that it's delivered with exactly the same motion and arm speed as a fastball, but it's released like a dart without snapping the wrist.

"It works a little differently for each kid," Wheeler says. "For Chris Drury, it drops and breaks a little to the left. Depending on how tightly you grip it, you can knock ten to twenty miles an hour off the speed." Keeping batters off balance, of course, is probably the single most important element of successful pitching.

When they assembled their team, the Trumbull coaches thought they had two strong starting pitchers. Paul, a right-hander, was strictly a fastball pitcher. His father wouldn't let him throw curves. Drury, also a right-hander, was a junk-baller. The team had a strong left-handed reliever in Matt Sewell. But he was injured during the state tournament, making the team even more dependent on the two starters. Galla had told his players: no stunt or trick bike riding. Sewell broke his left wrist when he fell off his bike while delivering newspapers.

During the regular season, Little League rules allow a pitcher to throw no more than six innings a week. In tournament play, however, the rule changes. A pitcher can throw as many as nine innings every other game. No one can pitch in consecutive games. "I didn't believe we could go to Williamsport with only two pitchers, but we did," Galla says. "There's no way those kids could have thrown so much without the Dart pitch. A kid could go out and throw it fifty times in a game and take absolutely nothing out of his arm."

Sewell, who played for Wheeler during the regular season, was already using the Dart pitch, but neither Paul nor Drury had used it before Wheeler taught it to them during the pretournament workouts. Drury took right to it, but Paul used it primarily to set up his fastball.

Trumbull won its first four games in the district tournament, but then lost, 2–0, in the double elimination event to a team from Bridgeport. It was their only loss in the sixteen tournament games. Galla had already scheduled a pool party for after the game and stuck with the plan. "That was maybe the best thing we could have done," he says. "The kids sulked for about fifteen minutes but then forgot about it. At practice the next day they were loose again." Trumbull came back to beat the same team, 7–0, to advance to the state tournament.

As the team advanced, the level of pitching and hitting it faced improved. To prepare the Trumbull hitters for the faster pitchers, Wheeler and the other batting-practice pitchers moved closer to the plate, 40 feet instead of the normal Little League distance of 46 feet. Some fourteen-year-old, former Little League pitchers were enlisted to give the hitters a different look. And, all the while, the Dart became more important. Drury began using the pitch more because it was much easier on his arm than curveballs. In the district final, for example, Drury allowed just one hit but threw his curveball too much. "My arm hurt for a week afterwards," he says. "The Dart pitch was great. It didn't hurt my arm." Both pitchers, like the pros, iced their arms after every game.

Trumbull won the state tournament and then scored 51 runs in the regional tournament, with just one close game — a 1–0, one-hit victory with Paul pitching, over a team from New Hampshire — before advancing to Williamsport. If the players were feeling any pressure, they weren't showing it. The coaches were a different story. Galla lost about twenty pounds during the tournament and Wheeler gained about fifteen pounds. "I didn't sleep. I just ate all the time because I was so damn nervous," Wheeler says. For Zullo, getting to Williamsport meant he could finally relax. "The goal of every all-star team is to get to Williamsport," Zullo says. "Once you get there, did anyone say you had to win? I slept every night."

There are eight teams in the World Series. Four teams representing different regions of the United States are in one bracket and four teams representing regions of the world are in the other. The U.S. champion then meets the so-called world champion for the World Series title.

Trumbull, with Drury pitching, opened with a 4–3 victory over Davenport, Iowa. Andy Paul hit a home run. The next game was against San Pedro, California, a team loaded with big power hitters. Paul was pitching. It was probably the biggest moment for the Dart. Three of the first six San Pedro batters hit home runs off Paul's fastballs. "I was kind of shocked," Paul says. Up until that point he had been able to blow his fastball past practically everyone, including a perfect game in one of the early tournament games.

In Little League, managers can't visit the mound or walk on the playing field. So Galla called his pitcher to the foul line twice in that first inning for conferences. The first time, after the second home run, he told Paul to keep the fastball low in the strike zone. His pitches had been up and too easy to hit. The second time, after the third homer, Galla's message was even more direct. "I told him to forget the fastball and just throw junk," Galla says. "I'd say from that point on, seventy-five percent of the pitches were Darts. That was a miracle. He had mainly used it as a setup pitch before. He hadn't really used it to get people out. He adjusted right there."

Paul didn't allow another run and Trumbull won, 6–3, advancing to the finals against Taiwan. When he throws the Dart, Paul, who turned thirteen the day after his victory over San Pedro for the American championship, holds the ball between his thumb and index finger and puts a little twist on his release to help control the pitch and get more movement on the ball.

Before Drury went to the mound in the final, Wheeler had some advice: "You can throw anything you want today, kid. We can patch you up afterwards."

Drury did just that. He mixed a few fastballs, change-ups, and knuckleballs with the Dart and allowed just five hits in the title game. He also drove in two runs. For the World Series he was 4-for-7, with three RBIs. His simple explanation of why the Dart pitch, which he holds between his thumb and two fingers, works: "It just fools them, I guess."

One of the most remarkable aspects of the World Series was that Trumbull committed a total of just three errors in the three games, just one against the Taiwanese. The Saudi Arabian team, by comparison, made six errors in its first-game loss to Taiwan, and Venezuela made five errors when it was routed 13–0. Taiwan was so concerned about Venezuela that it used its ace pitcher in that semifinal game instead of saving him for the final.

The dependable play of Trumbull was a testament to the coaching philosophy of expecting errors but not compounding them. The Trumbull coaches, in fact, instructed their players not to attempt to make spectacular plays, but to keep the ball in front of them all the time and make the routine plays. If an outfielder dives for a sinking line drive, for instance, the ball may get past him and go all the way to the fence, giving the runner extra bases. "We made all the routine plays," Zullo says. "When you do that, you win."

That philosophy also contributed to a style of team preparation that created no fear of failure. One of baseball's great attractions, and a reason it has remained so popular so long in American culture, is how it mirrors everyday life. Resiliency is central to both. A baseball player, Little Leaguer or major leaguer, can go from the ultimate humiliation, striking out, to elation, hitting a home run, within the span of just two at bats. Galla told his players not to get discouraged when they made an out, because they would soon be up again and have another chance. In the World Series, he told them that if they got one hit in a game, they had a great game. If they didn't get a hit, but played their defensive position well, they still had a great game. He didn't tolerate cockiness.

When the tournament began, Galla says he and his assistants had big hopes for how far the team could go. But they kept it to themselves. They tried to keep the players levelheaded and focused on one game at a time. During the regionals and the World Series, for example, the teams are housed at Little League compounds and stay with their coaches almost twenty-four hours a day. To avoid getting caught up in the tournament hype, Galla didn't let his players read newspapers or watch television news shows. Even when Galla yelled at his players he was careful to explain his motivation. After that hectic first practice at Williamsport, Galla took each player aside and talked to him individually. "Some of the other kids were surprised at how tough he was," Chris Drury says. "I've been on his teams five years. I knew what he was doing."

The coaching style was tough, but with its emphasis on communication, it put the players at ease. Ken Paul, Andy's father and a pilot for the Trump Shuttle, was amazed at how peaceful and calm the team remained during the tournament chaos. "There was a serenity, that everything was going to work out," he says. "And if it didn't, that wasn't the end of the world."

Tap the Power of Every Individual

Lee Brown

Linking the Police and the Community

When Lee Brown moved from Houston to become New York City police commissioner in early 1990, New York mayor David Dinkins spared no praise. "Of all the finalists, he seemed to be the absolute best in the country," Dinkins said. In an editorial, the *New York Times* called Brown "one of the finest police executives in the country" and lauded his innovative approaches. For his own part, Brown, who holds master's and doctoral degrees in criminology from the University of California at Berkeley, was typically low-key. "I take with me a process," he told reporters at a press conference in Houston, who wondered how he would fare in New York's 34,000-employee department, seven times the size of Houston's. "When I get there I will apply that process."

That he is doing. It is still too early to pass judgment on Brown's performance in New York, one of the toughest places in the world for police work. New York's criminals are tough and so is the press on its public officials. But based on Brown's success in Houston, don't bet against him. He has been through the pressure cooker before.

Consider the chaos when Brown became Houston's chief of police in 1982. The nation's fourth-largest city had gone through seven chiefs in eight years. A record 701 homicides occurred in 1981. The department was plagued by civil rights violations and had a reputation for frontier justice. In one notorious case, a suspect was found drowned in a bayou after being taken into police custody. Animosity festered between the police and the press. Reporters were sometimes arrested on manufactured charges as police officers got even for what they considered negative stories. In the history of the Houston Police Department, the highest rank ever achieved by a black person was sergeant. No outsider — read that as non–Texan good old boy — had ever been chief. Shortly after he was named chief, a cross was burned on Brown's lawn. Hate mail and threats against him were common, sometimes requiring twenty-four-hour protective surveillance for Brown and his family.

How, then, was Chief Brown, a black whose previous posts were on the West Coast, in Washington, D.C., and in Atlanta, able to turn the Houston Police Department into what is widely considered one of the best forces in the country, a model for modern urban policing in the 1990s? The Houston model, based on what Brown calls a marriage between the police and the community, is being used in cities across the nation like Washington and Los Angeles. How was he able to do this during the turbulent oil bust, when Houston budget pressures imposed long hiring freezes and rising unemployment sowed the bad seeds for increased crime? More simply, how was he able to survive for seven and a half years in such a volatile political climate?

The answer is Brown's approach. He operates much like a Japanese corporate manager, who focuses on quality and involves everyone in trying to attain it. The customer, in this case the community, comes first. "When I got to Houston, there was a separation of the people and the police," says Brown, who is in his early fifties. "It was the traditional us-versus-them attitude. Crime is not a police problem, it's a community problem. We have to solve it together." Changing those old attitudes toward policing takes patience and a constant eye on the long term, Brown emphasizes. "It is revolutionary, but we do it evolutionary."

The key element to Brown's process is neighborhood-oriented

policing. He writes and speaks about it frequently. The concept has slowly evolved since Brown's academic days. It became the official style of the Houston department in 1987.

Traditional police methods, for example, employ random patrols by officers. The theory is that criminals won't know when or where police might show up. The uncertainty, therefore, becomes a deterrent. But when the police do show up, they respond only to incidents and not to the underlying problems. "We say random patrols produce random results," Brown says.

One of neighborhood-oriented policing's main strengths is that it overcomes the feelings of helplessness to do anything about crime. It engages the community, patrol officers, and police administrators in defining the problems and devising solutions. "We bring in everyone and empower them to act," Brown says. "That's a pretty foreign concept." The patrol officer becomes the most important person in policing and in improving the quality of city life. He is encouraged to get close to the people in neighborhoods he patrols and be creative in approaching their problems. Everyone else's job in the department is to support the officer on his beat.

A good example of how neighborhood-oriented policing works is the Link Valley drug sweep that occurred in Houston in early 1989. Called "Death Valley" by the media, Link Valley is a six-block area of mostly deserted apartment complexes near the Houston Medical Center. With 2,700 vacant apartments (out of 3,000), the area in the last half of the 1980s became a haven for drug users and suppliers. Easy highway access made Link Valley the center of drug trade in Houston and for miles around. The area was like a drive-through fast-food restaurant, except that the main commodity was cocaine, not hamburgers. Year after year, literally hundreds of arrests were made, but dealers displayed little fear of the police because they could easily run and hide in the abandoned apartments. Drug-related crime began to spread to more affluent neighborhoods nearby. Property values plummeted. When an elderly woman living north of Link Valley was murdered in September 1988 by a teenager seeking money for a drug deal, the community said, "Enough."

Working together, police and community leaders developed a plan to attack the drug dealing and the underlying problem of a neighborhood in decline. The goal was not so much to make arrests of drug dealers as to give Link Valley a fresh start and a chance for economic redevelopment. In late January 1989, the police sealed off Link Valley, and about one hundred officers conducted an apartment-by-apartment search. No one was allowed into the development except residents. Since the action, by design, had been well publicized in the media, many of the drug dealers had already set up within a two-mile radius of Link Valley. Undercover police officers worked these new areas. For the next month, police controlled access to Link Valley with blockades. More than thirty officers patrolled the area twenty-four hours a day.

While the police protected the area, three hundred volunteers from the community cleared years of accumulated trash and debris, and mowed the high grass in empty lots. Housing officials inspected the apartment complexes and issued citations for code violations. County, state, and private attorneys tracked down property owners, informed them of their obligations, filed nuisance lawsuits against them, and acted to collect about $150,000 in delinquent taxes on the properties.

The result: Link Valley is no longer a haven for drug dealers. The cleaned-up area has become more attractive to economic development, an essential element in attacking the causes of crime and keeping places like Link Valley from becoming Death Valley again. "Drugs are our number-one domestic problem," Brown says. "They have the potential of destroying this country as we know it." About 65 percent of the criminal suspects arrested in Houston have drugs — not including alcohol — in their systems. The percentages are higher in places like New York and Washington, D.C.

Another successful neighborhood program — especially in re-

Lee Brown, former Houston police chief, now police commissioner of New York City

ducing fear of crime and building trust between police and citizens —
is the so-called storefront operation. (Fear of crime, Brown says, can
lead to neighborhood decline and contribute to further crime.) Think
of the storefront as a small police station with the atmosphere of a
corner grocery store or café. By late 1989, the Houston Police Department had established nineteen storefronts, with ten more scheduled
to open in 1990. As well as providing highly visible bases of operation
in neighborhoods, they also serve as community centers where officers
get to know the needs of the people. Officers in the storefronts can
help organize youth sports teams and scouting programs. Some storefronts can act as food banks for the needy, or can be used to collect
and distribute portable fans during the sweltering summer months.

Another example of Brown's neighborhood-oriented approach:
In 1985, to help reduce the high homicide rate among undocumented
alien Hispanic workers in Houston, Brown formed "cantina squads"
to patrol neighborhood taverns. Two years later, he called black and
Hispanic leaders together for what he called "summits" on crime in
their communities. The summit terminology illustrates another of
Brown's abilities: communicating effectively. "Who would want to
come to a meeting on crime?" he says. "My main motivation was to
get them thinking. 'What can you do, Mr. Businessman, to help fight
crime?' " Out of the summits came a program that organized citizens
on a block-by-block basis in some high-crime areas. Each block has a
resident captain who has access to a wide range of support groups,
much like what occurred in the coordinated Link Valley sweep. The
program has been so successful — reducing crime by as much as 40
percent in some neighborhoods — that Congress approved a $700,000
grant in late 1989 to expand the effort in Houston. "It can be a model
for other communities," says Representative Tom DeLay, a Republican who represents southwest Houston.

Bob Slater, an executive recruiter who conducted the search that
brought Brown to Houston, says one of Brown's main strengths is his

123

political adroitness — Brown has been called the maestro of bureaucracy. He has a high tolerance for criticism — even sniping — accepting it, then moving forward. "He can take disparate points of view and meld them into common objectives," Slater says. "He finds the sizzle in an issue and gets people to buy in." Houston Mayor Kathy Whitmire, disappointed at losing Brown but gratified by the national recognition he brought to the Houston department, says the appointment of Brown was the single most important accomplishment of her first term of office, and the most important factor in her landslide reelection in 1983.

Brown characterizes his career as a calculated, carefully planned series of steps in a long journey that eventually led to his appointment as police chief. His biography reads like pages from *The Grapes of Wrath*. He was born in Wewoka, Oklahoma, in 1937. Five years later his family, and several others, loaded everything they had in the back of a truck and drove to California to work in the farm fields. After graduating from Fowler High School, Brown attended Fresno State College on a football scholarship and majored in criminology. Because the scholarship amounted to just $50 a month, he also worked up to sixty hours a week at a local restaurant. In 1960, he moved to San Jose and became the second black police officer ever hired by the San Jose department. He established the department's first community relations unit and rose to the rank of sergeant, all the while continuing his education. He completed requirements for his bachelor's degree at Fresno State, earned a master's in sociology from San Jose State, and started work on master's and doctoral degrees in criminology at Berkeley, an hour's commute away.

In 1968, after deciding he would never be chief in San Jose, he became director of law enforcement programs at Portland State University. His doctoral thesis, completed in 1970, contained many of the ideas for community-oriented policing that he later developed in Houston. In 1972, he joined Howard University in Washington,

D.C., as associate director of the Institute for Urban Affairs and Research and as director of the criminal justice program. He returned to Portland in 1975 as sheriff and director of public safety for Multnomah County and then went to Atlanta in 1978 as public safety commissioner. He directed the task force that solved the Atlanta child murders case. "All the jobs provided a variety of experiences and familiarity with different regions of the country," Brown says. "I feel comfortable knowing what a good police department should be and what it takes to get there."

When Brown took over as Houston chief, there were about 3,200 officers and 1,200 civilians in the department. Now there are about 4,200 officers and 1,300 civilians. Despite a hiring freeze, Brown was able to put about 500 more officers on the street in 1988 and 1989 by reorganizing other department jobs. During his tenure the number of blacks and Hispanics on the force roughly doubled. Blacks now represent about 14 percent of the force and Hispanics about 11 percent. There were fifteen black sergeants when he joined the department. By late 1989, there were forty-five black sergeants, two black lieutenants, and one black captain. A third black lieutenant left the force to become police chief in another Texas city.

Brown makes good use of his academic training in his police work. As in Atlanta, his first task in Houston was a six-month assessment of the police department's strengths and weaknesses. He formed a department task force that included officers as well as administrators. "It was important to give a small number of officers a chance to experience what I had in mind for the department," he says. The findings, published and distributed in booklet form to the police department, Houston community leaders, and the media, were harsh. Brown said the department was understaffed and plagued by attrition. Many citizens of Houston, he said, feared the police because officers were disrespectful, slow to respond to calls, and prone to racial slurs and the use of excessive force, particularly in minority communities.

He followed the assessment with a published plan of action to correct the deficiencies. Later, Brown issued periodic progress reports on his action plan and other topics, such as a comprehensive narcotics plan, a crime control plan, and a report on integrating investigative operations through neighborhood-oriented policing.

Brown understands the importance of communicating both within the department and to the community. That became apparent his first day as Houston chief. He was touring police headquarters when he came across a group of visiting fourth- and fifth-graders. He talked to them about police work and even suggested that they someday consider becoming officers. Throughout his Houston tenure, he maintained a hectic speaking schedule, sometimes giving as many as four speeches a day to community groups. He also had a monthly cable television show, "Chief Brown's Journal." Consultants were brought in to advise the department on improving communication with the media. To increase the visibility of police, he quickly reestablished horseback patrols downtown and enlarged the police emblem on patrol cars. Within the department, he visited roll calls, rode along with patrol officers, and communicated through written and videotaped newsletters. A Toastmasters Club was established to help train other police officers to speak effectively to the community, the first police organization of its kind in the country.

"The clear message," Brown says, "is that you can't do too much communicating."

126

Sell Fantasy and Reassure People

four

Call it the Winnie-the-Pooh syndrome. At bedtime across the nation, kids are tucked in with their favorite stuffed toys. Maybe it's Ralph the bear, who wears one of his young owner's old soccer jerseys. Or maybe it's Chip, buck-toothed chipmunk and sidekick of Dale. When the lights go out — except for a night light, of course — kids hug a fuzzy friend for reassurance.

The toys may disappear as we get older, but the need doesn't change.

The people and the one company in the following three chapters have learned that the human need for fantasy and reassurance knows no age limits. They are successful, in part, because they

hold a mirror up to society — a mirror with a special coating that lets others see the softer, kinder images they mainly want to see. As the world grows more and more complex and the pace of change accelerates, as it certainly did in the 1980s and will continue to do in the 1990s, the need for the special mirror increases.

Everything at the Walt Disney Company, from movies to theme parks, reflects the same basic philosophy: Life is not that bad; people are basically good. The most reassuring highway signs in America have to be near Orlando, Florida, home of Disney World. No matter what job pressures or personal problems people face, when they see the

127

sign that says MAGIC KINGDOM 15 MILES, they just have to smile. Similarly, Roger Ailes, the image consultant who groomed Presidents Reagan and Bush, tries to get his subjects to feel comfortable so they can convey that same feeling to their audiences. "What I'm really doing is tearing away all the garbage to get them back to their natural state," he says. Richard Guy and Rex Holt, together known as GuyRex, the beauty pageant kings from El Paso, take the same approach with the women they groom for the Miss USA contest. "I'm trying to paint a picture that will please the people seeing it," Holt, a former artist, says of his work with beauty queens. A common theme for Disney, Ailes, and GuyRex is stressing the positive and purging the negative.

The differences in the three approaches are a matter of scale more than substance. Ailes and GuyRex work one on one. The Disney people work with millions of theme park visitors. But by training thousands of workers in the company's ideals, Disney can get some of the same personalized effects and try to make all visitors feel good about themselves. Each story shows that in today's world, success often comes through selling fantasy and reassuring people.

Disney

New Life for a 12,000-Year-Old Mouse

John Hench joined Walt Disney in 1939. Those were the days when almost nobody, including Hench, thought the company would survive. Nobody except Walt.

"Walt never doubted what he was doing, not one bit," says Hench, with the clearheaded certainty and knowledge of a fifty-year Disney veteran. "I've never once heard Walt say, 'I wonder if we're doing the right thing.' "

Hench says that what Walt knew, perhaps better than anyone before or since, was how to reassure people. How to convince them not to worry. How to convey to people of all races, ages, and beliefs a sense that "life's not that bad. You can make it. You're going to be okay."

If nowhere else, that's true in at least two places: California's Disneyland and Florida's Disney World.

"Walt's thing was survival, really," Hench explains. "Survival of the individual. That's our dynamic. It's all we have. Walt realized that the feeling of survival is what people want. It's the only thing we love, really. Everything Walt did was pro-survival."

Indeed, everything you see at Disney's theme parks — including Mickey Mouse — reinforces that belief.

"Disney represents the denial of death," says pop psychologist

129

Deena Weinstein of DePaul University. "Little Mickey proves that he can survive against all these bigger and badder things. All over the place, that's what you see — small things triumphing over big things."

According to Hench, Mickey is a universal symbol of life that's really a remake of a 12,000-year-old fertility symbol known as the Venus of Willendorf. Throughout history, a series of circles — akin to Mickey's playful ears and shape — has stimulated a warm, fuzzy feeling that even callous adults are drawn to. (The teddy bear is another example.) This symbol, known by various names, often was toted around by roaming tribes.

"Mickey triggers a nourishing instinct in humans," Hench says. "Like a baby's, Mickey's head is mostly forehead. At the bottom half of this oval, his eyes are set wide apart — like a baby's or even a young animal's. Walt knew all this a long time ago . . . Now we couldn't kill off Mickey if we wanted to."

Today, Disney World is the United States' number-one tourist attraction, by far. Every year, more than 25 million people — 80 percent of them adults — shell out $29 per day to see what Walt dreamed up nearly half a century ago. The reason they keep coming (65 percent are return visitors) revolves around creating the illusion that "everything's going to be okay."

The "real" world may very well be swamped with trash and drowning in decay. It is often filled with harsh, rude people, and insurmountable challenges. Not true at Disney. Once you're inside the Magic Kingdom's gates, the trash and the trauma simply melt away. As one Disney executive puts it, Disney World is like a medium-size U.S. city with no crime.

"We purposefully pose people with simulated threats and let them win over those threats," Hench explains. "In the big city, more often than not, they lose."

In the city, people tend to walk down a street and avoid looking anyone in the eye. That's the survival instinct at work. As Hench says, "They're trying to protect themselves by isolating themselves."

Disney World tries to present a world diametrically opposed to that. After you zip through Space Mountain, or plunge down a water slide, you walk away with the underlying notion, I'm not dead yet. I really felt that. I still have a capacity to feel something. "And there's something very reassuring in that," says Hench, who still works as senior vice president of Walt Disney Imagineering, the group that plans, designs, and engineers the theme parks' exhibits.

There is hard evidence of Hench's belief. Hollywood's golden age began during the worst years of the Great Depression. Disney got rolling in the late 1930s with *Snow White and the Seven Dwarfs*, the first full-length animated film. Now, whenever bad news looms on the horizon, Disney is one of the prime beneficiaries.

"Unfortunately, the rougher it gets, the more people want to have some exit from their environment," Disney CEO Michael Eisner told reporters in mid-1989.

Walt Disney died of cancer in 1966. On his deathbed, he would look up at the ceiling and tell his nephew Roy that he could see the entire park (Disney World) on the ceiling. "You know, Roy, we really need an east-west road across the center of the park," Walt said, pointing to a map that no one else could see.

Walt would never see his dream become a reality. (The company broke ground for Disney World in 1967; it opened in 1971.) But his spirit overhangs the parks as if he still made his home, as he once did, in an apartment atop the firehouse at Disneyland. In recent years, Eisner and President Frank Wells have gotten a great deal of credit and money (in 1988, Eisner earned $40 million and was the highest-paid American executive) for revitalizing the Walt Disney Company with hit movies such as *Who Framed Roger Rabbit* and *Three Men and a Baby*. But the theme parks still account for well over 50 percent of the company's revenues. "Eisner did revitalize the movies," says Dun-

131

can Dickson, Disney World's employment manager. "But the theme parks still belong to Walt."

A Walk in the Park

"A lot of people come here and ask us, 'What's the secret of your success?' " says Richard Nunis, the president of Disney World. "Well, Walt's been dead for twenty-two years. But everything goes back to his basic philosophies. Just two words, really: quality and pride. We design, we engineer, we build, we operate, and we maintain with quality. And that gives our people such great pride. If you don't have the pride, you never have the quality."

It was Walt who created Mickey, still the most popular Disney character. It was Walt who produced the Disney classics (*Snow White and the Seven Dwarfs, Bambi, Fantasia*) that become box-office hits every time they're rereleased. And it was Walt, along with Hench and a handful of others, who designed — and created the obsession with cleanliness and quality — at both theme parks.

When Eisner and his cohorts took over Disney, they contemplated changing the company's name to the Disney Company. As Hench recalls, they said, " 'Walt isn't here anymore. This is a new company.' " Then they did surveys and found out they'd better not change a thing.

"Sometimes people here don't buy that there's some kind of mystique about this place," says Hench. "They think this is just a business — that you just turn the crank and out comes this product in a neat little package. It's just not true."

The Early Days

When Walt began planning Disneyland, it was unheard of to ask people to pay to get into an amusement park. None of the nation's parks — Coney Island, Long Beach Park — charged admission. Walt turned that idea completely around.

Disney World

"Let's not be concerned with guests coming up to the gate and saying, 'Oh my God, I have to pay,' " he told Nunis. "Let's make sure that, number one, they have a good time. And, number two, that they receive their value."

Walt was convinced that people would pay for quality — something the Japanese have proved recently by commanding premium prices for Toyotas, Nissans, and Sony electronics. He also knew that Disney could never afford his grandiose plans unless they charged a hefty price at the gate.

Both parks were organized in a series of circles. In designing each building, Walt drew on stories and folk tales that everybody knew. Throughout his career, he steadfastly refused to capitalize on anything faddish or provincial. Walt wanted everything he did to have eternal and universal appeal. His culture, in a sense, would become everyone's culture.

At the center of the Magic Kingdom sits Cinderella's castle, developed from pictures that Walt made. At the center of the new Disney/MGM Studios is a classic reproduction of Grauman's Chinese Theater in Hollywood. Walt called these meticulously detailed centerpoints "wienies." They tend to draw people in because they identify with the old story or landmark. The only place this didn't work was at Walt's version of the future, Tomorrowland.

To keep the parks' magic alive, the Imagineers dream up something new to add about once every two years. Recent additions include a seventeen-minute *Captain Eo*, a 3-D video starring Michael Jackson, and Star Tours, a $32-million thrill ride at Disneyland. Hench personally scans fifty-two publications every month, looking for trends, which often are nothing more than the "rephrasing of an old message."

"We laugh about that," says Roy Disney, the head of Disney's animation department. "You find society evolving, but the basic themes and stories are pretty much timeless."

In designing each exhibit, Hench and one thousand fellow Imagineers draw from their experience in creating, step by step, Disney's animated films. Hench explains, "Just like a movie, you have to show them scene one, scene two, scene three, and so forth. And scene three has to take some of its meaning from scene two. It's like writing chapters in a book, really."

It may sound straightforward now, but when Walt first approached him with the idea, in late 1953, Hench was nervous. He thought, I'm no engineer. I'm an artist. Then Walt, as he was prone to do, would stick his long, bony finger into Hench's chest and tap it, bang, bang, bang, and say, "You're going to do this and you're going to like it."

As the Imagineers developed each exhibit, they were extremely careful not to duplicate anything else in the park. Millions of tiny parts became part of a gigantic puzzle. And every single piece, be it a castle or a park bench, had to enrich and support everything else. Everything is color coordinated and, to avoid notions of mystery or emptiness, the artists use very little black.

Walt insisted on top quality in every detail. Early on, during the construction of Disneyland, the Imagineers were adding miniature figures to an exhibit at Storybook Land. One of the art directors, who was trying to cut the budget, asked, "Why don't we just use regular glass instead of importing it? Nobody will know the difference."

Walt said, "I will . . . Look, the thing that will make Disneyland stand above everything else is the detail. And when we've lost the detail, we've lost everything."

Many of Main Street's buildings were modeled after turn-of-the-century landmarks. All the architecture is pushed in the same direction — usually slimmer than it should be, and soaring upward, to convey a sense of optimism. Hench and his colleagues borrowed from medieval cathedrals the idea of using a door within a door. It helps to bring a giant structure down to less threatening, human size.

Sell Fantasy and Reassure People

"We carry every single thing down to the last detail so there are no ambiguities," says Hench. "Our number-one survival technique is to see something and recognize it for what it is. We ask, subconsciously, 'Is this going to enrich my life experience, or the reverse?'"

To underscore this notion, Hench offers the analogy that you often see something, such as a pretty girl, that looks good at a distance. That's the easy part. But if it doesn't look just as authentic close up, "Forget about it. You're dead."

Through the years, various people, including hotel baron William Marriott, Sr., and ex–Disney executive C. V. Wood, have tried to create rivals to Walt's parks.

At Disney World's grand opening, Marriott approached Nunis at a reception at the park's Polynesian Resort. As they looked out at the castle, Marriott said, "You know, Dick, what I need are some of those castles around some of my hotels. What does it take to do one?"

Nunis looked at him and said, "Well, sir, a lot of guts and a lot of money."

Shortly after that, Marriott plunged into the theme park business by opening parks near Chicago and San Francisco. But it didn't work. Says Nunis, "They started out with a great concept, but they ran out of the guts to spend the money. You just couldn't take pride in it because it was just half there. You'd come down to the end of a very 'themed' street, and come up to an octopus ride that was not themed. They just didn't have the detail."

The Magic's the Magic in You

Walt realized early on that you can't run a top-notch park without top-notch people. He also was smart enough to realize that if you went to the park's popcorn stand and got cold popcorn, you'd blame Disney — even if the stand was independently operated.

The solution: make each and every person who works at the park a Disney employee. Then train that person to do his or her job as if the company's survival depended on it.

"Walt wanted all his people to be ambassadors for him," says Nunis. "Our whole concept of training was focused on the idea that 'you can create happiness.' "

Finding first-class professional workers isn't a problem. Each year, Disney World receives a whopping one hundred thousand applications to fill just four hundred white-collar jobs.

Finding good hourly workers isn't so easy. Every day, up to nine hundred people walk into Disney World looking for an hourly job. (The hiring ratio for hourly work used to be ten candidates for each job; now it's three to one.) Disney's hiring staff attempts to spend at least thirty minutes with each candidate.

The staff looks for candidates who are basically cheerful and optimistic. Says Disney training manager Shelley Lauten, "We look for how they respond to people. We create scenarios to explore that."

To weed people out, Disney warns candidates about its golden rules: No facial hair. One ring per hand. One watch, and it must fit into an exhibit's theme. No necklaces. Neutral fingernail polish. Make-up must complement skin color. And earrings must be no bigger than a penny. After hearing those rules, about 25 percent of the applicants drop out.

Once they're hired, Disney employees go through an extensive training process, beginning with a get-acquainted session known as Traditions 1.

There, they learn that Disney World's thirty thousand employees are not hired for a job; they are to be "cast" in a role and behave like "hosts" and "hostesses." They will wear "costumes," not uniforms. Everything they do at the park is designed to make their "guests" (as park visitors are known) forget the nasty world outside.

"We look at it as putting on a play for our guests three hundred and sixty-five days a year," Lauten says.

At Traditions 1, employees learn a sense of teamwork the minute they arrive. The instructor tells tables of five to introduce themselves to one another, then he leaves the room. Upon returning, he asks each new employee to introduce someone else (their name, home town, etc.) to the rest of the room. Then new employees are walked through the history of the company. They work in teams to answer quiz questions such as "Name the seven dwarfs," and "What does EPCOT stand for?"

In classes, as well as in a film featuring the theme song, "The Magic's the Magic in You," employees hear tales about real-life miracles at the parks. The tales tend to reinforce management's rules or suggestions.

For instance, employees learn always to volunteer to take a photograph. They hear about two nuns who had their last picture taken together at Disney World weeks before one of them died.

They learn that people wait seven to ten years to come to Disney World, then spend roughly $500 per person (per week) for the privilege. Then they're told about a boy in a wheelchair who spoke just one word before he died, "Steve," the name of a Disney host who had paid special attention to him.

"The real secret is modeling their behavior and perpetuating the Disney culture with stories," says Lauten.

The instructors tell employees: Look for guests' name tags. Speak their names whenever possible. Anticipate guests' needs. Never say "I don't know." Be accurate. Never argue with a guest. Never complain to a guest.

"We don't do smile training," says Lauten.

But managers do keep a close eye on the hourly workers. "You have to put the fear of God in people," admits Nunis.

After Traditions 1, employees spend anywhere from eight hours to three weeks learning about a specific job. One of the most extensively trained is a Jungle Cruise skipper. He or she has to memorize a hundred-page script, including a list of "approved" variations to occasionally break up the monotony. Everyone masters more than one job. On a given day, a Jungle Cruise skipper might rotate through six different jobs. Even management gets into the cross-training act. Two or three days each year, every employee must work in the park, doing anything from sweeping to dancing around the park in a hundred-pound character costume.

Like Walt, Disney executives make a point of leading by example. Nunis is often seen stooping to grab a piece of trash.

Eisner is well known for dropping into the parks — in a station wagon, not a limo — unannounced. Hench remembered one steaming hot day when he was changing a color at the entrance to the Magic Kingdom. He turned around and there was Eisner with no hat, his face bright red. Hench asked, "What the hell are you doing here?"

Eisner said, "Well, I've been talking to people and you know, we don't have enough signs for directions out here."

"I liked that," Hench recalled. "Walt would have done that."

On any given day, only about two hundred cast members are "in character" — dressed as Mickey Mouse, Donald Duck, Snow White, or whoever. Their roles are critical to maintaining every child's sense of make-believe. To become such a character, would-be cast members must pass through a series of painstaking auditions. Again, the rules onstage are hard and fast: Always be in character. Never eat, chew gum, smoke, or talk. Never tell anyone outside Disney World what character you really are.

To keep Snow White, or even an unfamiliar gnome, from appearing in the wrong place, Disney World's characters make their way around the park through a maze of underground tunnels. That's where they eat, socialize, and dress up with costumes from the world's largest (two-million-piece) theatrical wardrobe. To maintain the illusion, they make their way into the park through inconspicuous doors and hidden panels.

139

Disney World's cleanliness and friendliness are frequently rated by guests as the park's best attributes. Those two things, more so than Journeys into the Imagination or Adventureland, keep them coming back for more.

The first year Disneyland was open, the lot was filthy. Walt told Nunis to hire as many people as it would take — and buy as many trash cans — to keep it clean.

"Next time you walk through one of our parks, notice how many trash cans there are," says Nunis. "We've trained our guests to help keep it clean."

The trash is swept away by the most meticulously trained and groomed $5-per-hour work force in the world. According to Disney president Frank Wells, every park surface is cleaned every fifteen minutes. Some two thousand custodians work around the clock. Every day at dawn, a "banzai" cleaning crew steam-cleans every wad of chewing gum off the park's seats. Every window is washed — every day. At Disney's 1989 annual meeting, Eisner said that Bette Midler ran into a problem shooting a film at Disney/MGM Studios. The script was supposed to feature a trash-strewn New York street. But before Midler got there to shoot the scene, anxious sanitation crews had already cleaned up the mess.

Keeping Walt's Dream Alive

Disney uses a few psychological tricks to keep its hordes of guests placated. For instance, the waiting times — often an hour or more — are purposely overestimated so that guests feel grateful they didn't wait as long. The lines are formed in a series of tight loops, to make them appear shorter.

The parks have also benefited from Eisner, who, just like Walt, has a knack for picking a winner and pumping new ideas into everything the company does.

"Michael is really just a big kid who has ideas coming out of him at an incredible rate of speed," says Roy Disney. "Unless you're constantly generating new ideas, you're running a movie theater of the past."

But, whether it's Walt's Mickey or Eisner's Roger Rabbit dancing down Main Street and into everyone's memory lane, the intent will eternally remain the same.

"The parks make people realize that life can still be pretty decent," Hench concludes. "They're life-enhancing, and I don't know when we'll be sick enough in this country to ever prefer pain or extinction to that."

Roger Ailes

The Remaking of Two Presidents

It was early October, 1984, and President Ronald Reagan, the "Great Communicator," was having trouble communicating. The seventy-three-year-old president had appeared tired and confused in a nationally televised debate against Democratic rival Walter Mondale. Reagan's handlers knew they were in trouble. If Reagan didn't bounce back in the second debate, Mondale might walk away with the presidency.

Then a call went out to Roger Ailes, a relatively obscure media consultant who had played a small role in the reelection campaign. Ailes was asked to fly to the White House, observe what was going on, and make suggestions for the second debate. However, he was to discuss his ideas only with Jim Baker and Michael Deaver, Reagan's top aides, not with the president himself.

Late one afternoon, Ailes arrived at the little theater in the Executive Office Building next to the White House. The stage was set up for a mock debate. There were two lecterns: one for the president and one for budget director David Stockman, who would play the part of Mondale. To Ailes, Reagan looked uncomfortable, detached, and uninterested. When a panel of Cabinet members began firing questions at the two men, Reagan ad-libbed and fumbled around for answers. Stockman offered perfect responses, usually read from a notebook prepared by Ph.D.'s. Ailes recalls that when Reagan erred, one of his aides would always correct him: "Mr. President, the tonnage on that warhead is wrong . . . The date of that treaty was so-and-so."

Ailes knew the president was in a terrible bind. He warned Deaver and Baker, "If you think he was bad in Kentucky, wait till he gets to Kansas City. It'll be a disaster if you keep this up."

Ailes knew what was wrong. Reagan's aides were trying to pump the president full of facts. "His so-called handlers got him all screwed up and off his game . . . They'd gotten him into information overload," Ailes explained at the New York headquarters of Ailes Communications, Inc. "His handlers were saying, 'Hey, you've got to know *all* the answers.' And Reagan was saying, 'Holy shit. I can't learn thirty years of stuff. I only know what I know.' "

Ailes realized that if the president was going to win the debate, Reagan's handlers had to let Reagan be Reagan — that is, let the president go back to basics and quit worrying about little details. With that in mind, Ailes told Baker and Deaver to cancel the mock debates and get everyone off the president's back. He asked to spend a couple of hours alone with Reagan and to spend the last half hour with him before the second debate.

When Ailes and Reagan sat down to talk, Ailes did his best to "unplug or deprogram" the president. He said, "Look, Mr. President, people know you don't know the tonnage of that warhead, or the date of that treaty. Nobody cares about that. What they care about is what you believe in. That's what got you here in the first place. And they also want to be reassured that you're not too old for the job."

With that in mind, Ailes began to pepper the president with questions. But this time, Reagan was advised to channel every question into one of his basic themes. The president had spent twenty-five years in politics running on a handful of simple beliefs: government's too big; taxes are too high; we need a strong national defense; communists are bad. Ailes told Reagan, "What I want you to do, Mr. President, is to go back to your instincts. Just say what comes to you out of your experience."

With Ailes in charge, the president's team hit Reagan again with tough questions. But this time, Reagan the actor and consummate communicator was back in charge. Every time he started to stumble, Ailes would ask, "What do your instincts tell you about this?" His confidence renewed, Reagan breezed through the preparations. He also heeded Ailes's advice to prepare a short, pointed answer to the "age" question.

As agreed, Ailes spent the last half hour before the debate with the president. Alone in a Kansas City hotel suite, Ailes pumped Reagan up with a last-minute pep talk. "You can't hurt someone's confidence right before they go out," Ailes explains. "That's why I insist on spending the last hour or so alone with my clients before they go in front of the public. You can't have someone walking up and saying, 'By the way, your dog died.' It just won't work."

Reagan was magnificent. Cool and confident, he used quips and gentle barbs to steal the show. Asked about his age, Reagan said he felt up to the job and that he wanted the public to "know that I will not make age an issue of this campaign. I am not going to exploit for political purposes my opponent's youth and inexperience." As Ailes notes, it was not just the president's words that drove the message home. It was his timing, facial expression, and body language. That simple retort gave the media their lead quote for the next day's news — and greased the skids for the march to another Reagan White House.

It also crowned Ailes as the champion among political consultants and media manipulators. After a long career in television, including producing "The Mike Douglas Show" for many years, Ailes had finally hit the big time. His understanding of the American psyche

144

Roger Ailes, architect of the Reagan and Bush media campaigns

and his mastery of conveying messages on television were unsurpassed.

Hedrick Smith, in his book *The Power Game: How Washington Works,* noted that when the U.S. Senate agreed to televise its proceedings, at least a third of the Republican senators met Ailes secretly to get his advice. Smith wrote, "Ailes lectured the senators like a parent talking to children." As he had with Reagan, Ailes scolded them into realizing that what they had to say didn't matter nearly as much as how they said it: how they looked, how they spoke, how comfortable they seemed.

One notable politician who used to have a very difficult time with television was George Bush. Despite his relationship with Reagan, Ailes didn't get to know Bush until 1986. At that time, Bush was trying to develop a TV persona with help from speech coaches, but it wasn't working. He still didn't feel comfortable. He asked Ailes for help with his upcoming campaign. (Ailes, incidentally, was approached by five presidential hopefuls. But he worked only with Bush, because he was convinced that the public could be charmed into liking the guy.)

Ailes began to work with Bush and, over time, became one of his trusted advisers and confidants. In 1988 and 1989, before Bush spoke to the nation about drugs, and conducted his live interviews with David Frost and Dan Rather, he met privately with Roger Ailes. In fact, Ailes convinced Bush not to settle for a half-hour taped interview with Rather. He warned him that a tape would allow CBS to edit out sections where Bush defended himself. The result: Bush agreed to the famous live interview, in which he turned the tables on Rather for walking off the "CBS Evening News." That segment, shown in its entirety, helped Bush to wreck the "wimp" image that threatened to derail his presidential aspirations.

As with Reagan, Ailes helped Bush to become more comfortable and confident on TV. "The toughest thing for Bush was following the

'Great Communicator,' the great John Wayne character that Reagan was," Ailes explains. "George is more like Gary Cooper in *High Noon* — not as articulate, quieter, but the kind of person who has a steel core if he's pushed too far."

Ailes prodded Bush to relax and converse with the media, just as he would with anyone else. It may sound simple, but simplicity is one of Ailes's core philosophies. "People assume I'm out there adding some sort of crap or tricks," Ailes says. "What I'm really doing is tearing away all the garbage to get [my clients] back to their natural state."

Ailes was also the key person behind the TV advertisements that helped Bush win the presidency. As the *Washington Post* noted on January 17, 1989, Ailes was the "archetype of the master manipulator whose creations may have been more important than anything said by the candidate on the stump." The *Post* went on to describe the "brilliant exploitation of political technology" that Ailes used to get Bush elected. For instance, he and his colleagues assembled people into focus groups and supplied them with "people meters" — little dials that they could turn up or down to show when they were emotionally touched by what they saw on the screen.

While Ailes's team made use of such state-of-the-art technology, the reality is that his creations have more to do with Main Street than sophisticated research on Madison Avenue. Ailes flew by the seat of his pants, with a hodgepodge team that included, in his words, a "Hispanic from Los Angeles, a crazy sonofabitch from New York" who'd been fired from his agency, a Milwaukee woman who'd never done a national ad before, and a Young and Rubicam veteran in New York. They were a "bunch of wackos but they were great copywriters," says Ailes. "Nine of their ideas would be crazy but the tenth was right on."

This unusual team came up with about forty TV ads. One of the positive ads, showing Bush with British prime minister Margaret

Thatcher and Polish solidarity leader Lech Walesa and his grand-daughter, was picked as number one by the American Association of Political Consultants.

Three of Ailes's ads were widely criticized for their negative and critical slant. But they successfully cast Dukakis as a free-spending liberal who was soft on both crime and the environment. One showed a childish-looking Dukakis bouncing around a field in a battle tank. Another showed criminals in Dukakis's home state reentering society through a revolving door. A third pointed a finger at Dukakis for the intolerable pollution of Boston Harbor.

"The negative ads cut through quicker," Ailes explains. "People tend to pay more attention to them. People may or may not slow down to look at a beautiful pastoral scene along the highway. But everyone looks at an auto accident."

In a sense, Ailes was using the ads to package both candidates. When voters walked into the voting booth, he wanted them to think four things about each candidate. For Bush, he wanted them to think, "This guy's not a genius, but he's smart enough; he's traveled all over the world; he won't raise my taxes; and he's a kinder, gentler, family guy." For Dukakis, "Well, that Massachusetts 'miracle' seems like bullshit; he's soft on crime; he's never even been to Europe on a vacation; and he never smiles, so I don't know if I like the guy."

"A lot of it comes down to who you like," Ailes says. "People basically liked George Bush. They figured if they have to watch one of these guys on the tube for four years, it might as well be him."

In the final analysis, Ailes excels because he knows how to press the hot buttons better than almost anybody. "You have to give people information but you also have to get them to feel something about it," he says. "With all the computers, all the direct mailing, all the focus groups, that's what it comes down to: getting the data and coming up with a very simple message that makes them feel something. Only then do you have a chance."

148

GuyRex

The Sultans of Sash

"Be sure you eat something before you come over," Richard Guy warned someone on the phone whom he invited to a party. "We don't have any food in our house, just liquor."

Sure enough. Later, during a tour of the El Paso, Texas, home he shares with business partner Rex Holt, Guy opened the refrigerator. The only items it contained were bottles of champagne and a tub of Cool-Whip. Guy then opened the dishwasher. The instruction pamphlets were still in the top rack. "It has never been used," Guy said. "The only reason I put in a kitchen is because I might want to sell the house someday."

Guy and Holt, better known as GuyRex Associates, or simply GuyRex, have been called the Kings of Beauty Queens, the Gurus of Glamour, and the Sultans of Sash. They have an unparalleled record in a unique business: running beauty pageants and molding contestants. In the 1980s they virtually owned the Miss USA title, grooming five straight winners of the national crown in the last half of the decade. All of the winners were from Texas. "Any competition where you have a dynasty is unique in the 1980s and 1990s," says Michael Clark, president of Miss Universe, Inc., and Madison Square Garden Television Productions, which run the Miss USA pageant. "To me, they're like the Yankees of the fifties or the Celtics of the sixties.

149

They've brought a tremendous amount of attention to the pageant because of their success. It has enhanced what we're doing."

Guy himself uses just a bit less hyperbole to describe the two of them. "We're the old star-makers, that's what we are," Guy says. "We're like the old-time Hollywood producers."

What is the secret of these two men in their fifties who advise young women just above the age of consent? It's a partnership approach, polished over thirty years of working together, where each complements the other. "We argue and we fight," Guy says. Then Holt breaks in, finishing the thought: "But we've got to be able to criticize and take criticism."

Holt, tall and bearded, is a workaholic. He never drinks except for an occasional taste of his own brand of champagne, GuyRex, made from Texas grapes and bottled in El Paso. An artist by training, Holt is a quiet philosopher type, equally comfortable designing dresses and the sets for pageants and discussing the diminishing role of the small businessman in America. He concentrates on what he calls the outer beauty of a girl. "A true artist paints a picture for art's sake," Holt says, using an analogy from his past to describe his current role. "I'm trying to paint a picture that will please the people seeing it."

Guy, short and with rough facial features like Johnny Cash's, is part salesman, part public relations whiz, and part psychiatrist. He's always finding an excuse for a party, like the time he chartered a cruise ship from New Orleans for the 1989 Miss Universe pageant in Cancún. He helps design dresses and costumes, but concentrates on trying to bring out what he calls the inner beauty of a girl. "The world has been brainwashed by *Vogue*," Guy declares. "The real difference in a GuyRex girl is in the eyes and the confidence."

Holt often acts like a governor on the runaway train his partner Guy can sometimes be. Once, when explaining how the pair first started working together, Guy quickly jumped into a monologue of how they had changed the pageant business, taking it much more seriously and with more attention to detail than anyone else. "You're getting off the track," Holt said, interrupting his partner. "Finish the story first."

The story began in 1959 in El Paso, the West Texas city trapped in the desert between mountains and the Rio Grande. Here the modern world clashes with the wide-open frontier of neighboring Juarez, Mexico. And here GuyRex would begin to change the concept of the modern beauty pageant. Guy, a self-described army brat, and Holt, the son of a railroad engineer, met while teaching at an Arthur Murray dance studio. They soon tired of working for someone else so they opened their own studio. "We didn't sell golden dreams and promises," Holt says. "We taught dancing."

They also opened a shop to sell Christmas decorations. That led to decorating El Paso businesses for Christmas and then to building floats for the annual Sun Bowl festivities. In 1971 they entered the beauty pageant business, taking over the Miss Texas franchise of the Miss America contest and running the Miss El Paso contest, then affiliated with Miss America, a rival of the Miss USA organization. While the Miss America organization's main goal is to raise scholarship money for its winners, Miss USA is a for-profit enterprise. "I overdosed this town on Miss America, let me tell you," Guy says.

The GuyRex style, however, clashed with those fostering the American ideal. "I was trying to change the system and they kicked me out," Guy says. Soon after, the Miss USA people called, and GuyRex was in business again. The annual Miss El Paso contest, now affiliated with Miss USA, is still the largest local beauty pageant in the United States.

In addition to Miss El Paso, GuyRex runs the Miss Texas–USA, Miss California–USA, Miss Texas Teen–USA, and Miss San Antonio pageants. The Miss Texas contest, one of the top-rated television shows of the year in the state, brings in the most money. It costs $350,000 to produce, and GuyRex charges more than $20,000 a minute for advertising. To bolster ratings, the number of contestants from each area of the state is based on the population of the respective television markets. The Dallas–Fort Worth and Houston areas, therefore, account for about half of the one hundred contestants. The winner receives up to $100,000 in cash and gifts from sponsors.

Guy and Holt and a dozen employees also operate a dressmaking business and recently introduced their own brands of champagne and cosmetics. They also offer independent consulting for beauty pageant contestants elsewhere in the nation, even in Mrs. contests for married women. For $6,000, a woman receives a specially designed gown, a cocktail dress, a costume, and two days of intensive sessions from Guy and Holt. "The first thing I do is sit them down in my office, close the door, and ask them to tell me about what they really want to be," Guy says. He has consulted with some older female executives, trying to improve their speaking styles and personal presence, and has developed a video stressing the same techniques.

After the Miss Texas and Miss California contests, the winners come to El Paso for about six months of training before the Miss USA pageant. "If I had to have a girl go to Miss USA the day after the Miss Texas pageant, she wouldn't even make the top ten," Guy says. In El Paso, the girls receive counseling in physical fitness, nutrition, and makeup, and they're given tips on how to dress, do their own hair, and even walk down stairs. "I take care of everything for that girl so she feels good about herself," Guy says. The girls learn to handle the public by attending parties in El Paso and doing promotional appearances for sponsors. Subaru, for example, sponsors the Miss Texas–USA pageant. The winners go to school for three days to learn everything they can about the car, even how to make minor repairs and change tires. Then they frequently sit in a Subaru booth at county fairs, pitching the car to visitors.

Guy also tries to get the contestants to appear on the syndicated television show "Star Search" and puts them in front of the media as

Richard Guy and Rex M. Holt — GuyRex — with recent beauty contest winners

much as possible. In the fall of 1989, for example, both Miss Texas and Miss California held a press conference in New York and then appeared in bathing suits, barefoot, in Times Square for a photograph. "You should have seen how the traffic in Times Square stopped," Guy says.

The single most important aspect of the Miss USA pageant, Guy and Holt contend, is the interview. In fact, they say the entire pageant can be viewed as a job interview. "The woman of today is not a baton twirler," Guy says. "I'm training my girls to be businesswomen." Much of their training is aimed at making the girls feel comfortable in such situations. Says Marilyn Sietz, who runs the Miss New York and Miss New Jersey pageants, "Guy and Holt instill a tremendous sense of well-being in their girls, and it shows."

While Guy stresses the positive and tells his girls to avoid the negative — "You're worried you have big feet, forget them," he says — his basic method of training seems to be: tear them down and then build them back up. For instance, one of the first things he told Courtney Gibbs, the 1988 Miss Texas who went on to become Miss USA, was "You dress awfully." On a visit to El Paso in 1989, Guy was overheard telling one future contestant, "Your face is beautiful but your hair looks like shit."

Yes, there's crying, Guy admits. And, yes, there's fighting. But the process eventually builds confidence. That confidence will remain with the girl throughout her life, whether she becomes Miss USA or not. "Our philosophy is that it's not the crown that makes you a winner," Holt says. "We get the winner before we go to the pageant. That can apply to any type of business."

Guy and Holt didn't always have that approach. For a period of several months in 1976 they even thought of getting out of the beauty business. They wanted to win the national title. Badly. But never did. The low point for Holt came during the 1976 Miss USA pageant in Niagara Falls. "I figured, what we're doing is coming up here to lose," he recalls. "Why go through the frustration?" From that disappointment evolved a much more stoic attitude. Now they do the best they can to prepare a contestant. If she's meant to win, they say, she will. In 1977, they won their first Miss USA crown.

In their preparations, no detail is overlooked. During the 1988 Miss USA pageant, GuyRex gave portable telephones to both Miss Texas and Miss California. That way, the contestants could be in instant contact with Guy or Holt for advice and support. (The pageant later outlawed portable phones.) Before the 1985 Miss USA pageant GuyRex advised Laura Martinez-Herring to undergo chiropractic treatments in order to add nearly an inch of height to her five-foot-six frame. They also designed a gown with chiffon and beads draped to her ankles to enhance the illusion of height. And they got her to slow her rapid speaking style and reduce her heavy Spanish accent. Martinez-Herring won, beginning the run of consecutive Miss USA titles. The other winners were Christy Fichtner in 1986, Michelle Royer in 1987, Gibbs in 1988, and Gretchen Polhemus in 1989.

No one else devotes as much time to their contestants as GuyRex, says Marilyn Sietz, who has run her pageants for about twenty years and has known Guy and Holt since they started with Miss USA. "They are colorful characters, they have a tremendous sense of promotion, and they know how to create excitement," Sietz says. "Their girls who win deserve to win." This sentiment is shared by Michael Clark of Miss Universe. "If anything, their success has put pressure on other states to pay more attention and do their jobs better," Clark says. Sietz also thinks girls from what she calls the glamour states of Texas, Florida, California, and Hawaii have an advantage in the national contest. "You expect a certain look from them," she says. "Beauty pageants are a way of life in those states."

Even after GuyRex's contestants have won the Miss USA title, the firm's attention continues. While in El Paso viewing Mexican newspaper photographs of Polhemus before the 1989 Miss Universe contest, Guy became concerned that Polhemus was too tan and her hair too long. He sent a GuyRex employee to Cancún to talk with her. She eventually finished third behind Miss Holland and Miss Sweden. "Nobody's as professional as those guys," Polhemus's father told reporters in Cancún, speaking of Guy and Holt.

That reputation makes some contestants seek them out. Cynthia Nelson, who won the Miss California–USA title in 1989, had previously competed in two state pageants affiliated with Miss America. "I did everything wrong," she says. "I listened to everybody and did what they told me instead of searching for what was me and going from there. I decided Miss America wasn't for me." Then she tried Miss California–USA and won. "I was myself," she says. "I gave the best interview I've ever been through because I was so honest." She likes GuyRex because of their flexibility. "They are not trying to fit me in a mold," Nelson said as she prepared for the 1990 USA contest. "They are trying to figure out what's best for me, pulling out my strong points. That's why they are so successful."

Because of their methods and success, Guy and Holt have been the constant target of criticism by rivals, mostly aimed at the merchandising and alleged manipulation of the girls. A rumor circulating in mid-1989, for instance, was that Polhemus had a rib surgically removed to give her a better waistline. Guy laughed when he retold the story. "She'd never be able to wear a bikini again because of the scar," he said. Later, he emerged from the fitting rooms with another contestant in a new gown. Guy was holding an old-fashioned merry widow, a corsetlike garment that creates a smooth line at the waist and hips. "Look, I just took a rib out of her," Guy said, holding up the merry widow. "That's my secret, but don't tell anybody."

Guy and Holt will recommend that a girl get her teeth bonded, if the gaps between them are too noticeable, or her hair woven if it is too thin. If a girl wants cosmetic surgery to correct a perceived blemish, their standard answer is, "If it will make you feel better about yourself, do it, but it's not necessary." The most important thing any contestant wears, they maintain, is her expression. "My girls are not plastic," Guy says. "And they are not boring."

The headquarters of GuyRex are on a busy street on the edge of downtown El Paso. Actually it's a three-house compound, surrounded by a high iron fence. The house with the little-used kitchen, which Guy and Holt purchased about twenty years ago for $17,500, is in the middle. On the left is a now remodeled house, originally purchased for $9,000, with rented storefronts and apartments for contestants. On the right, at the corner, is the house containing the GuyRex offices, purchased more recently for $225,000. The three present a weird mix of Spanish, Victorian, and thoroughly modern styling.

The front door of the office house has a stained glass panel with the GuyRex logo on it. Inside are hardwood floors, Oriental carpets, and a fireplace in the main reception area. Country music plays on the speaker system. The walls are covered with photographs of Miss USAs, Miss Texases, Miss Californias in gowns and costumes. Most are signed by the contestants, with thanks to GuyRex. Holt, in his office upstairs, has a rolltop desk. Guy's desk, in his office down the hall, is a giant slab of glass supported by two metal ram sculptures.

In the middle house, where a metallic GuyRex sign is mounted over the entryway, the decor is more outlandish. The front double doors are made of bronze-toned steel plates welded together. Large candlesticks serve as door handles. Inside, near the front of the house, one wall is covered with pennies. "Forty-seven thousand of them," Guy says. Nearby is a chess table with medieval-style, foot-high pieces. Mirrors, huge candlesticks, and thick shag carpeting are everywhere. Upstairs, one bedroom has been converted into a bathroom, with a large round tub in the middle. Another room, which runs across the back of the house, is a huge closet filled with dresses, gowns, and stored paintings. It also has a bathroom.

Then there is the bar and party room, a newer addition just off the kitchen. It sits on practically the entire rear portion of the lot. Its centerpiece, behind the bar, is a century-old, church-size stained glass window salvaged from a brewery in Mexico City. It shows a reveler with a mug sitting near a wooden barrel of *cerveza*. Two wooden horses from an old carousel in Juarez are mounted along one wall near the middle of the room, as if bounding toward the bar. The party room steps up to another lounge area and then out to an enclosed swimming pool behind the remodeled office and apartment house next door.

For Guy and Holt, their home and work lives are inseparable. They follow no set schedule. During some periods they will work around the clock, seven days a week. "But it's not work," Holt says. Some days they sleep until almost noon before going next door to the office.

One day after work, Guy invited a group of Mexican journalists from Juarez to his house to interview Stephanie Kuehne. She had stopped off in El Paso on the way home to Houston after winning the Miss Wonderland title in Taiwan. (Kuehne would later win the 1989 Miss Texas–USA contest and be GuyRex's hope, along with Cynthia Nelson, for a sixth straight Miss USA crown in 1990. Neither, however, finished in the top ten.) In the hierarchy of beauty pageants, Miss Wonderland — "Isn't that an awful title," Guys says — is on a level with Miss Universe and Miss World. It's big in Asia, South America, and Mexico, but still little known in the United States.

After the Mexican photographers posed Kuehne at the chess set and poolside — "He wants you to show more leg," Guy hollered, translating one photographer's request — Guy, behind the bar sipping champagne, acted as an interpreter and coach for Kuehne, who also was drinking champagne. "I allow my girls to drink, but they can't get drunk," Guy says. Indeed, one of the Texas pageant's big sponsors is Miller beer, which the winners promote. A Mexican reporter asked Kuehne why Texas girls were winning so many Miss USA titles. Her answer, basically, was Texas braggadocio: she said Texas girls are prettier. "That's negative," Guy warned her before translating her answer. "That detracts from girls from other states. Now remember, nothing negative." Later, he would admonish her again. "Be humble," he said.

The amazing thing about the low-key press conference for Kuehne was that at the same time Guy was negotiating a sponsorship agreement with a Mexican construction contractor. Doing quick calculations on a piece of paper, the contractor agreed to sponsor the Miss Texas pageant for $10,000, and Kuehne personally for $7,000. He also wanted to be a judge. "No, no. If you sponsor Stephanie you can't be a judge," Guy said in Spanish. The contractor was disappointed, but left smiling.

As the Mexican press left, other friends and co-workers wandered in on this Friday night. Some kind of impromptu party always seems to be going on at the GuyRex home. It has almost become an unofficial stop on any tour of the city's attractions. About midnight, several journalists from an El Paso newspaper brought in guests from Dallas newspapers. More GuyRex champagne. And another tour of the house. The journalists came back shaking their heads in disbelief at the decor.

The surroundings do seem out of line with one of Guy's dicta to his girls: Don't overdose. Don't do anything — hair, dress, makeup — to excess so that it detracts from the real person. Asked about the seeming contradiction, Guy admitted, yes, maybe the house was a little overdone. "But it's still comfortable," he said. "If it wasn't comfortable, then it would be wrong."

By two A.M., Kuehne had retired to her apartment, Holt had called in from New Orleans where he was on business, and the American journalists had departed. Guy was sitting on the floor, talking to

159

a small group of friends around a coffee table. When he spoke, he fixed his eyes on the person he was talking to, not in a way to make the person uneasy, but as a vigilant observer always looking for that inner person. He took another sip of champagne and said, "I believe in beauty queens."

And that, perhaps, is the most important reason for GuyRex's success.

Tap the Power of Information

five

As the world goes increasingly on-line, and desktop computers rival the power of mainframes, the problem is not getting information but using it. Information that will give the answers to all kinds of marketing, distribution, and manufacturing problems is probably in a computer somewhere — maybe even your own. All you have to do is find it.

In the following chapters you'll meet three companies that literally filter the universe for data useful to them, and then focus what they find on specific areas. They are successful because they take information and use it to its fullest potential. One company, Frito-Lay, taps the power of information to sell snack foods. Another, Nintendo, sells video games. The third, Information Resources (IRI), makes a pure play. It sells nothing but information.

Frito-Lay and Nintendo, one American and the other Japanese, could be twin enterprises. Each employs elaborate research and product testing to stay in touch with the changing tastes of predominantly young customers. Frito-Lay's ten thousand salesmen submit daily reports on hand-held computers. Nintendo monitors the point-of-purchase data from twelve thousand retail outlets so it knows what games are selling where. Frito-Lay has a special phone number for customers who have nutrition questions about the company's products. Nintendo has a special number for video game players to receive advice.

161

IRI, by contrast, considers companies like Frito-Lay to be its main customers. But the approach is the same: know everything there is to know, then figure out a way to sort and sift the data to find the answers to the marketing and promotion problems that face package goods companies. IRI chairman John Malec compares the process to mining gold. In a mountain of rock and gravel there are a few nuggets worth keeping. Tapping the power of information means finding a way to locate those nuggets faster.

Frito-Lay's Recipe for Success

Permission to Indulge

S mack your lips. The secret to success in the snack food business is so close you can taste it. Indeed, if the chips don't taste right, if they don't look and feel right — factors closely associated with taste — people won't eat them. George Crum discovered that when he created the potato chip in 1853 at a hotel in Saratoga Springs, New York. A customer ordered fried potatoes, but kept sending them back because they were too thick. Crum finally sliced the potatoes in thin wafers and cooked them crisp. His effort satisfied one customer and started a whole new snack rage called Saratoga chips.

At Frito-Lay, Inc.,* the world's largest maker of salty snacks, the management techniques are a bit more sophisticated. But the guidelines are still vintage George Crum: Stay close to the customer and concentrate on taste. "We can't compromise in the flavor, texture, and appearance of the product," says Bob Longan, the company's vice president of product development.

In 1986, that uncompromising approach helped Frito-Lay launch one of the most successful new snack products of all time, *Cool Ranch* flavor *Doritos* tortilla chips. In the industry, *Cool Ranch* flavor is a

163

* The following are owned by Recot, Inc., and licensed exclusively to Frito-Lay, Inc.: *Frito Lay*®, *Doritos*®, *Cool Ranch*®, *Lay's*®, *Chee-tos*®, "*Betcha can't eat just one.*"®, *Fritos*®, *Salsa Rio*®, *McCracken's*®, and *Ruffles*®.

legend. With comedian Jay Leno acting as the main pitchman, consumers bought $218 million worth of the chips in 1987, only their second year on the market. Sales surged another 30 percent in 1988, to $270 million, and hit $300 million in 1989. That's the equivalent of creating a Fortune 1000 company on the basis of one flavor of one style of chip.

In 1989 and 1990, Frito-Lay was ready to repeat the magic. Capitalizing on a trend toward so-called light food and drink, the company introduced to the nation's snackers tortilla chips that contain one third less oil and slighly fewer calories than the company's regular items. Light potato chips and cheese snacks soon followed. As a group, the revenue potential of the low-oil line could substantially exceed that of *Cool Ranch* flavor *Doritos* tortilla chips, predicts Dwight Riskey, vice president for new products.

Whether it's a new flavor of an existing product or an entirely new concept like low oil, Frito-Lay's success is the result of a combination of taste engineering by lab scientists and the company's well-polished flair for consumer testing, pinpoint marketing, and efficient manufacturing processes. Better than any other snack food company, Frito-Lay understands what the customer wants and then delivers the product. Emanuel Goldman, a PaineWebber securities analyst who is probably the leading authority on snacks and soft drinks, calls Frito-Lay the Mozart of the snack food industry. No company is better at themes and variations of established product lines, he says. No company is better at composing new product ideas and conducting product campaigns. Adds Martin Friedman, who tracks new products as editor of *Gorman's New Product News:* "Frito-Lay is definitely on the leading edge, as far as light snacks. This whole light market is really a magic button."

Light snacks, along with light beer and diet soda, give health-conscious consumers more permission to indulge. *Doritos* light tortilla chips, for example, have four grams of fat per serving, compared with seven grams for regular *Doritos* tortilla chips. A major motivation for food companies entering this new market is the simple logistics of demographics and eating habits. As people get older they tend to eat less in general — about 2 percent fewer calories a year — and fewer salty snacks. Over the past decade, however, people have maintained their snacking habits longer. A thirty-year-old today still eats fewer salty snacks than a

Frito-Lay understands what the customer wants and delivers the product.

twenty-year-old, but more than a thirty-year-old of ten years ago. In the past few years, per capita consumption of salty snacks has increased about one third of a pound per year, to more than thirteen pounds. By making their products less filling — to borrow a phrase from Miller Lite beer — companies hope to continue that trend. And the best feature of the new light snacks, says Riskey, is that many traditional nonsnackers are buying them. That means new sales for Frito-Lay, rather than just cannibalizing sales from the company's other products. "It's a different kind of market for light snacks," Riskey says. "The people tend to be older, have fewer kids, higher incomes, and are better educated."

While tinkering with established brands does hold some risks, as Coca-Cola discovered with its New Coke formulation, it also can offer high rewards. "Light oil enhances Frito-Lay's brand equity because it's a response to human needs," says Carol Moog, a psychologist and independent marketing consultant in Bala-Cynwyd, Pennsylvania. "Really, it makes so much sense, unless they taste bad." Moog says well-known brands become almost like extended families and friends to some people. That allure is one of the reasons companies like RJR Nabisco, with a huge stable of established brands, have been such popular buy-out targets. Their brands are already a part of modern culture and almost impossible to re-create.

165

Dallas-based Frito-Lay, a division of PepsiCo, Inc., controls about a third of the $10 billion salty snack market in the United States, according to surveys by the trade journal *Snack World*, and about half of the snack chip market. Its nearest rival is the Borden Snacks Group of Columbus, Ohio, a division of Borden, Inc., with about $1 billion in domestic sales. Frito-Lay was formed in 1961 with the merger of the Frito Company known mainly for its *Fritos* corn chips, and the H. W. Lay Company, known for its *Lay's* brand potato chips. The new firm merged again in 1965, with Pepsi-Cola, to form PepsiCo. Today, Frito-Lay accounts for roughly 25 percent of PepsiCo's worldwide sales and 40 percent of its operating profits. Frito-Lay's forty plants, in more than twenty states, use about two billion pounds of potatoes a year, about 5 percent of all potatoes grown in the United States, and about ten million bushels of corn, 1 percent of all the corn produced in the United States, to make more than ten thousand packages of snacks per minute. The company has four of the ten best-selling dry-grocery brands in the United States — *Doritos* tortilla chips, *Ruffles* potato chips, *Lay's* potato chips, and *Fritos* corn chips, and six of the top ten snack chip brands. *Doritos* tortilla chips, by themselves, are a billion-dollar business.

Frito-Lay first flirted with the low-oil, light concept in the early 1980s, but couldn't get the taste right so abandoned the project. Borden went ahead with its own low-fat potato chip about the same time and it flopped. More recent advances in taste technology, however, made the new Frito-Lay project feasible. Consider the problem with *Chee-tos* cheese puff snacks. Cutting the oil content also cut down on the cheese solids, and, therefore, the taste. Frito-Lay researchers were able to compensate with enzyme-modified cheese.

All of the company's laboratory research is conducted in a 150,000-square-foot research and development center in Irving, a suburb of Dallas. The center employs more than three hundred researchers, including seventy Ph.D.'s. They use the most sophisticated equipment available, including a mass spectrometer, to make sure the flavor components in any new or existing product are present in precisely the right amounts. The site also has its own pilot plant, which can produce twenty pounds of potato chips an hour for use in some of the taste tests. By comparison, a full-production chip machine produces five thousand pounds an hour.

When developing new products, Longan is most concerned about eliminating a heavy aftertaste and taste buildup. "We want a big flavor impact, a pleasant aftertaste, and not much flavor buildup so the consumer wants to go back and have another," Longan says. That taste philosophy was probably stated best in an advertising campaign for *Lay's* potato chips that began in the 1960s: "Betcha can't eat just one." It's still true for the low-oil line. "I think they're terrific," says PaineWebber's Goldman.

Longan, who has been with Frito-Lay almost twenty years, says new-product ideas come from a variety of sources, including the company's sales force, competition, trend watching in restaurants and grocery stores, consultants, and upper management. At any given time, Longan's researchers may be pursuing between thirty and forty different ideas — between one hundred and two hundred over the course of a year. Out of every hundred ideas, between ten and fifteen become what he calls "projects." These ideas fit the company's business, are technically feasible, and make sense commercially.

Many of the ideas are what Frito-Lay calls line extensions, new flavors, or taste twists that capitalize on the popularity of the company's main brands. Some research shows that brands that dominate their markets are 50 percent more profitable than those of their nearest competitors. The *Fritos* corn chips name, for instance, is more than fifty years old. But in 1986 Frito-Lay introduced a new flavor, *Chili Cheese* flavor *Fritos* corn chips, that had more than $60 million in first-year sales. "It gave the whole corn chip category a real boost," says Mike Maloney, who heads one of Frito-Lay's regional business groups.

When it comes to new products, Frito-Lay, with its national

167

presence, generally has bigger ambitions than other snack food companies. It usually won't consider an item unless it can generate $40 million or more a year in sales. It considers $100 million a major success. Martin Friedman of *Gorman's New Product News* says fewer than 1 percent of the roughly one thousand new snack and candy products introduced every year generate more than $25 million in first-year sales. Conventional wisdom in the industry used to indicate that 80 percent of new products fail. Newer studies suggest more than 90 percent fail, meaning they don't hit their profit or sales targets. "I've been tracking this business for more than thirty years, and it's harder now than ever for manufacturers to get new products established," says Robert McMath, who has assembled one of the world's largest collections of package goods — more than 75,000 items — in Canandaigua, New York. "That's why we're seeing more line extensions and variations of established products."

Once a potential new product, like *Cool Ranch* flavor or the light snacks, passes the initial taste test in Longan's center and becomes a "project," it then faces a barrage of further testing and refining, which could eventually involve more than 100,000 consumers and take years before being launched nationally.

When you ask Frito-Lay officials the real reasons for their success, they credit their entire system — from the way products are conceived and manufactured to the ten thousand salespeople who make nearly 400,000 calls a week on stores around the country. The company even sponsors an annual competition for its truck drivers and mechanics, with more than $10,000 in prizes awarded to the winners, to promote their skills and professionalism. But just as with George Crum so long ago in Saratoga Springs, the main reason is the continual product testing and contact with customers. Frito-Lay researchers and marketers are constantly tinkering with new tastes and promotional methods based on the responses they receive from test customers. A product is not released for general distribution until all the feedback says it is right.

In its hometown of Dallas, for instance, Frito-Lay pays community groups (scouts, churches, soccer clubs) to test products and product ideas. They sample from five to ten different products, entering their taste opinions directly on portable computers. The compiled results are available to researchers the next day. "That overnight turnaround is great feedback for the scientists," says Longan. "It really gets their attention."

As the project ideas are refined using that overnight feedback, the company also tests products with consumers in shopping malls and with target consumers in homes around the country. In those tests, for example, each of the low-oil products scored equal to its sister (normal-oil) product, meaning consumers couldn't tell the difference or, when they did, had equal preference. If the results of the tests are positive and the product's sales potential is high enough, the next step is a market test. At any one time, the company could have between five and ten different products in test markets.

A year is probably the optimum length of time for a full-scale market test, to get a good idea of the long-term potential of a new product, Riskey says. Frito-Lay, however, can get a good fix on some of its products in five or six months because they turn over so fast, often at the rate of once a week. The company designs its products with a shelf life of forty-nine days, but codes them for removal from the shelves after thirty-five days to ensure their freshness.

Occasionally, however, products can go right from the home test to full-scale distribution because the results are so encouraging. Example: *Cool Ranch* flavor. The only problem was the name. Up until just before the new product was launched, it was called *Malibu Dip* flavor. Some late consumer sampling, however, indicated confusion about what "Malibu Dip" really meant, so the name was changed. All *Doritos* tortilla chip flavors have two words in their name. One indicates the flavor and the other provides what Frito-Lay calls a good "romance descriptor." Thus *Nacho Cheese* flavor, *Cool Ranch* flavor, and *Salsa Rio* flavor.

169

Sometimes all the testing leads to a decision not to launch a promising product. Such was the case with *McCracken's* apple chips, actual slices of apple, cooked crisp and then seasoned. Because it had never sold anything like them before, Frito-Lay tested the apple chips concept for more than three years before deciding to kill the project. The product was unique and was received well by consumers in taste tests. But a major problem was deciding where to sell the new chips in the supermarket. In bags in the salty snack section? In boxes in the fruit snack section? Frito-Lay tested both approaches and wasn't satisfied with either solution.

In 1985 and 1986, Frito-Lay did introduce several new nonsalty snacks that failed. Some industry experts thought Frito-Lay had introduced the products much too fast, overloading and confusing the company's sales representatives without enough regard for one of the company's main strengths, its established brands. Since then, the company has returned to an emphasis on new flavors of existing brands and other line extensions like the low-oil snacks. The problems with the new products may have contributed to the decision about *McCracken's* apple chips. Another problem with the apple chips was the capital investment required. They needed an entirely new line of manufacturing equipment.

The low-oil snacks, by comparison, are manufactured by modifying existing equipment. They also offer considerable savings through lower production costs. PaineWebber's Goldman says oil is the single most costly ingredient in Frito-Lay's salty snacks, equaling about 9 percent of the company's $4.5 billion in revenues. Each penny a pound saved in manufacturing costs, Frito-Lay says, translates into an additional $10 million in profits.

170

Frito-Lay began test-marketing *Nacho Cheese* flavor *Dorito Light* tortilla chips in January 1988. In mid-1988 it began market tests for low-oil *Ruffles* potato chips and *Chee-tos* cheese snacks, all the while monitoring consumer feedback. In 1988, with the taste components of the new products pretty well locked in, Frito-Lay began a BehaviorScan test of all its low-oil items in one market, Grand Junction, Colorado. Offered by Information Resources, Inc., a Chicago market research firm (see page 186), BehaviorScan allows a manufacturer like Frito-Lay to test its new products in conjunction with different marketing and advertising programs. Among the questions Frito-Lay seeks to answer in its market tests: How do the different products work together? What sizes, packaging, and pricing work best? How exactly should the products be marketed and promoted in the stores?

Riskey says the BehaviorScan technique has revolutionized marketing. Through computerized scanning of purchases at supermarkets, it allows Frito-Lay to monitor the buying patterns of each participating household in a market area. (Each family has its own ID card, to be presented at checkout time.) Frito-Lay can then immediately judge the impact on sales of any marketing changes it makes. A new service from IRI called InfoScan, also based on supermarket scanning data, helps Frito-Lay and other companies judge the performance of products once they are launched into the general market.

For optimal use of all this information against its national and regional competitors, Frito-Lay installed a new computer system at its Dallas headquarters and reorganized its manufacturing and marketing operations into four regional business groups in mid-1989. Each unit now focuses on the particular consumer tastes, competitors, and trade differences in its area. Salt-and-vinegar-flavored *Lay's* potato chips, for example, are much more popular in the Northeast than the Southwest. The six hundred top decision makers in the company have instant access to data compiled from hand-held computers carried by Frito-Lay's ten thousand salespeople and from IRI.

"We'll probably know more about what the competition is doing than they do," says Frito-Lay president and chief executive Robert Beeby. "This data is as close as we'll ever get to real time. It enables

171

us to change course in midstream, to rev up a campaign when we need to, to counter the competition when it looks like they're on to something smart, to rethink a trade promotion when it doesn't appear to be working."

Some marketing experts are still wary of the enormous amount of data available through scanners, saying it amounts to an information overload. Companies don't know how to use all the information. Riskey, however, says Frito-Lay has designed its computer system to do the work. The computer is constantly trolling through the data, and it sets off an alarm anytime there is a significant change in market share, positive or negative. Then company executives try to determine why.

The next frontier for Frito-Lay and other snack food companies in their efforts to give consumers even more permission to indulge is rather obvious: diet snacks. "You don't have to be a rocket scientist to figure out that no-cal potato chips would have a helluva big market," says investment analyst Ron Fielding, who is president of the Rochester Funds. While low-cal is a possibility, no-cal is probably unrealistic, Riskey says. "Food has calories," he says. "And as long as potato chips are made out of real potatoes, there will be calories." That's one worry George Crum didn't have.

Nintendo-mania

Selling a National Obsession

At first glance, it looked just like any other consumer electronics trade show. Weary-legged attendees, many of them retailers looking to pack their shelves for the Christmas shopping season, milled about exhibits plastered with colorful decor and company names like Atari, Panasonic, and Casio.

The closer they edged to the far corner of Chicago's cavernous McCormick Place, the louder the rumble got. The "oohs" and "aahs" coming from this particular corner sounded vaguely familiar, reminiscent of the way adults giggle and squirm when they're acting like kids. Sure enough. Nintendo, the video game craze turned national obsession, was what normally sane adults were making such a fuss about.

For Nintendo, the June 1989 Consumer Electronics Show was a crowning achievement. In endless droves, some four thousand attendees a day inched their way into Nintendo's booth, a display area the size of a football field filled with everything from video game boxes and laser guns to infrared remote controls and a game you play by dancing around in your bare feet. Nintendo shelled out $1.5 million to erect the most extravagant display in trade show history. The company was beating its chest in proud recognition of the fact that Nintendo, not Atari or Panasonic or Casio, is now the undisputed champion of the home entertainment world. In both 1987 and 1988, Nintendo was America's number-one-selling toy. In its heyday, the Cabbage Patch doll reached $600 million in annual sales. In 1989, Nintendo and its licensees surpassed $2.6 billion.

Behind the scenes at the trade show, six of the engineering wizards most responsible for Nintendo's rise to glory quietly made their own way around the showroom floor. These game designers hadn't flown from Japan to Chicago to celebrate or even to pitch Nintendo products to retailers. Their full-time job is to scrutinize American culture, to study the way typical Americans normally behave. From the electronics show they moved on, traveling around the United States to absorb the trends and fads that are permeating the popular culture. A typical trip might include a day at Disneyland in California, an afternoon of shopping at a K mart, an evening at a baseball game in Pittsburgh, a visit to a local library, and a walk through New York City's Central Park.

"While they're here visiting, they communicate very little with us," says Peter Main, the marketing vice president of Nintendo of America, Inc. "But obviously they're very sensitive to what's going on in America. It's like osmosis."

The Japanese come here to look for ideas that they can take back to Japan, incorporate into a video game, and ship back to America. In Japan, it has become a great honor for a video game designer to design a game that sells a million cartridges or more in the United States. Several Japanese have done just that: The Legend of Zelda has sold 3 million copies; The Super Mario Bros., created by thirty-five-year-old Shigeru Miyamoto, 9 million copies.

It's no quirk of fate that Nintendo video game machines can be found in one of every five living rooms in the United States today. They're there because a group of Japanese came up with the sophisticated games and an ingeniously clever marketing scheme, to make Nintendo virtually irresistible to America's youths.

"Nintendo has become the icon or mascot of this generation, in much the same way that AM radio was in the 1950s or FM radio in the sixties," says Brian Stonehill, a social critic and professor at Pomona College.

Teenagers today talk and trade Nintendo games the way baby boomers swapped Top Forty singles and baseball cards. They play for hours on end. One fourteen-year-old, Rasheed Hall of West Palm Beach, Florida, played for two days straight. (Some of Nintendo's complicated adventure games take up to one hundred hours to complete.) Why are they so obsessed?

Nintendo can tell you, at any given moment, exactly who's playing its games: their age, sex, and skill level.

"There's always going to be a must-have item for kids," says David Surrey, an anthropologist at St. Peter's College in Jersey City. "Remember when people used to twirl a hula hoop twelve hours at a time?"

Video games, particularly Nintendo's, are perfectly suited to be today's must-have toy. They reflect many traits of the American psyche: competitiveness over cooperation, aggressiveness, xenophobia, and individuality. In a sense, Nintendo's adventure games are the high-tech equivalent of age-old games like Cowboys and Indians. You, the protagonist, find yourself making your way through underworlds and overworlds filled with traps and dungeons as you fight off enemies blinking their way across a television screen. Describing the phenomenon, *Newsweek* said Nintendo "speaks to something primal and powerful in [kids'] bloody-minded little psyches."

Throughout history, mankind has had a need to confront danger and overcome it. When the dangers aren't real, people tend to dream them up. "Video games fulfill a mythological need to do battle without danger," Stonehill says.

Video games are, of course, perfectly suited for a generation that

175

is growing up with computers in the classroom and with their eyes glued to the television at home. TV is a passive medium. It talks to you but you can't talk back. Computers and video games are active and are, therefore, much more powerful media. Notes Peter Kline in his book *The Everyday Genius*, "Whereas children have to wait days or weeks before finding out how they did on a test, video games (just like TV game shows) tell the story instantly."

Children, particularly boys, love to solve problems. And that's exactly what Nintendo's adventure games revolve around. In games such as The Super Mario Bros. 2, the gamemakers don't tell you what to do. You have to discover for yourself how to direct the heroes (two Italian janitors) past man-eating plants and red-hot lava balls. The farther you go, the more difficult it gets. Making your way through the maze to save the Mushroom Princess can take weeks, even months. And even then you might never get to see the princess.

"You become totally engrossed in the characters and how you're going to get through this room, that room," says George Hersh, a Nintendo novice and analyst at Daiwa Securities, Inc. As you get closer to the end, your heart rate jumps, you perspire. As fourteen-year-old Dylan Gordon told *Newsweek*, "Afterwards you just want to drop dead."

As any adult who plays Nintendo knows, video games have a curious side effect that kids love: they reverse the household hierarchy. Notes Jack McLain, a Nintendo game counselor, "Sometimes kids feel their lives are controlled by everyone else. Video game play is an area where a kid can show his or her expertise and feel in control."

Nintendo's climb to the top of the video game charts started in Kyoto, Japan, back in 1983. Nintendo, a century-old maker of playing cards, was looking for ways to diversify. Its engineers came up with Famicom, a home video game system designed to leapfrog game machines sold by Atari and Coleco in the United States. Nintendo

176

knew from day one that it must develop more sophisticated, arcade-quality games that would appeal to everyone in the household, not just kids.

Famicom fit the bill. It was packed with a powerful microprocessor that could run rings around the technologically obsolete Atari machines. And it could be used to play games containing up to 3 million bits of computerized information, compared with machines that played games containing 8,000 bits or fewer. The added muscle allowed Nintendo to offer games with close to arcade-quality graphics — and adventure games that could challenge anyone's imagination.

In Japan, Famicom caught on like wildfire. In just two years, Japanese consumers purchased more than 6.5 million Famicom systems. Meanwhile, in the United States, video game sales were going into an unstoppable tailspin. In 1983, sales dropped 33 percent, to $2 billion. Games that had sold for $35 plummeted to $5 or less. In 1984, Coleco and Mattel quit the business entirely. Warner Communications sold its Atari subsidiary at a fire-sale price. The U.S. companies had made a fatal mistake: thinking they could do no wrong, they flooded the market with virtually every game that gamemakers came up with. Companies with no experience or expertise also began to produce video games.

Before attacking the U.S. market, Nintendo "studied the others' failures long and hard," says Main. "Basically, they deserted their players by failing to recognize what kinds of games they wanted. Video games have to have more than nice packaging and a great title. They have to have depth of play. Somehow Atari and the others lost sight of that in their frenzy to bring out another blockbuster."

In 1985, video game sales in the United States hit rock bottom, barely topping $100 million for the entire year. Nintendo smelled an opportunity. But the Japanese were wary; they decided to proceed very slowly and cautiously.

They began by testing the Famicom system in focus groups.

177

Nintendo asked youngsters to play the games and describe what they liked or didn't like about them, and why they had abandoned Atari and Coleco games.

"We found that they never really walked away totally from video games," says Bill White, Nintendo's director of advertising. "But their parents [who foot the bill] had become really disenchanted."

The focus groups convinced Nintendo to test-market a video game system in the New York City area in late 1985. It wasn't easy to convince retailers, who had already been burned once when the video game fad fizzled, to add Nintendo to their store shelves. In fact, Minoru Arakawa, the president of Nintendo of America, Inc., got thrown out by more than one account when he tried to swing a deal. In some cases, he and other Nintendo salesmen wound up making irresistible "guaranteed sales" offers. That meant if, on December 26, a retailer had any machines or games left in his warehouse, Nintendo would have to buy them back. To give their pitch to retailers an added flair, Nintendo came up with "Rob," a twelve-inch-tall robot that could be controlled with the video game machine. (Impressing retailers was Rob's only task: he was yanked off the market a year later.) Nintendo also convinced retailers to sell the game machine for little or no profit. The argument: Just like the razor blade business, the big bucks would come not from the hardware, but from selling millions of games. (For instance, a retailer makes about a 17 percent margin on a Nintendo game machine. Operating costs eat that up entirely. But a video game that sells for $45 costs only $7 to $8 to make. Nintendo and its retailers pocket the difference.)

The New York rollout was a big success. It convinced Nintendo to attack the U.S. market in full force. In the fall of 1986, Nintendo introduced its game system ($79 to $149) and a host of $25 to $45 games, including The Super Mario Bros. and The Legend of Zelda, created by a team of 140 game designers in Japan. Zelda introduced players to a new level of role-playing sophistication. It invited them to assume the role of Link as he made his way through a series of challenging mazes in an electronic adventure filled with pitfalls.

Why are kids — and a growing number of adults, including superstars like comedian Jay Leno and Los Angeles Rams halfback Eric Dickerson — so captivated by these new Nintendo games?

1. *Quality is one obvious reason.* Nintendo didn't want the sad history of video games (and other fads, such as Cabbage Patch dolls) to repeat itself. So it took steps to prevent any other company from flooding the market with cheap, low-quality games.

Nintendo invited other companies to design games to run on its machines. But Nintendo reserved exclusive rights to manufacture the computer chips that act as the electronic "brain" of every video game. That meant no company besides Nintendo could manufacture video games for Nintendo's machines. To further protect itself, Nintendo placed a "lockout" chip in its game machine that prevents all but Nintendo-authorized games from playing on its system.

Keeping such strict control over manufacturing was one of the major reasons for Nintendo's success. It meant that nobody could sell a Nintendo video game without Nintendo's approval. It also meant that Nintendo alone could decide what games to manufacture, and how many of each type should be produced. (That capability has caused Nintendo's competitors to cry foul. In late 1988, Atari and a subsidiary, Tengen, Inc., sued Nintendo for $250 million. Atari claimed that Nintendo's 80 percent market share, coupled with its lockout strategy, amounted to an illegal monopoly.)

"This sort of control lets us be very selective," says Main. "We probably have examined two hundred games that have never seen the light of day."

The process works like this. One of about 40 third-party game developers, such as Mattel or Milton Bradley, comes up with a rough idea for a game. Then Nintendo checks to see if anything similar is

179

being developed elsewhere. If not, three or four of the third party's engineers spend anywhere from six months to two years incorporating the idea into a video game.

"It's like producing a film. One person writes, one edits, and so forth," explains Don James, Nintendo's director of product development. "Every game goes through fifteen or sixteen revisions before it's through."

Even when it's finished, there's no guarantee the game will ever be sold. Nintendo stacks the game up against its internal marketing plan. Say the company is looking for a game to market to American girls under the age of eight, or to adults who watch "Jeopardy." If that game fits the bill, it becomes a candidate to move on to the next stage.

That next stage, perhaps the most important of all, involves rating the game's appeal on a 40-point scale. James and two other professional game players at Nintendo's Redmond, Washington, headquarters, sit down and grade every game. They consider everything, from the uniqueness of the story line to the quality of the graphics and the number of elements in each scene.

"It's kind of like reading a book," James says. "You read a chapter and you get a sense of whether it will succeed."

Their grading system is remarkably consistent. Usually the three judges' ratings don't vary more than a few points from one another. Any game that scores in the 20s goes back to the drawing board. If it scores in the high 30s, as did Zelda and Super Mario Bros. 2, Nintendo knows it's destined for great things. Says James, "We don't miss very often."

2. *The timing is perfect.* Nintendo is very careful not to introduce any game before its time. For instance, Japanese game players are considered to be about 2.5 years ahead of their American counterparts. They've had that much extra time to advance their eye-hand coordination and gain a better understanding of complicated adven-

ture games. In the fall of 1987, Nintendo of America asked a focus group to test two games, called Dragon Quest I and Dragon Quest II. The games already were smash hits in Japan, but the focus group gave them low grades (4 or 5 on a scale of 10). As Nintendo executives watched through one-way mirrors, they failed to see the spark of excitement and fascination that they always look for in a child's face.

The Americans were disappointed. But Arakawa reminded them that the Japanese (with game machines installed in 35 percent of all households) were already well acquainted with adventure games such as The Legend of Zelda and Zelda II — The Adventure of Link.

Arakawa was right. A year later, Nintendo of America test-marketed the games again. This time they scored 8 or 9 on a 10-point scale. "We realized that now the players were ready for that next great adventure," says Main. "We learned that if we launched a product out of sequence, our focus groups told us, 'Don't do that to me.' "

Nintendo also discovered that some regions of the United States are behind others. For instance, game players in certain parts of the South and Southeast are up to 2.5 years behind their counterparts in New York. That helps determine where and when different games are marketed.

3. *Nintendo sells to Junior, Sister, Mom, and Dad.* In the early 1980s, 80 percent of the nation's video game players were six- to fourteen-year-old boys. Nintendo began to push home video game versions of popular TV shows, such as "Wheel of Fortune" and "Jeopardy." It added adult games such as Anticipation (a Pictionary clone) and pushed sophisticated baseball, tennis, and hockey games for adult men. A cross-promotion with Procter & Gamble's Tide detergent and Ralston Purina's cereals helped put the Nintendo name in front of Mom in thirty thousand supermarkets. By mid-1989, 25 percent of Nintendo's avid players were female, and 30 percent were over eighteen. That's important, because adults, especially mothers, usually decide where the family's money is spent.

Kids under seven often lack the motor skills for many video games, but they do have decent eye-foot coordination. So Nintendo developed a game you play with your feet on a "power pad." The percentage of players under age six jumped from 1.8 percent to 3 percent in one year.

Another major reason for Nintendo's success is its unsurpassed ability to follow and, to some extent, control the sales of its video games in twelve thousand U.S. stores. Main and his staff closely monitor sales by tracking the sales reports from thousands of point-of-sale computer systems. "We measure sixty percent of the nation's retail base on its weekly sell-through [the total video game purchases at retail stores]," says Main. "Each week, we begin by analyzing the sales data. We know instantly what changed last week, what this new game is doing to the others in the same category, and so on."

Nintendo backs this data up by sending a field force of 145 of its own people on nationwide scouting missions. These scouts visit 7,500 accounts every month. They photograph the video game displays, check prices, and examine inventory levels. Then, using a hand-held Panasonic computer, they feed the information via phone lines to an IBM System 38 computer at the Redmond, Washington, headquarters. Main can sit down at a terminal and find out what's happening anywhere in the United States.

"If some retailer is running a special promotion, I know that," he says. "And we let our retailers know what's going on at this store or that store."

Monitoring sales this way enables Nintendo to:

1. *Decide how many games to produce.* Again, the company tries to avoid putting too many games on store shelves. The well-publicized scarcity of Nintendo games, real or contrived, creates the illusion that they're almost a priceless commodity. In many areas, the shortage has sent kids scouring the countryside for a hot Nintendo game, further fueling Nintendo-mania.

182

"They could always sell a lot more games, but the secret is supplying 95 percent of the market's needs, not 100 percent," says Al Chaikin, CEO of Circus World, a chain of 324 toy stores in twenty-nine states.

Nintendo maintains that game shortages are caused by a world-wide scarcity of computer chips. In 1988, according to Main, Nintendo sold thirty-three million video games. "We were short about twelve million games because we couldn't get the chips."

Nintendo's competitors, and some industry watchers, say the shortage is a fake. When Tengen, Inc., sued Nintendo, Randy Broweleit, senior vice president for operations at the Atari subsidiary, told the *New York Times*, "They've created an illusion of a chip shortage. They are keeping supply low to keep prices high."

Intentional or not, the scarcity of games has enabled Nintendo to avoid what happened to Atari. Notes John McDonald, the president of Casio, "Atari didn't keep its products in short supply, so its games very quickly became a loss leader for everybody. I had friends calling me to get them an Atari game at wholesale. I said, 'Go out to K mart and you'll get it cheaper than that.' "

Finding a hot-selling Nintendo game can be almost as challenging as the games themselves. Any kid who gets his hands on one is the envy of the block. And if he doesn't find the game he wants, he's apt to buy a slower-selling, second-tier title.

2. *Kill games before they die.* By studying the sell-through data, Nintendo knows exactly when to yank a game off the store shelves. Sometimes that happens long before the product's expected life cycle ends. When Nintendo withdraws a game, it doesn't do it in just one city or region; it disappears from stores nationwide. This strategy prevents retailers from slashing prices and keeps customers thinking that a hot Nintendo game is a precious commodity. The message: Buy it now before it disappears.

3. *Keep an eye on retailers.* Nintendo suggests a retail price, but

183

generally retailers sell the games for slightly more than that. Occasionally a retailer will put games on sale. When that happens, Nintendo finds out about it almost immediately. "The best policemen on that are the retailers themselves," says Main. "We'll hear very quickly about his 'friend' down the street selling at a discount."

A bigger concern are gray-market dealers who mark the games up in price, not down. In several cases, Nintendo discovered that New York City dealers were camping out at out-of-town retail stores. They would buy ten to twelve games at $39 each, bring them back to New York, and sell them for $99 each. Nintendo does everything it can to discourage that.

Another important factor behind Nintendo's success is keeping a steady eye on its customers. In their best seller, *In Search of Excellence,* Tom Peters and Bob Waterman's number-two principle was: Stay close to the customer. Learn his preferences and cater to them.

Nobody does that better than Nintendo. "We have the biggest continuous customer-tracking study ever done in the United States," White says. "It really lets us keep the pulse of the players."

Nintendo can tell you, at any given moment, exactly who's playing its games — their ages, sex, and skill level — what games they own, and what kinds of games they would like to purchase.

There are several components of this research. As a service it calls *game counseling,* Nintendo offers a toll-free hot line that lets game owners call in with questions, complaints, or comments. Each week, eighty video game "counselors" handle up to a hundred thousand customer calls. Besides fielding questions, they ask each caller a series of questions. The answers are fed into a customer data bank.

In addition, Nintendo does an annual "usage" study. This survey of game owners, many of whom subscribe to the company's 1.5-million-circulation *Power* magazine, tells Nintendo what games are the most popular in each region of the country. For example, Nintendo knows that 82 percent of the games sold in New York in late

184

1985 are still in active use. Players also can call in to a toll-free hot line and listen to a recorded "tip of the month" — from Captain Nintendo himself.

This wealth of information enables Nintendo to know exactly what's going on, not only in the marketplace, but in nineteen million living rooms across America. It's ironic that the Japanese — through their meticulous research, their strict dedication to quality, and even their short visits to Disneyland, ball parks, and trade shows — have picked up a better understanding of their U.S. customers than their American counterparts.

"What they've done is learn to reflect our culture," says Surrey, the anthropologist. "If the games didn't reflect our culture, they'd never work."

Information Resources

A Revolution in Marketing

In business, it might be considered one of those ultimate ironies. Leonard Lodish, an entrepreneur and marketing professor at the Wharton School of Finance and Commerce, had a small management consulting company that was doing about $15 million a year in business back in 1978. One day, another entrepreneur and teacher from the Midwest, John Malec, showed up, pitching an incredible idea. By linking electronic scanning data at supermarkets with the flexibility of cable television, Malec thought he could offer package goods manufacturers a powerful new tool, called BehaviorScan, for testing the effectiveness of advertising and promotions on the sale of new products.

"We studied the proposal for a month and said it was unbelievable," Lodish says. "But it was impossible to do because of the computing power necessary. So we rejected it."

Lodish wasn't alone in his opinion. Malec approached thirty banks, looking for financing to launch a new company. All rejected him. He and his partner, Gerald Eskin, another academic, also offered their idea to the biggest companies in the research field, A. C. Nielsen and SAMI. Neither was interested. Malec especially remembers the reaction of a senior Nielsen executive after a two-hour lunch where

Malec and Eskin outlined their concept. "He put his arms around each of our shoulders and said, 'I like you boys, so I'm going to be blunt,'" Malec recalls. "'This is the dumbest idea I've ever heard.'"

That quote is now framed and on a wall in Malec's house.

Just a few years later, all of those doubting opinions would change. Lodish's company, Management Decision Systems, merged into Information Resources, Inc., the company founded by Malec and Eskin. Lodish became a director of IRI.

In modern commerce, where information is the main currency, it's the ultimate competitive weapon.

"I knew their data was going to be real cutting-edge," Lodish says. Many of the same banks that once rejected Malec now happily lend money to the company. And the parent company of Nielsen, Dun & Bradstreet, offered almost $600 million to buy IRI. The impossible idea revolutionized the market research industry. "The theme most important to me is to keep loose and keep your senses working all the time," Malec says of IRI's success. "I don't know anyone who has gotten it right the first time."

In the span of a decade, Chicago-based IRI has been the main force in completely changing the way package goods companies test new products and sell existing ones. In 1984, the Association of National Advertisers called BehaviorScan "the most important advance in the history of marketing research." Since then, IRI has introduced a number of other innovative research products, including a syndicated national tracking service. All of IRI's offerings are based on a simple idea with powerful implications: Give manufacturers more timely and accurate information about what's selling and why. In modern commerce, where information is the main currency, it's the ultimate competitive weapon. "IRI is still the pioneer and innovator," says Dirk Godsey, an analyst with Hambrecht & Quist, an invest-

187

ment-banking firm in San Francisco. "It's been that way forever. IRI stays ahead of the curve and customers tend to catch up."

Don Schultz, a professor of advertising at Northwestern University, says IRI, with its scanner-based technology, has not only changed the concept of market research, but is also causing schools to reevaluate how research is taught. "It used to be the accepted method to take a small sample and project it to the whole," Schultz says. "With scanners, you've already got the whole. The main question now is how you manipulate the data. The answer you're looking for is probably in there somewhere."

Armed with an informational gold mine about shopping behavior, some supermarkets, for example, are beginning to profile their customers' habits and offer incentives for frequent shopping, or shopping on slower days or times of the week. Stores and package goods manufacturers are beginning to understand just how precious each cubic inch of shelf space is. Slotting fees — charged by stores to manufacturers to carry products — can run as high as $4,000 per item. Research data that once had the freshness of weeks-old snapshots is now the equivalent of full-color video, running practically at real time.

"Did IRI invent all of this or just come up with the concept?" muses Schultz, who has followed the company since its beginning. "Or is everyone taking what IRI has done and extending it in different ways?" A little of each, he says, answering his own questions.

When Malec and Eskin wrote the original business plan for BehaviorScan in the late 1970s, they viewed it as a business in itself. At the same time, however, they also saw BehaviorScan as a building block in a nationally syndicated data base. No longer would companies have to wait weeks for sales reports from distributors and retailers which would already be outdated. No longer would companies have to depend on the fickleness of test consumers filling out paper diaries detailing their supermarket purchases. Eventually they wanted to link

188

the scanner data from thousands of stores and tens of thousands of test consumers. This would be instant data, no longer dependent on slow paper trails.

That original plan became a reality in the late 1980s when IRI introduced InfoScan. "The second step, InfoScan, was a much bigger gamble than BehaviorScan," Malec says, speaking in his office at IRI headquarters in a remodeled loft building on the edge of downtown Chicago. "We bet the company. If we had failed, we would have gone into bankruptcy."

Today, IRI's scanner-based system continues to change the way package goods companies test and sell the new products that millions of Americans eventually see on their supermarket shelves. It helps shape the advertising and promotional approaches companies use to sell those products. And it helps manufacturers, as well as supermarkets, track the market share and sales volume of products once they go into general distribution.

"It's dynamite stuff," says Robert Beeby, president and chief executive of Frito-Lay. In fact, one of the reasons Beeby's company revamped its own computer system was to take better advantage of InfoScan and BehaviorScan. Now each of Frito-Lay's top six hundred decision makers have instant access to IRI's data and from the snack food company's ten thousand route salespeople, who carry hand-held computers. As noted in an earlier chapter, Frito-Lay can react to new competition or adjust unsatisfactory product campaigns and promotions within days.

"Prospectors find gold by starting with a pile of gravel, sifting, winnowing, screening, and straining away the irrelevancies until, with luck, a nugget of gold appears," Malec wrote in a company publication. "The initial effect of the new single-source data [scanners] has been to make the pile of gravel larger. Isn't it about time to improve the technique of finding gold?" The answer to his question is IRI.

"If you buy the premise that most, if not all, of the answers to marketing questions are in the data, companies are just now beginning to learn how to use it," Malec says. "I think IRI today can get ten percent of the value out of the data. Some companies are right on our heels, but most are down around one percent to two percent. To get full value, a company needs to make changes in its organization and approach as well as in computers and software." By the end of the 1990s, he thinks companies will be getting 50 percent of the value in the data.

Learning to use the data effectively will become increasingly important as new products continue to crowd available space in supermarkets. A typical supermarket carries about twenty thousand different items and introduces as many as two hundred new items a month. Gian Fulgoni, IRI president and chief executive, says shelf space at stores has increased 10 percent in the past five years while the number of new items has increased 80 percent. "Time pressure in the market is tremendous," says Fulgoni. "Companies want to get a good read on their products in a matter of months, rather than a year or more. And some retailers say, 'If this thing doesn't move in three months, I'm not going to keep it around.' "

Malec, in his mid-forties, carefully guards his privacy. He agreed to be interviewed only when he was assured the focus would be on IRI and its success. Malec is the idea person at IRI and is quick to credit others with the implementation. "I had the macro idea for BehaviorScan and Gerry Eskin figured out how to do it," Malec says. Company folklore, he says, holds that Eskin discovered the potential of targetable cable TV when he saw the wide variety of programs, including X-rated movies, available in hotel rooms wherever he traveled. Another founder, Bill Walter, worked twenty-hour days, seven days a week over a nine-month period in the late 1970s developing the software-processing systems for IRI that allowed the company to handle their huge data base. Some of that system is still in use today.

"I don't think we ever invent technology here, just ways to use

190

technology," Malec says. "We concentrate on applications." Malec says IRI is one of the world leaders in the use of computer-expert systems, mainly to help manage the mountains of data coming into the company. More than 400 billion bits of information are on-line. That's the equivalent of 600,000 books, each about 400 pages long. To check and correct the data added to IRI's system each week would take thirty man-years. Instead, that job is done automatically with a neural network that mimicks how a person thinks and solves problems. For example, some store scanners record sales of six-packs of soda as a single item, rather than six. Based on price differences and awareness of each store's habits, IRI's computers adjust for this accounting practice to give more accurate information on unit sales.

The concept behind BehaviorScan, the basic building block of IRI's system, the idea Lodish first thought was impossible to execute, is quite simple: Know exactly what shoppers in an isolated town buy, and when, and then manipulate advertising, pricing, packaging, promotions, and even the positions on store shelves to see if sales change. Manufacturers seek the best combination to move the most merchandise at the lowest cost.

The execution of BehaviorScan, however, is complicated. First of all, IRI selected self-contained geographic areas with high cable TV and local newspaper penetration to establish its test sites. Those cities are Midland, Texas; Grand Junction, Colorado; Eau Claire, Wisconsin; Marion, Indiana; Pittsfield, Massachusetts; Rome, Georgia; Cedar Rapids, Iowa; and Salem, Oregon. "We picked the markets to be a cross section of mid-America," Fulgoni says.

Manufacturers can test in one city or several. A typical testing contract, running for a year in two markets, costs a manufacturer between $250,000 and $300,000. The manufacturer receives data only in the product category being tested.

In Midland, for example, IRI has the cooperation of all ten supermarkets and five large drugstores, representing the vast majority of grocery items and health and beauty aids sold in town. Midland County's 120,000 residents spend about $180 million a year at food and convenience stores. Each of the test stores is equipped with a scanner checkout system that electronically records the items from their bar codes. IRI maintains a dictionary containing two million universal product codes, uniquely identifying each product by its manufacturer, brand, weight, and price. If the store didn't previously have scanners, IRI helped install a system. IRI's contracts with the stores vary. Some compensate the stores with cash and sales reports. Others may allow a store to do its own testing of private-label brands.

Because the stores themselves are so competitive with each other, IRI pledges strict secrecy. Terry Tayrien, IRI's district manager in Midland, recalls a situation early on when one of the stores had not yet joined with IRI, so it didn't stock some of the hottest test items. Not wanting to be at a competitive disadvantage, the store sent representatives to buy the most popular test items off the shelves of the other stores to stock its own shelves.

Each time one of IRI's test panelists makes a purchase, he or she shows an identification card, allowing IRI to track precisely the buying patterns of each household, often for many years. "Almost nothing goes on in those towns that we don't know about," Fulgoni says.

Although collecting the sales data is important in test marketing, the real fun begins when IRI tinkers with advertising and promotions. "BehaviorScan has really made promotion more important than advertising," says Northwestern's Schultz. "IRI found that the response to promotion so overwhelmed the response to advertising [that] it has forced many of us to rethink advertising. It's more of a defensive weapon. You have to advertise to hold on to what you have."

Through arrangements with the local cable television companies in each BehaviorScan city, IRI can direct different commercials to different panelists. Each of the panelists' television sets is equipped with a special receiver. "We can have three households sitting in a row and each home could get a different commercial," says Donna

Gibson, IRI's media supervisor in Midland, where the research firm has 3,500 test panelists.

In Midland, the research company maintains its own TV studio in a building adjacent to Times Mirror Cable Television of Midland. For IRI's panelists, the cable signal is routed through IRI's studio and then back to the cable company before it is transmitted to the homes.

TV monitors cover the walls of the IRI studio. Armed with approximate airtimes of commercial spots and storyboards for accurate recognition, an IRI technician watches the appropriate monitor and manually punches in the test commercials instead of the regular ones. Substitutions can only be made during airtime purchased by the testing manufacturer.

Studio technicians need patience and quick reflexes. During a prime-time show they know roughly when commercial breaks occur. But during a sporting event they're at the mercy of the game. Sometimes spots run at different times than scheduled, so the technicians are trained to recognize commercials from their first frame on the screen. If they make a mistake, they can restore the original commercial within the first second.

On a busy day, Gibson says her Midland studio makes as many as one hundred commercial substitutions. Her technicians can cut into any of the cable system's forty channels. "I have no way of knowing what those test commercials are," says Peggy Bailey, who has been an IRI panelist since 1982. Panelists' TV sets are automatically monitored every four seconds to check the channels being watched. IRI still can't be sure that a particular commercial is seen, but it can get a good idea.

The commercials may test the effect of different copy with the same visuals. Or the effect of less advertising saturation on a certain product by substituting public service announcements. In an extreme case, Tayrien says the testing service was once able to demonstrate how a $10,000 spot on an alternate channel would have been more effective than a $500,000 spot during halftime of the Super Bowl.

IRI has similar testing arrangements with local newspapers in the

BehaviorScan cities and some magazines. For example, certain house-holds might receive coupons for 50 cents off on an item, while the rest receive coupons for 25 cents off. In-store promotions and the effects of different shelf positioning are also tested. "Virtually any type of marketing strategy a manufacturer wants to try we can replicate," Tayrien says.

InfoScan, which IRI began offering in 1987, specializes in analyz-ing sales in the general market. It links data from about three thou-sand stores and seventy thousand households nationwide. The data is available almost immediately to user companies through computer links with IRI.

IRI, founded in 1977, is a publicly traded company with annual revenues approaching $175 million. (Malec is the largest individual shareholder, with about 12 percent of the company's stock.) Its chief competitor is Nielsen, a division of Dun & Bradstreet, which tried to buy IRI in 1987. IRI originally agreed to the D&B deal, for about $600 million in stock, but the purchase was nixed at the end of 1987 because of antitrust opposition from the Federal Trade Commission. Malec estimates that Nielsen has about 40 percent of the $250-million-a-year grocery-related syndicated tracking business; IRI has 30 per-cent. In 1990, IRI is moving into the $150 million market for drug and mass merchandise tracking, an area previously controlled com-pletely by Nielsen.

Since 1986, the scope of the scanning research field has expanded dramatically. After Nielsen announced it was shifting from diaries to scanners, IRI quickly followed with its own announcement of Info-Scan. IRI had 150 supermarkets on-line in August 1986. Six months later, 1,100. Another 1,300 were added by the end of 1987. IRI's total investment in establishing the new service exceeded $50 million, equal to the company's net worth at the time. "We weren't ready to do it that quickly," Malec says, "but the moment Nielsen announced, we knew we had to announce our system or be also-rans."

Later, when D&B made its offer to buy IRI, Malec says his

company's new business stopped dead for six months. Why buy from IRI when it would soon be a division of Nielsen? "I think D&B thought, 'We can't lose,' " Malec says. " 'Either we buy IRI, or it is mortally wounded.' Our lawyers thought the deal would be approved. It was a tough period around here." Business started to revive again toward mid-1988, and annualized sales for InfoScan reached more than $75 million by the end of 1989.

Another Malec invention, VideoCart, is being expanded beyond a few test supermarkets in 1990 and could go national in 1991, Malec says. Through small, interactive computers mounted on shopping carts, VideoCart offers product advertisements, in-store product maps, meal planning, and nutrition advice to shoppers. The advertisements, for example, are automatically tripped when the shopper reaches the appropriate aisle in the store. "I compare it to driving a car," Malec explains. "You look at the road and every now and then you glance down at the speedometer. We've failed if the consumer views this as technology." Malec foresees great potential in VideoCart because about 85 percent of brand-buying decisions are now made in stores. In some test markets, sales of products featured in VideoCart advertisements and promotions have more than doubled.

The investment necessary for VideoCart — "We're talking about a million computers nationwide," Malec says — will be more than that needed for InfoScan. But unlike InfoScan, VideoCart's rollout can be phased in city by city.

While scanning is the central technology in IRI's system, another important element in the company's success is the test panelists, such as Peggy Bailey, whose tastes and preferences represent the typical shopping patterns of Main Street America. "If you wanted to talk to an exciting person, it's not me," Bailey says. At work, she monitors a half-dozen oil-well service trucks for the Midland office of Schlumberger. On her own time, she likes to travel, bowl, and read romance novels. "Not the trashy stuff," she says. "Just a good love story."

New panelists are recruited as old ones move or drop out. IRI always looks to fill specific needs in its demographics, such as retired people or families with dogs. The Midland office has a waiting list. Panelists aren't offered much inducement. Bailey, for instance, receives a monthly check for either $1 or $2, depending on how often she uses her shopper's identification card. She is also eligible for monthly drawings that offer free vacations and other prizes. Bailey says she has never won anything big. She pays for her own cable TV service, but she did receive a free remote control. "To be truthful," Bailey says, "the main reason I became a test panelist was so I could get the remote control."

Grit, Guts, and Genius

Master Quality

six

If there's one concept that accounted for Japanese manufacturing dominance in the 1980s, it was quality. If there's one concept that will determine who wins the economic race of the 1990s — Japan, the United States, or a united Europe — it is quality.

Quality is more an attitude than anything else. It can be used to manufacture products, provide services, or run an office or home. The basic belief is that any job or task can be done better. The goal is not so much perfection as it is continual improvement — improvement that can best come from the bottom up, from the workers who know their jobs best, rather than from the top down, from the

executives who sometimes lose touch with what's really happening in their businesses.

In tours of factories or other industrial sites it's easy to see who has the quality attitude. Japanese plant managers, for example, are proud of their ultraclean and efficient operations. Yet, invariably, one of the first things they tell visitors is, "If you see anything we could be doing better, or know someone who is doing it better, let us know."

The companies in the following chapters are two of America's premier quality companies: Motorola and Florida Power & Light. They have learned that if you make a quality product and provide quality service, you will

197

succeed. FPL is the only non-Japanese company ever to win Japan's Deming Prize for quality, the top industrial award in that country. Motorola won the American equivalent of the Deming, the Malcolm Baldridge award. While one company, FPL, sells service — electric power — in a regulated industry, and the other, Motorola, makes and sells products such as cellular phones in the hypercompetitive global marketplace, both have the same approach to quality. They know their customers and their own competitors. And they empower their employees with the means to identify problems and fix them. As both stories show, the effort to attain the quality attitude is not achieved overnight. It can take years — a decade for FPL. And even then the quest for improvement doesn't stop. It becomes a way of life.

198

Motorola

Making "Perfect" Products

P rominently displayed in Secretary of Commerce Robert Mosbacher's office are four of his most prized possessions: a two-foot-high photograph of his stunning wife, Georgette, a shot of Mosbacher with his pal George Bush, a one-foot-tall glass statuette, and a cellular phone that can be slipped into a shirt pocket.

The first two obviously belong to Mosbacher. But the latter two are the property of Motorola, Inc. The statuette is the Malcolm Baldridge National Quality Award, a prestigious new prize designed to honor the U.S. companies that produce the highest-quality products in the country today. (Congress created the prize in 1987 after Baldridge, President Reagan's close friend and commerce secretary, was killed in a rodeo accident.) The phone, Motorola's 12.3-ounce Micro TAC, is the first Dick Tracy–style model ever produced. It's 50 percent smaller than anything the Japanese have produced, and proof that Motorola has not only caught up with but is now leapfrogging over its Japanese competitors. In 1989, Motorola captured the number-one share of the Japanese pager business — a business that six U.S. companies, including RCA, had surrendered to Japan.

Motorola also leads the world with 25 percent of the market for cellular telephones. And the company even charged back into the computer memory-chip business in 1989.

199

Winning the Baldridge Award was Motorola's most spectacular achievement. In 1988, a total of sixty-six U.S. firms, including divisions of IBM, Kodak, and Hewlett-Packard, applied to be considered for the award. Only Motorola won it — and not just one division but the entire company.

The payoffs, particularly for Motorola's morale and corporate image, have been phenomenal. First came the publicity: President Reagan presented the award to Motorola Chairman Robert W. Galvin on November 14, 1988, at a widely televised ceremony in the Rose Garden. On January 30, 1989, 98,000 "Motorolans" celebrated Quality Day at twenty-three plants worldwide. In Tempe, Arizona, 650 employees formed a huge Q for an aerial photograph. In Tokyo, 800 more marked the eyes of a *daruma* doll in a ritualistic dedication to quality. In Kuala Lumpur, Malaysian employees danced the ceremonial Lion Dance in celebration. Capturing the rekindled spirit, Motorola's Patricia Richey, a cellular-phone account manager, wrote in an unsolicited letter: "I can honestly tell you that Motorola inspires dedication. [Once you] hear the factory employees' pride as they tell you how many units they have produced defect-free, it becomes very easy to work a 16-hour day in a city many miles from home and family."

The financial rewards were also phenomenal. In 1988, superior quality enabled Motorola to save $250 million by all but eliminating costly rework and repairs. That savings went to an eye-popping bottom line: that year, Motorola's profits soared 44 percent, to $445 million, a record high. Its revenues jumped 23 percent, to $8.3 billion. In 1989, revenues leaped another 17 percent, to $9.62 billion, and profits were up 12 percent, to $498 million. A 1989 Dataquest survey of 168 U.S. companies concluded that Motorola's semiconductors were superior in quality to anybody's, including Japan's.

As word spread that Motorola had discovered how to manufacture virtually perfect products, companies worldwide began to besiege the company to learn its quality secrets. Motorola set up monthly

200

Quality Days to host managerial teams from AT&T, General Motors, Xerox, Procter & Gamble, Italy's Fiat, and other firms. In the first three months of 1989, more than 160 companies made the trek to Motorola's sprawling Schaumburg, Illinois, corporate headquarters. At one point, twenty-two IBM executives came to hear the gospel firsthand. In 1990, IBM began to transfer Motorola's quality secrets to its own factories. The Motorola name became synonymous with quality. "Winning the Baldridge Award," said Gary Tooker, Motorola's chief operating officer, "had an effect that money just can't buy."

Ten years ago, or even five, winning a national quality prize would not have seemed like such a big deal. Sure, everybody talked about quality. They even tried to emulate everything from Japanese quality circles to Theory Z. But most companies, Motorola included, spent more of their time complaining about unfair Japanese competition than learning how to compete with it. Motorola had surrendered to Japanese manufacturers of TVs (in 1974), stereos (1980), and computer memory chips (1985). It had reacted largely by pointing the finger at Japan's unscrupulous trade practices, ultimately convincing Uncle Sam to slap 106 percent duties on Japanese pagers and cellular phones. It had joined other semiconductor companies lobbying for protection from Toshiba, Hitachi, and other Japanese semiconductor suppliers.

But then Motorola, as well as other U.S. companies, began to realize that quality is the only way to compete with foreign rivals. In April 1989, *Fortune* asked two hundred CEOs, "What are the most important steps U.S. industry can take to improve its world competitiveness?" The number-one response, with 30 percent of the votes, was "Improve quality." The mad dash to improve quality — and win the Baldridge — was on. Typical was the effort at Corning Glass Works in 1989. About a dozen Corning executives disappeared for weeks, including Easter Sunday, into what became known as the War Room. There, they laid detailed plans to seek the Baldridge Award.

To become a quality master, Motorola underwent one of the most grueling and extensive transformations in recent history. Then it organized a perfectly executed campaign to convince the Baldridge judges that it deserved the award. "I always thought my company was pretty good," recalled Ralph Rosati, quality director at Eastman Kodak and a Baldridge judge. "Then I spent four days at Motorola. That convinced me that Motorola is simply the best this country has to offer."

Motorola's quality crusade dates back to a 1981 meeting of the company's eighty corporate officers. Business appeared to be going well at the time, but Arthur Sundry, a twenty-two-year company veteran, stood up and began to criticize the quality of Motorola's goods compared with products made in Japan. Others began to chime in. Their criticisms shocked everyone, especially chairman Galvin.

"It just electrified us," said Galvin. "At that one meeting, everything started to change."

Galvin named Jack Germaine the quality director. Germaine set a corporate goal: a tenfold reduction in defects by 1986. Germaine's staff spent close to two years scoring the quality performance of Motorola's twenty-four plants. Factory managers answered 250 questions such as, What percentage of products are defective? How many do you produce? Managers were scored and given five-year targets. For instance, if a line of cellular phones contained 5,000 defects per million parts, the manager was forced to reduce the figure to 500 or jeopardize his raise, his shot at a promotion, even his current job.

"Suddenly, quality was ranked ahead of everything else," Tooker said. "We started holding up shipments if the quality wasn't there."

To compare itself to the world's best, Motorola borrowed a page from Xerox Corporation and began a process called "competitive benchmarking." Basically, this is keeping up with the Joneses, corporate-style. It involves finding the companies that are simply the

202

Motorola Chairman Robert W. Galvin receives the Malcolm Baldridge National Quality Award from President Ronald Reagan on November 14, 1988.

world's best at what they do — and then beating them at their own game.

Motorola sent teams on scouting missions throughout the world. Its manufacturing experts visited Matsushita's TV plant, Seiko's watch plant, and seventy-five others, trying to determine how many defects their assembly lines produced.

"It's a course in logical thinking," says Richard Buetow, Motorola's current quality director. "You walk in and you ask, 'If you build a thousand of these, how many go through without repair or rework?' If I get to spend an hour or so in a plant, I'll get my answer. And that was the key. That became the driving metric for us."

As the five-year deadline approached, Bill Smith and other quality managers in Motorola's cellular division became convinced that they were missing something. Quality was definitely improving. But the Japanese still enjoyed an edge. Smith believed the problem must lie somewhere deep in the manufacturing process. So he and his staff built a computer model to pinpoint the source of each and every cellular phone defect, be it a bad design, mechanical foul-up, or human error. They discovered that the phones were defective because of faulty connections, bad solders, and other mistakes made very early in the manufacturing process. At a meeting in December 1984, Smith told his managers, "If we don't eliminate the defects in the factory, the products are going to fail in the field."

Like other U.S. companies, Motorola mistakenly believed that quality inspectors could catch the defects before the products were shipped. But that can be a fatal error. "That's dead wrong," says Buetow, "because you always miss something. And customers end up with one or two service calls in the first year. That ruins your reputation."

The key to fixing the manufacturing process was a plan that came to be known as Six Sigma quality. To eliminate the likelihood of mistakes, engineers altered the product's design to allow for considerably more variation in the size and shape of the parts being produced. Basically, this allows more leeway in the manufacturing process. It's similar to widening your garage door to give you more room for error when you park your car.

"If you're driving a Lincoln Town Car that's ten feet wide, and the door is only ten feet three inches wide, you're probably going to nick it," Smith says. "But if the door is twenty feet wide, you'll almost never nick it."

Simple. But it worked.

To further reduce the chance of errors, engineers slashed the number of parts in each phone from 1,378 to 523. The company retrained hourly workers, then made them responsible for identifying defects, rewarding them handsomely when they did. (In 1988, the cellular unit's four hundred workers received bonuses equal to 30 percent of their salaries for meeting quality goals.) Suppliers were directed to improve quality or lose Motorola as a customer. As Charles Gonsior of St. Paul Metalcraft told *Fortune*, "If we can supply Motorola, we can supply God."

The result of all these efforts? Defects per phone plummeted 90 percent, from 1,000 per million to fewer than 100. Smith's group began to set its sights on the seemingly impossible: virtual perfection, or just 3.4 defects per 1 million parts produced. That would mean that 99.9997 percent of phones produced would be defect-free — the equivalent of Six Sigma quality.

When Motorola executives saw what the cellular unit had accomplished, "we realized that we hadn't set our company-wide goals high enough," said Tooker. "We had been doing incremental things, but what we really needed was radical change."

In short, it was time to take Six Sigma corporation-wide.

To prepare for that step, in late 1986 Galvin hit the road, touring the country and talking to customers. He sat down, not with CEOs, but with the engineers, buyers, expediters, and others who really use

205

Motorola's goods. They basically told him, "We like doing business with you, but we'll do 20 percent or 30 percent more business with you if you serve us better."

Galvin came back and, on January 15, 1987, wrote a letter to all employees. He challenged them with new goals: a tenfold quality improvement by 1989, a hundredfold by 1991, and Six Sigma quality (3.4 defects per million) by 1992. "Things from this point forward cannot be normal," Galvin wrote. "We must move to a point of perfection in the eyes of our customers." The letter was signed "Bob."

Wallet-size cards stating Galvin's goals were given to all employees. Even outside suppliers were clued in. Then, to drive the Six Sigma message home, vice chairman William J. Weisz meticulously prepared a videotape. In it, he explained why providing error-free quality 99 percent of the time just won't cut it. He said that if everyone in the country provided quality 99 percent of the time, we would suffer at least 200,000 wrong drug prescriptions each year. More than 30,000 newborn babies would accidentally be dropped by doctors or nurses each year. We would have unsafe drinking water almost four days each year, or no electricity, water, or heat for about fifteen minutes each day. "Pretty scary, isn't it?" Weisz said. Then he reminded employees that every business day, a policeman entrusts his life to a Motorola walkie-talkie. Millions of consumers depend on the Motorola chips that operate today's electronic car engines and color TVs.

In the factory, Motorola put in place systems to find the source of each and every defect — and then showed employees how and why the error had occurred. For instance, factory manager Rick Chandler's plant makes the supercomplex, refrigerator-size base stations that process cellular telephone calls. One station contains 17,500 parts. If you add up all the places where a defect could occur, the sum would surpass 144,000 per base station. "At ninety-nine percent quality, we would have 1,440 errors per product," Chandler says. "And we'd have to add 1,800 employees just to correct the errors and retest them."

Instead, management finds the errors and, within a day or less, locates the source of the defect and corrects it. The payoff: two years ago, Chandler's plant averaged 130 defects per base station. In late 1989, the level was down to 5 or 6. That's 99.9997 percent quality. By 1992, it will drop to fewer than 2 per station. Says Chandler, "The worker is not the issue. More than 80 percent of the responsibility for errors rests with management. I have to tell my people what we're trying to do and why, and then provide the tools to get us there."

To prove that they, too, were dedicated to quality, Motorola executives attached beepers to their belts so customers could reach them anywhere, day or night. Following Galvin's lead, other officers began to crisscross the country, calling on customers. When Tooker visited a Forth Worth construction site, a foreman there showed him places where the Motorola pager didn't work properly. A crane operator told him that his radio's battery didn't last long enough. Tooker attacked those and other problems when he returned.

At executive meetings, quality was moved from last to first on the agenda. Sometimes, when the quality discussion ended, Galvin would get up and leave the room because he felt the company's most important mission had already been taken up. Says Smith, "That kind of symbol I've never seen at another company."

Competitive benchmarking began to sweep through the entire company, and not just the factories. The finance department began to study how Chicago's First National Bank treated its customers. Delivery and warehousing managers scrutinized L. L. Bean, and distribution personnel went to school on the Spiegel catalog.

The benchmarking process even led to an entire superfactory. In November 1988, Motorola dedicated a fully automated pager plant in Boynton Beach, Florida, that arguably is the country's most sophisticated factory. The $9 million plant is dubbed "Operation Bandit" because it stole so many of its production secrets from sixty of the world's top manufacturers, including the Japanese. Twenty-four engineers spent eighteen months touring the globe. Parts management was cribbed from Detroit automakers. The robotics came from Seiko and other Japanese watchmakers. The result is that Bandit robots produce in just one and a half hours what would take humans up to twenty-seven days. The plant responds to orders for its products ($220 Bravo pagers) faster than any other U.S. factory. In most cases, the factory's twenty-seven one-armed robots — run by forty-two computers — can crank out a pager just two hours after the order is received at Motorola's Illinois headquarters half a continent away. If you order a Bravo pager, it will be air-shipped to your office by ten A.M. the following day. Says plant manager Scott Shamlin, "We're the only U.S. pager maker left. We survived because we discovered that manufacturing is a competitive weapon." Ed Bales, chief of Motorola's training center, notes that four years ago, before Bandit and other plants attacked quality with a vengeance, "we'd have built the Bandit plant overseas."

With its quality act so painstakingly put together, going for the Baldridge Award was a relative breeze.

"For us to apply for the award and compare ourselves to other companies was a piece of cake," says Smith, now a Motorola vice president.

"Frankly, we didn't find it difficult to respond to the Baldridge requirements," said Buetow. "We had the infrastructure already in place."

But the Baldridge Award rests as much on leadership and customer satisfaction as it does on statistical process control. In other words, Motorola had to convince the Baldridge judges that quality permeated the entire organization, from the chairman's office to the suppliers making every widget, bolt, nut, and screw. Motorola managers spent several weeks, working until four A.M. some nights, filling out 250 pages of documentation for the Baldridge questionnaire. The company's application was enough to convince the judges that Motorola merited a four-day site visit.

A site visit meant that Motorola had reached the finals. But winning the Baldridge was by no means guaranteed. The rules state that up to six organizations — two large manufacturing concerns, two large service organizations, and two small businesses (those with fewer than five hundred employees) — can win a Baldridge award each year. But there is no minimum: the judges can award zero prizes. The Tuesday morning after Labor Day in 1988, Motorola erased that possibility almost immediately.

"The first day, the four Baldridge site examiners arrived at our board room, and sitting there was our chairman, our chief operating officer, our CEO, and the heads of every Motorola business unit worldwide," Buetow recalls. "There were no absentees and no substitutions."

Each one of the officers stood up and talked about Motorola's quality improvement process. Then every sector manager got even more specific. Says Buetow, "That showed an absolute top-down commitment, and everyone knew what they were talking about. That really set the example."

As Kodak's Ralph Rosati, the chief site examiner, remembers it: "That's what really impressed me — that they were driving it directly from the top down. There was no way they could have practiced to be as ready as they were. They only had two weeks to prepare and they had absolutely no idea what we were going to ask. Motorola went through as difficult a site visit as I can imagine."

Then the site examiners split into two teams. One team went to Phoenix to study the semiconductor operation; the other went to Florida to see the Bandit plant. After that, the examiners regrouped to tour several operations near the Schaumburg headquarters. Throughout the process, Buetow said, "We purposely left them free to ask any questions they wished. They were free to go onto the factory floor, into any meeting."

At each plant, the general managers talked about their quality programs and how they related to Galvin's Six Sigma goals. In every conference room where the judges met, Motorola managers stacked file boxes full of evidence about Six Sigma. The site examiners popped their heads into meetings where assembly-line workers were talking quality control. They even talked to customers and Motorola suppliers. In every case, they heard the same message.

At the cellular radio plant, the examiners asked to talk to some suppliers. One supplier, Jim Schwartz of Omni Circuits, was asked to describe Six Sigma. He responded, "I know Six Sigma quality is what I must get to or else I'll just keep on feeding the Motorola dumpsters."

What the examiners saw and heard clinched it. Motorola walked away with the only prize awarded to an entire company. Two others also won: a Westinghouse division that makes commercial nuclear fuel and Globe Metallurgical, a small alloy producer in Beverly, Ohio.

For Galvin, that victory was just a start.

Shortly after capturing the prize, the sixty-six-year-old chairman ordered ten thousand Motorola suppliers: "Tell us by June 30 [1989] when you're going after the Baldridge" or lose Motorola as a customer. Galvin feels that applying for the Baldridge teaches you where you stand, qualitywise, and where you need to get to, to remain a Motorola supplier. That's a precious commodity, since, over the next few years, Motorola plans to eliminate seven thousand suppliers. Galvin even pinned down IBM chairman John Akers at a Washington conference, pointed a finger at him, and asked when IBM, a significant supplier, was going to apply. He wants other U.S. companies to discover, before it's too late, how to solve the quality puzzle.

"We'd always assumed you could only get so close," Galvin says. "We came to the conclusion that we human beings can produce something that is virtually perfect."

Florida Power & Light

Providing "Perfect" Service

In early 1981, Marshall McDonald went to Japan with a group of executives from American utility companies to meet with top executives from Japanese utilities. As the head of Florida Power & Light Company (FPL), his personal agenda was to learn as much as he could about the total quality process. He wasn't too successful until he cornered several officers of Kansai Electric, then embarking on their own quality effort, during a geisha party in Kyoto. One of the officers promised to send McDonald training materials that Kansai had prepared. He did, but they were written in Japanese. "That wasn't too helpful," McDonald says.

Later, however, those geisha party contacts would prove invaluable. With Kansai's guidance and plenty of American hard work, FPL in late 1989 became the first non-Japanese company to win Japan's coveted Deming Prize for quality. Named after American quality expert W. Edwards Deming, who helped Japanese companies emerge from the rubble of World War II, the Deming Prize is widely considered to be the Nobel Prize of industry. It certifies that a company's practices and business methods are at the pinnacle of achievement. The devotion to quality that the Deming symbolizes is the reason that Toyotas, Hondas, and Sony television sets rarely break down. That same devotion is the main reason Japan is challenging the United States as the most powerful economy in the world.

211

Before FPL, no non-Japanese company had ever dared compete for the Deming Prize. Before FPL, quality was considered attainable mainly by manufacturing companies whose products could be standardized by measuring and testing. Just defining quality was a problem for service companies. For example, what exactly is quality electric power? But today, after a decade of effort that totally transformed Florida Power & Light, the company's fifteen thousand employees find themselves at the center of the quality movement in America, an unlikely spot for a monopoly power company whose profit margin is set by the government. Some experts, in fact, say no American company practices the total quality process better in everyday work.

"They are the best example I have seen," says Xerox chief executive David Kearns, who has personally visited FPL to study its progress. "I have not run into any company where senior executives spend as much time on quality as they do at FPL." Adds author and quality expert J. M. Juran, "To my knowledge, among the service companies, FPL is farther along than anybody."

Other managers and company executives are flocking to Florida to learn FPL's secrets. Since 1986, when FPL began offering seminars to outsiders one day a month, more than four thousand executives from 750 companies, municipal governments, and even the Internal Revenue Service have made the trip to see what can be accomplished when quality becomes more than just the management fad of the month.

At FPL, the fourth largest and fastest-growing electric utility in the nation, quality is anything but a fad. Instead, it's a way of business life that has been passed down through three chief executives: McDonald, John Hudiburg, and Robert Tallon. Often, the process was slow. People had to see results before they became true believers. As in many companies, quality became almost a religious experience. Hudiburg compares it to getting "struck by lightning on the road to Damascus."

A visitor to Hudiburg's plainly furnished office at FPL head-quarters in Miami in mid-1989, just before he retired, quickly learned why Jack Grayson, head of the American Productivity and Quality Center in Houston, calls Hudiburg a "fanatic" about quality, precisely the trait necessary in a chief executive to make the process work.

Some experts say no American company practices the total quality process better than FPL.

"Have you seen those charts?" Hudiburg asked his interviewer after a few minutes of conversation. "The names are camouflaged, so I don't mind showing you." He opened a loose-leaf binder and turned to a page listing what FPL considered the sixteen top electric utilities in the United States. Each company was ranked according to a blend of critical quality indicators such as price increases, Nuclear Regulatory Commission (NRC) violations, employee injuries, and customer complaints. In 1987, FPL ranked eleventh among the sixteen; in 1988, fourth. Every company is improving, Hudiburg explained, but FPL is improving fastest. His goal was to be the undisputed best by 1992. But he quickly conceded that his company was already at or near the top.

Framed stock certificates of failed companies, most of them utilities, covered Hudiburg's walls. His tie clasp was a miniature version of the so-called Deming wheel, developed by Deming. A circle is divided into four quadrants, each with a different letter: *P, D, C, A.* The letters stand for the four elements of Deming's quality process: Plan, Do, Check, Act. "Americans are good at Planning and Doing," Hudiburg said, "but they're not so good at Checking and Acting." Hudiburg and Grayson were instrumental in establishing the American equivalent of the Deming Prize, named after the late commerce secretary Malcolm Baldrige.

The total-quality process has slowly evolved in the United States since the late 1970s, more than two decades after the Japanese em-

213

braced quality as the primary avenue of industrial success. The process is based on the work of American experts like Deming, Juran, and Philip Crosby, but each company puts its own twist on the concept. Generally, instead of a traditional product-oriented approach to quality — make it, inspect it, ship it — advocates of total quality teach that it is a never-ending process that involves everyone from top management to the factory floor or service center. Every worker's effort is important and intimately linked to the ultimate success of the company.

Rather than carrying a connotation of luxury, the term "quality" instead is defined by customer expectations. If the customer wants a Chevrolet, advocates say, don't give him a Cadillac. Those customers can be internal, the people who receive production reports and financial data, as well as external, the people who receive the final products and services. "My secretary is one of my customers," McDonald points out. The role of top management is to evaluate its most important priorities and then set policies to achieve them. At the worker level, the tasks become very specific but they still are focused on company goals.

The trick is to get everyone in the company believing. And that takes time. In the beginning, only McDonald was a true believer, and there were times when even he had doubts. Sometimes success comes only after failure. McDonald recalls how, early on, outside specialists primed his top managers with enthusiasm and armed his first-line workers with sophisticated analytical tools, communications skills, and training in group dynamics, all the weapons necessary for successful duty on Japanese-style quality teams. But something was amiss.

"We just about split our pants," McDonald says. "We had spent all this time and money on training, and all of a sudden it became apparent that we were getting significant problems from middle management."

Those managers had been ignored during the initial training. They were told to leave the teams reporting to them alone, but they were never taught how to harness the many good ideas percolating out of the teams to accomplish their own responsibilities. So instead they worried about protecting their turf and became even more resistant to change, exactly the opposite of what McDonald and his then chief deputy, Hudiburg, wanted. The training regimen was quickly changed to include everyone, but the mistake was costly. It took about a year for the quality process to regain its direction and momentum.

In addition to initially ignoring middle managers, another early mistake McDonald and Hudiburg say they made was unleashing their teams before they established the company's priorities, a process they call policy deployment. Now FPL has nearly two thousand individual teams of workers, all seeking to solve particular problems in order to accomplish specific company objectives, such as reducing customer complaints or employee injuries. Team participation is voluntary, unlike Japan, where it is mandatory. A main emphasis is on management by fact, not opinion. FPL, for example, teaches college-level statistical analysis to some of its unionized high school graduates. In meetings, no one is allowed to say, "I think . . ." or "I feel . . ." Instead, the emphasis is on rigorous analysis of the causes and cures of problems.

The specifics of the quality process can quickly glaze the eyes of all but the most devoted disciples, but the theory remains amazingly simple. Take the problem of lost-time injuries to workers. A team in one of the company's regional divisions would ask the specific question, What's the main cause of injuries to meter readers? After analyzing all of the injury reports, the culprit is found to be dog bites. How can they be avoided? Since each reader carries a hand-held computer that lists the resident and usage information at each address, an extra line is added, where appropriate, warning of a dog. And for insurance, each meter reader receives a tetanus shot upon his employment. Then further analysis is done to see if the same procedures can be used at other sites.

The story of quality at FPL, and how the utility company won

215

the Deming Prize, is really a story of how McDonald and Hudiburg were able to overcome their own skepticism and then slowly make believers out of the rest of the company. Both men are southerners, but their business backgrounds vary markedly. McDonald, known for his eagerness to try new management ideas, holds a law degree from the University of Florida and an M.B.A. from the Wharton School. He worked as a CPA, an attorney in private practice, and an executive at several oil companies, including Sinclair, Pure, and Union, before joining FPL as president and chief executive in 1971. He retired at the end of 1988, at the age of seventy, as president and chief executive of FPL Group, the holding company that includes FPL, Colonial Penn Group (an insurance company that has its own quality program), and several small subsidiaries. FPL, with three million customers, accounts for most of the group's $6 billion in annual revenues.

While McDonald was the idea man, Hudiburg, in his early sixties, was the technician and implementer. He joined FPL, the only company he ever worked for, in 1951 as an engineer directly out of the Georgia Institute of Technology. He became chief executive in 1983, and chairman in 1986.

McDonald remembers his first exposure to the real power quality has to change an organization. It was during a presentation at the Drake Hotel in Chicago in late 1979 or early 1980, he says. This was a particularly troubled period for FPL. Costs were increasing more rapidly than the rate of inflation, primarily because of the price of oil. In 1978, FPL generated a kilowatt hour of electricity for 3.7 cents. By 1981, the cost had nearly doubled, to 7.1 cents. Customers began complaining about the high prices. The utility's voracious power generators burned forty million barrels of oil a year, accounting for 60 percent of total capacity. The price of oil in that three-year span jumped from $12 a barrel to $28. Soon, McDonald's projections revealed, the company would burn fifty million barrels a year.

At the same time, FPL was in the midst of adding nuclear capacity. This was right after the disaster at Three Mile Island. Many utilities around the nation were battered by long construction and licensing delays. Seeking to avoid the same problems, FPL's nuclear unit established some quality teams to coordinate construction and maintain close contact with the NRC. Their main job was to plan for the critical periods during construction and anticipate problems before they occurred. The strategy worked. FPL's St. Lucie 2 nuclear unit, which began operation in 1983, was completed in six years, three years under the industry average, saving $600 million.

The Chicago speaker presented a case study of a Motorola plant that greatly improved productivity with Japanese help. McDonald was impressed because he had never heard of such major advances by American workers. The speaker also plugged Philip Crosby's best-selling book, *Quality Is Free*. After returning to Florida, McDonald bought thirty copies and sent them to his top executives. The book focused on manufacturing, and hardly anything in it applied to a service company. But McDonald wondered if there wasn't a way to adapt the manufacturing methods to FPL. "The initial reaction from the vast majority of people at the company was, 'Here's another wild hare of Marshall's,' " McDonald says and adds, "I've had my share."

Hudiburg agrees. "Down through the years we've tried them all," he says of McDonald's ideas. Education and training. Short courses for management at Harvard. Management by objective. High-powered consultants. Most didn't work. And those that did never permeated the entire company. That was about to change.

By 1982, quality was still a vague concept at FPL. Some teams had been formed in some divisions by workers and managers. The St. Lucie 2 project was winding down, with great success, so the quality team specialists there began to look at problems at the company's fossil fuel plants. But the efforts were still isolated. By the end of the year, only 160 quality teams had formed throughout the utility, many of them looking at electrical transmission problems. No company-wide strategy had yet emerged.

Kent Sterett, who was then FPL's quality director, remembers bringing in Deming, Juran, and Crosby for presentations to FPL's senior management. Each quality mentor had good ideas but no one had the complete answer. Juran's concept of continuous improvement, for example, seemed much better suited to a service company than Crosby's concept of zero defects. "We decided that a blend or hybrid was the best approach for us," says Sterett, who left FPL in mid-1989 for a similar position at Union Pacific in Omaha. His department began the long process of developing FPL's own training materials.

Then, what is probably the key event in FPL's quality quest occurred. Kansai, after years of preparation, won the Deming Prize in 1984, proving the concept could work just as effectively in a service company as it did in a manufacturing company. McDonald immediately renewed his Kansai contacts from the Kyoto geisha house. He asked to send a group of FPL's top officers to Japan for a thorough study of Kansai's methods. "When we really got rolling was when Kansai allowed our top people to go over there and open up their records," McDonald says. "Before that it was only my faith. Then it became a certainty."

Hudiburg led the first FPL group to Japan in late 1984. By that time, almost seven hundred teams were operating at FPL. He returned a few months later, in early 1985, from a trip that convinced him teams were just one part of a much larger strategy that included policy deployment and quality in daily work, a common-sense term that means every person's job is important and can be done better. He was captivated by the progress Kansai had made during its challenge for the Deming. In some areas, such as "scrams" — emergency shutdowns of nuclear reactors — the Japanese utility went from not being as good as FPL to being much better.

Earlier in his career, at one of FPL's regional offices, Hudiburg had struggled with a chronic nemesis in the utility industry: errors by meter readers. FPL meter readers made one error in every 2,000 meter reads. Kansai meter readers, Hudiburg discovered, had reduced the error rate to one in every 150,000 reads. The Japanese, in analyzing their own problem, found that most mistakes were made on dial meters, rather than digital meters. They replaced the dial meters over a three-year period and mistakes declined dramatically. "That's when I could see what was possible," Hudiburg says. "Until then, I thought the process had limited potential."

With Hudiburg's newfound enthusiasm, the number of FPL teams mushroomed to 1,300 in 1985. From then until he retired, Hudiburg returned to Japan about three times a year to personally monitor new improvements at Kansai and other Japanese companies. Kansai also provided FPL access to some of the most sought-after academic experts on quality in Japan: Tetsuichi Asaka, Yoshio Kondo, Hajime Makabe, and Norichi Kano. They continue to consult regularly with FPL.

At the same time the company's top executives were becoming convinced of the power of quality, others at FPL also had their own "road to Damascus" experiences, some sooner than others.

Wayne Brunetti, an executive vice president, was a skeptic until the summer of 1982 when he saw a presentation by a team of FPL union workers who installed equipment on power poles. They were frustrated by the cumbersome brackets used to attach transformers. The brackets were too heavy and unsafe, and took too long to install. Using a time and motion study and other statistical tools, the team devised a bracket of equal strength that weighed one third less, contained one tenth as many parts, and required less than half the time to install. The total cost in labor and materials was one third less than with the old bracket. "At the time, I didn't think our work force had that kind of capability," Brunetti says.

219

C. O. Woody, an executive vice president who heads the nuclear division, became a believer in the fall of 1984 when he went into the hot locker room at the St. Lucie 2 nuclear unit near the completion of its first refueling. The hot locker room is where workers change into and out of their anticontamination clothing. Until then, the average length of time a nuclear plant was shut down for refueling was seventy-five days. The St. Lucie team, on its own initiative, attempted to cut the period in half, and succeeded, saving $28 million. "I knew if I could get into the locker room away from the plant managers, I could get the real story on how this process was working," Woody says. The workers told him they had never worked so hard or had so much fun. Woody's realization: Don't underestimate the power of self-initiative. Instead of management dictating the schedule, let the workers, who know best, help decide.

St. Lucie 2 remains one of the company's biggest success stories. In early 1989, it was shut down for another refueling, this time after a remarkable run of 427 consecutive days of operation, averaging 100.7 percent of capacity. It was one of the leading nuclear units in the world during 1988.

While some areas, such as nuclear, are more critical than others, no department at FPL is ignored in the quality effort. The public relations staff has devised a method to quantify how effectively it deals with the media. Every telephone call from a reporter is logged, coded, and then computerized. Quality has one simple measure: Are correct answers provided in time to meet a reporter's deadline? In telephone operations — FPL receives more than six million calls a year — the main quality elements are considerate service and accurate answers. Operators are taught how to ask questions that will elicit important information and to listen without interrupting.

And in what must be the ultimate analysis of quality, FPL has devised what it calls a Table of Tables defining customer needs. Based on surveys and other judgments, it charts 127 different attributes of quality, such as safety and easy-to-read bills, each with a separate rating based on the importance to the particular customer, in eight categories ranging from residential customers to the NRC and environmental agencies. Residential customers, for instance, consider quality repairs the single most important factor. Commercial and industrial customers favor the quick restoration of power after outages. FPL can use the data to determine the most important needs of customers in a specific geographic region — even down to a neighborhood — or group, such as computer users. All of these elements then feed into an overall ranking of corporate quality elements. Public safety is number one.

Hudiburg admits there are still a few skeptics in the company, maybe 10 or 15 percent of the work force. "But the data is so overwhelming, no one can come out directly against it anymore," he says. McDonald is even more blunt about the potential of the quality process. "For managers," he says, "this is the best tool to get your job accomplished that management science has created." Both quickly add that the process takes time. "Any large company is going to have to devote years to it," Hudiburg says.

Many of the major improvements FPL has made have come since Hudiburg's first trips to Kansai when he expanded the quality effort. Since 1984, customer complaints to the Florida Public Service Commission, which regulates the utility, have dropped by two thirds. FPL used to have the highest complaint rate of electric utilities in the state. Now it's the lowest, and it continues to improve. Service unavailability, the average number of minutes a customer is without power annually, has declined from seventy minutes in 1986 to about forty minutes. The number of NRC violations dropped from fifty-eight in 1986 to forty in 1988, despite stubborn problems at FPL's older Turkey Point nuclear facility. New targets are set for each succeeding year. The goal for NRC violations in 1992, for instance, is eleven.

Equally dramatic is the increase in employee participation

through suggestions. From 1983 through 1987, FPL averaged about a thousand employee suggestions a year. In 1988, the policy was changed to allow these ideas to be approved and implemented at a local level, rather than at the company level. In 1988, the number of suggestions mushroomed to more than eighty-five hundred; in 1989, more than twenty thousand, exceeding the cumulative total of the previous sixty years. Most suggestions are implemented.

In filings with the Florida regulators, FPL said it spent $7 million on its quality program in 1988 and realized direct benefits — primarily money saved — of about $70 million. An even more important measure in the capital-devouring electric generating business is the effect on the need for expensive new plants. Because of the effectiveness of FPL's quality program, Woody says top management has decided to postpone construction of a new plant until 1993. Turning to his own set of charts — performance charts are everywhere at FPL — Woody shows how $100 million spent on one improvement program has added the equivalent capacity of a new 700 megawatt generating unit costing almost $1 billion.

That's good news for FPL's customers. Dan Rudakas, an industry analyst at Duff & Phelps in Chicago, says FPL's residential electric rate is just 5 percent above the national average, an unusually small difference considering most of the company's customers are located at the end of a five hundred-mile peninsula with no access to cheap hydroelectric or coal power. A fast-growing utility such as FPL, which adds 130,000 customers a year, would be expected to seek regular rate hikes to help finance new power plant construction, Rudakas says, but FPL hasn't appeared before the Florida Public Service Commission with a general rate increase request since mid-1984.

All of this improvement does not come without a price. Some FPL managers retired early to avoid the extra demands of the quality effort. One of the main costs is increased executive time. Juran says adoption of the total quality process requires a 10 percent increase in

222

the work load of executives. He may be a little conservative, especially when a company is striving for the Deming. In 1987, Sterett says company parking lots were virtually deserted at night and on weekends. In 1989, as the company prepared for the Deming audits in the summer, the lots were crowded, even on Sundays. Hudiburg says he worked all but three Saturdays in 1988. The next year he took more Saturdays off, but he also delegated more responsibility. He appointed Brunetti to be the point man on the Deming effort. Brunetti, who used to work fifty to sixty hours a week, cranked up his work load to eighty hours.

Even McDonald couldn't escape the changes he had initiated. At company social functions, spouses complained to him about the late work hours. One Sunday evening he tried to visit an old friend who was a vice president at FPL. The executive wasn't home. He had gone to work. And he had worked the previous Saturday, too.

In the weeks before the Deming audits were completed in August 1989, workers postponed vacations. Some worked through the night. But the spirit was contagious. "I've never seen the morale and enthusiasm as high as what we experienced in the last four weeks before the audit," says Tallon, FPL's president. "Everyone was walking around with smiles on their faces." During the audits, Japanese judges could ask any question anywhere in the company. FPL workers had to be able to supply the data to support their answer within three minutes. "It's overwhelming," Brunetti says of the Deming process. "You realize there is always more to do."

After the audits, Tallon expected a letdown, but it didn't occur. He said the presidential review at the end of October was the best the company had ever had. "I thought I'd have to give them all a pep talk and get them back up to speed," he said. "But I didn't need to. Quality is not an additional system anymore. It's a way of doing business. We use the quality tools in our everyday work."

To help maintain the intensity of FPL workers, the company

223

established an internal competition to reward those teams that best meet their goals. The highest recognition is the President's Cup, awarded once a year. In November 1988, in what was the most significant endorsement of FPL's methods until the Deming Prize, the company's top team became the first American team ever to participate in Japan's National Quality Control Conference in Tokyo.

After four months of training in team dynamics and more than a year of specific problem analysis, seven blue-collar linemen from FPL's Stuart Service Center addressed an auditorium crowded with more than a thousand Japanese quality masters. They explained how they had designed and constructed a wooden template to hold underground protective pipe firmly in place, avoiding extensive delays during the installation of wiring. The total annual labor savings for one service center was $5,300. "We've made over two hundred of these templates for other teams," team leader Jeff Vigrass said proudly. "We found out everyone else in Florida has the same problem."

Hudiburg, McDonald, and Tallon were criticized by some for making such a wide public display of FPL's Deming challenge and other quality efforts. Philip Crosby says much of the attention FPL received is because of self-promotion and "breast-beating." A lot of companies, Crosby says, are making progress in quality. They just don't talk about it as much. The company stopped using Crosby as a consultant several years ago. Others have been critical of the money FPL spends to send employees to Japan to study quality.

The critics miss the point, Hudiburg and Tallon answer. Investing in quality is like investing in research and development. Small expenditures up front can have a tremendous payoff in the future. Quality is a long quest. Overcoming employee skepticism is one of the main obstacles, so a manager looks for any tactic he can use to motivate, including talking about accomplishments. Likewise, the main reason any company strives for the Deming Prize — judged not in competition with other companies but rather against a demanding

224

array of quality criteria — is the accelerated improvement it brings in your own operations. The documentation supporting FPL's Deming application covered one thousand pages in ten bound booklets. "We had people working sixty-, seventy-, and eighty-hour weeks to perfect their own success stories and knowledge," Hudiburg says.

Tallon says the great danger in adopting a quality program is reaching a plateau where progress stops and actually begins to decline. An important element of quality, remember, is the concept of continual improvement. That improvement-then-decline cycle has occurred at other American and European companies. "I attribute that to the fact they had nothing dramatic to work for, like the Deming Prize," Tallon says. "Without the incentive, they never got up to the Japanese level."

As for the future, FPL is using the total-quality process to prepare for a changing industry and changing customer expectations. It's not inconceivable that utility transmission lines could someday be deregulated, putting FPL in the same position as the telephone companies. Already, more and more industrial clients are building their own co-generation plants. Ten years ago, a short power blip would never be noticed by residential customers. No more. Now any failure causes customers to race around their homes resetting those blinking clocks, VCRs, and microwaves.

Likewise, expectations are changing in every industry. Those new expectations demand a new approach. FPL's success in winning the Deming Prize should be a breakthrough for other American companies searching for ways to compete. "I think it will make a difference," Tallon says of the Deming Prize. "We're seeing the emergence of a tremendous interest in the quality concept."

225

Anyone thinking about beginning a quality program at their company should be prepared for a long haul, Florida Power & Light and other quality experts warn. There is no quick fix. It may take several years before real results are achieved, because a commitment to quality involves a fundamental change in a company's culture.

There are, however, several early steps to take to ensure that the journey begins in the right direction.

- Know what your competitors are doing and how they are improving. "The only measure that counts is your relative rate of improvement against your best competitor," says George Graham, director of quality at Texas Instruments. At Xerox, the process is called benchmarking. The copier giant compares itself to the other copier manufacturers and what it considers the best practitioners in specific disciplines, such as L. L. Bean in warehouse distribution.

- Study your customers, using technniques such as surveys and focus groups to learn exactly what they expect from you. FPL traces the reason for every customer complaint to the Florida Public Service Commission.

- Put quality in the business plan along with the normal revenue, profit, and market-share objectives. That, says J. M. Juran, puts quality into a framework managers understand. They can begin to think about quality planning, quality control, and quality improvement in the same way they think about financial planning, financial control, and financial improvement.

- Get the full support of top management, "otherwise you're going to have a very frustrating life," says Kent Sterett, former quality director at FPL who now has a similar job at Union Pacific. If top management isn't committed, employees won't care either.

226

- At every opportunity, communicate the importance of quality to workers in newsletters, meetings, and speeches. Open up the books and show them exactly what's at stake.
- Make suppliers and vendors your partners. Many companies are winnowing suppliers to a select list, promising them business if they also adopt quality practices. Motorola is asking its suppliers to compete for the Malcolm Baldridge Award, the American equivalent of Japan's Deming Prize.

Target, Target, Target

seven

The so-called yuppie market has been an easy target for sexy, sleek, big-ticket items like Porsches, BMWs, Sony Trinitrons, and Braun coffeemakers. The conventional wisdom has been: Design the product with a European flair, engineer it to perfection, slap on electronics features, and charge a hefty premium.

In the late 1980s, a funny thing happened. Yuppies began to sour on big, selfish indulgences (exotic vacations, fur coats, and Porsches) in favor of less expensive, more home-oriented indulgences like Absolut vodka, Corona beer, catfish, and Kodak's Ektar film.

It was no accident.

As you'll see in the following four chapters, the makers of the little indulgences knew precisely what consumers were looking for. Their products were each specifically designed and marketed to cater to upscale, youthful (yuppie) tastes. The marketing geniuses paid close attention to design and quality. To promote a sense of novelty, they kept prices high, and their products became big hits with the trend-embracing college crowd.

The experts at the Catfish Institute targeted meticulously planned media events and advertisements at upscale consumers. Kodak, from day one, referred to Ektar as the "yuppie film." To emphasize purity, another big concern with the yuppie

229

crowd, Corona and Absolut
packaged their beverages in clear
bottles with painted labels. They
made coughing up an extra buck
for Absolut or Corona with lime
the in thing to do at metropolitan bars.

Their stories differ in some
ways. Absolut succeeded largely
because of flashy advertising.
Corona, until recently, didn't do
any advertising. Kodak had
huge resources to develop and
market Ektar. Corona and Catfish succeeded with almost no
money.

But what each did was target,
target, target. And they stuck to
their audience, refusing to
branch out even when demand
outside their niches began to
soar.

The message: If you try to be
all things to all people, you lose
the magic you deliver to a
few.

230

From Hush Puppies to Mousse

Going Upscale with Catfish

The nation's catfish farmers, most of the largest of them located in Mississippi, were worried. It was mid-1986 and they had too many of the whiskered fish swimming in their ponds. Eighty million pounds too many. Along with the oversupply, the farmers had an image problem as well. Most Americans thought of catfish — when they thought of them at all — as dirty bottom-dwellers good only for skinning and frying.

How could the farmers avoid a catfish calamity?

They already had several organizations, like the Catfish Farmers of America, whose purpose was to promote the industry. But this problem demanded an extraspecial effort.

So they banded together again and hired Bill Allen, Jr., a former cotton farmer and commodities broker who grew up in Belzoni Mississippi, the heart of the Delta, to head their newly formed Catfish Institute. About 80 percent of the catfish grown in the United States comes from within a forty-mile radius of Belzoni.

Allen's specific mission was to create a market for all those excess fish. That meant he had to devise a new image for the creature. Then he had to keep demand steadily growing from the new plateau.

"We knew coming into 1987 that we had close to 300 million pounds of fish swimming, and the most that had ever sold before was

213 million pounds," says Allen, a 1973 graduate of the University of Mississippi.

It was the beginning of one of the most visible, entertaining, and successful marketing campaigns in recent memory, all in an effort to turn an ugly fish, best known as a deep-fried companion to hush puppies, into a delicacy that could be served as a mousse, in a salad, with hollandaise sauce, or even stir-fried. "We changed the perception of the fish from a mud-sucking, bottom-dwelling rascal to something that was sweet-tasting and good for you," says Brad Todd, the advertising and marketing specialist who developed much of the strategy for the institute's campaign.

The success of the marketing and promotion effort is probably best judged by the numbers. In 1987, the critical year as far as the farmers were concerned, more than 280 million pounds of farm-raised catfish were processed in the United States, a record increase of 67 million pounds over 1986. In 1988, as seafood consumption by Americans dropped for the first time since 1982 because of concerns about pollution, more than 294 million pounds of catfish were processed. More important, revenues to catfish farmers in 1988 increased by more than $50 million, a record, as prices paid to farmers pushed 75 cents a pound because of increased demand. Sales increased another 16 percent in 1989 to 340 million pounds. As the year was closing Allen had a more pleasant dilemma: "We're going to run out of fish," he said.

The catfish effort is also remarkable because it illustrates what can be accomplished with limited funds and manpower. Allen and a secretary are the institute's only full-time employees. He knew he would need plenty of help from outside agencies, which he actively solicited.

The institute's home is a small office on the main street in Belzoni. Its money comes from a special fee of $6 per ton on catfish feed, raising about $2 million a year. Since farmer cooperatives own the feed mills, the farmers, in effect, tax themselves. Of the money available, $1.3 million was spent on advertising in 1987, and $880,000 in 1988. Ad spending increased to $1.3 million again in 1989, a level the institute hopes to maintain.

Since that's hardly enough money to buy sixty seconds of exposure during such prime-time events as the Super Bowl, Allen and his advisers knew they would have to be selective and make their carefully aimed rifle shots count. Television was out, because of the cost. Instead, they chose regional editions of national magazines with upscale consumer audiences. A main reason was the availability of full-color quality photography to show off the catfish in its unusual culinary company. In addition, with the help of Golin/Harris Communications, a New York public relations agency, the institute focused on media contacts. That effort re-

The institute's first task was to determine who the target audience should be.

sulted in winning a 1989 Big Apple Award from the Public Relations Society of New York.

"It was a perfect example of how PR did the job, dollar for dollar, much better than any ad campaign could hope," says Phil Ryan, a Big Apple judge who runs his own public relations firm in New York. "It was a modest-size New York agency working with an obscure trade organization. What made it work was the power of the ideas and creativity. That's the essence of PR, not brute force. Anyone can make a campaign work if they put enough money behind it."

One constant in both the public relations and advertising efforts was a sense of humor, even while pushing the product upscale. "You just can't get too serious about a damn catfish," Allen says.

An early ad, for instance, was headlined "In Praise of the Lowly Catfish." Another, trying to emphasize the healthful aspects of low-cholesterol, high-protein fish versus red meat, featured a full-color picture of a catfish and said, "Think of It as a Chicken That Doesn't Cluck."

233

On the public relations side, the institute courted star chefs and congressmen, diplomats and disk jockeys, as well as food editors and reporters at newspapers and magazines around the nation.

At one point, the institute's advisers even flirted with changing the name "catfish" to help upgrade the creature's muddy image. "You never discount a good option," says Lee Ballard, naming specialist at the Richards Group in Dallas. "And changing the name was a good option."

At a crucial meeting with the institute's board of directors — who were all catfish farmers and catfish feed manufacturers — in late 1986, Ballard offered several alternatives, including "springfish," "Deltafish," "cleargill," and "snowcat." Instead, the directors chose a more conservative approach. They selected a mark of certification or a quality stamp — Mississippi Prime — that could be added to packages of the finished product and to all of the institute's promotional materials.

Since there are no mandatory seafood inspection requirements, the institute devised a special program with the help of the U.S. Department of Commerce. At the same time the department inspects the sanitary conditions at catfish plants, it also takes samples of the fish. Every aspect of the fish is then scored on a scale of 1 to 100: meat, bone, and skin. Only those processing plants that score an average of 80 or above can use the Mississippi Prime stamp. The institute monitors the program by receiving weekly quality reports from the inspections.

With all the concerns about ocean pollution and seafood contamination, this effort has become a cornerstone of the institute's current marketing efforts. It wants to spread the message that there are no worries about Mississippi Prime because of the strict inspection procedures and taste requirements. "Every catfish you eat tastes just like the one before because they're raised in drinking-water–pure water," says Lester Myers, Jr., a catfish farmer and feed mill opera-

234

tor who is on the board of the institute. From each truckload of live, swimming fish delivered to the processor, two fish are randomly selected for a taste test. The samples are cooked in a microwave oven and then eaten. If the taste is the slightest bit off, the entire load is rejected and the fish are returned to their pond until the taste improves.

All of the institute's marketing and advertising efforts were substantially initiated in the second half of 1986 and early 1987 as the catfish in the ponds kept eating their expensive, high-protein, floating feed and kept growing. At $200 a ton, a typical Delta catfish farmer can spend $200,000 or more on feed over a nine-month growing season. That's in addition to the typical start-up costs of $4,000 to $5,000 per acre for ponds and wells, totaling up to $1.5 million for the average farmer.

"We got the message fast," says Todd of the Richards Group. "If we didn't sell fish, we wouldn't be around long."

The institute's first task was to conduct a survey of consumers to determine perceptions about catfish and exactly who the target audience should be. "Everything we do is based on research," Allen says. No surprises here. When the results came back to the Richards Group, it was evident that most people who had heard of catfish thought it was usually hooked in a dirty river and then fried. About 70 percent of the nation's catfish are eaten in a ten-state area extending from Texas to the Florida panhandle and from Illinois to the Gulf of Mexico. "Our job was to take the fish out of the frying pan in the heartland and say it could be eaten anyplace," Todd says. The main messages he tried to communicate were the versatility of the fish, its nutritional value, and its taste. The target became seafood-loving consumers aged twenty-five to forty-four, with household incomes over $30,000.

For its advertising, the institute concentrated on regional editions of magazines such as *Time, Newsweek, People, Better Homes and*

Gardens, Reader's Digest, Good Housekeeping and *Woman's Day*. Since Lent is the major fish-eating time of the year, the ads began in March and ran through October. "We decided not to compete against the poultry and pork months of November and December," Allen says. The institute always requested that its ads be in the front of the magazine, on a right-hand page and, if possible, adjacent to the lead editorial story. When the Jim and Tammy Bakker scandal broke in *Time,* for instance, the institute's ads were right next to the story. "That positioning was a coup," Allen says. Each ad was accompanied by a coupon, promoting a catfish recipe booklet for $1.50. More than twenty-seven thousand consumers sent in coupons. "Given my Mississippi background, I still think one of the finest creations on earth is the deep-fried catfish," cookbook author Craig Claiborne is quoted as saying on the opening page of the booklet.

As the ads were breaking, Golin/Harris went to the media with the story. Famous chefs cooked catfish on television shows around the country. Willard Scott wore a catfish hat on the "Today" Show. "I would like to be known as the person who convinced the American people that catfish is one of the finest eating fishes in the world," Scott, also a cookbook author, says in a promotional blurb for the institute. Allen, who has a flair for communicating in easily understood terms, and other spokesmen went on speaking tours. Suddenly, stories on catfish — as a food and as a novelty — were appearing in major daily newspapers and magazines everywhere. *Glamour* magazine ran a catfish recipe with a full-color photograph. The *New York Daily News* devoted an entire page to catfish.

Charles Hillinger, roving columnist for the *Los Angeles Times,* was driving through the Delta en route to another assignment. He saw a huge billboard proclaiming the region the Catfish Capital of the World and immediately pulled into Belzoni, where he tracked down Allen. Hillinger's story ran in the business section of the *Times* and went out on the wire service shared by the *Times* and the *Washington*

Post. "I was surprised to find out what they had," Hillinger says. "The industry has really blossomed."

According to tracking reports compiled by the Richards Group, more than 2,100 print, television, and radio stories about catfish appeared in 1987, worth a comparable advertising value of $1.57 million. That value is calculated by determining how much it would cost to buy the same space or airtime.

"1987 was a Cinderella story for us," Allen says. "We found out catfish was as much a new story as it was a food story."

One of the most productive single efforts for the institute was an elaborate luncheon for the media in New York, arranged by Golin/Harris Communications, during the late spring of 1987. The institute rented a midtown loft where, with a musician playing a grand piano, waiters in tuxedos served champagne, catfish mousse in snow peas, and pasta with catfish and artichokes to thirty editors and reporters from magazines and newspapers. The lunch, which cost $35,000, generated eighteen media placements worth $300,000 in comparable advertising value, Allen says. "We figured that once people tasted catfish they'd be hooked on it," says Diane D'Ambrosio of Golin/Harris.

Allen also credits the lunch with defusing a potentially damaging story. Through his contacts, Allen understood that *Newsweek* was preparing a story about the working conditions in the catfish processing plants in Mississippi. Indeed, the conditions are harsh. The plants are wet and cold, about 50 degrees — they have to be, to ensure the freshness of the fish. From the time a live catfish comes into the plant until it is beheaded, gutted, and chilled in ice to 40 degrees takes about four minutes. Water, used to wash the work stations, is everywhere. Most of the workers are black and are paid just above minimum wage. Turnover is high. One plant, for example, needed to hire about fifty new workers a week just to maintain a total work force of four hundred fifty.

237

When the *Newsweek* story appeared, however, it featured a photograph of the elaborate table setting and food at the luncheon and concentrated on the new, upscale image of catfish. The industry's wages and conditions were mentioned at the end of the article.

Representative Mike Espy, a Democrat, whose Mississippi district encompasses the Delta, acknowledges the low wages in catfish processing, but calls it a "saving industry" for his economically depressed region. "The industry employs twenty-five thousand, sixteen thousand in my district," Espy says. "There are hardly any alternatives, only welfare and we don't want that."

When Espy took office in 1986, he began promoting the industry and the work of Allen. "The institute has been vital to getting the word out about catfish," Espy says. As a result of meetings the congressman held with procurement directors and other heads of the armed services, the Department of Defense increased its purchase of catfish by 65 percent. On most military bases around the country, catfish is on the menu once a week. Espy sponsored a bill to create a National Catfish Day in 1987. That's when Willard Scott wore his hat. Espy also sponsors an annual catfish feast in Washington for 1,500 people. "We serve it fried, with hush puppies and French fries," Espy says. "We feed half the Congress."

Catfish farming in America began in Alabama and Arkansas, more as a hobby than anything else. It really wasn't big enough to be called an industry until the mid- to late 1970s. In 1970, for example, just 6 million pounds of catfish were processed.

But in the past decade the industry has boomed, steadily increasing production from 46.5 million pounds in 1980. As the industry grew, it became concentrated in Mississippi, which has more than 100,000 acres of ponds. In the Delta, uninterrupted catfish ponds, averaging seventeen acres in size, run for a dozen miles or more at a stretch.

The flat land with clay soil, once great for cotton farming, is now bulldozed into seven-foot-high banks to hold water pumped from underground wells. In the Delta region there are 250 catfish farmers, eight processing plants, and three feed mills. Many of the farmers are partners in the cooperatives that run processing plants and feed mills. Agricultural banks in Belzoni helped fund the development. Every year, Belzoni hosts the World Catfish Festival, which attracts thirty thousand people.

Catfish make a good crop because they are efficient at converting feed into fish. It takes about 1.8 pounds of feed to grow a pound of catfish. That compares with roughly 20 pounds of feed for every pound of beef and 3 to 4 or more pounds of feed for every pound of chicken. Rainbow trout, mainly raised in Idaho, are even more efficient than catfish, converting about 1.5 pounds of feed into a pound of fish. But rainbow trout aren't nearly as popular. About 50 million pounds a year are processed. Sales of flounder, cod, and tuna are also considerably lower than those of catfish.

Aside from the novelty of the catfish, why did the institute's merchandising campaign work so well?

D'Ambrosio of Golin/Harris credits the fish itself and its adaptability to unconventional recipes usually associated with tuna, swordfish, and even chicken. "It has become more of a posh fish," she says. She also credits the quality of the photography used in advertisements and the visual materials her agency was able to supply media outlets.

Todd of the Richards Group credits Allen's salesmanship and the timing. "It was the era of the emerging American restaurant," the former Frito-Lay executive says. "And we hit at the same time these chefs were looking for an American product."

Allen admits the novelty of catfish is wearing off, so it's more difficult to get the same attention from the media. "We have to come up with something new because these people are sick of hearing our story," he says. That something new includes a club, the Loyal Order

239

of Catfish Lovers, and sponsorship of studies by nutritionist Joyce Nettleton showing that farm-raised catfish is high in protein, low in cholesterol, calories, and sodium, and presents no measurable risk to human health from pollutants. Institute surveys in 1989 revealed that some consumers had reduced their seafood consumption by as much as 30 percent because of pollution and contamination concerns.

Convinced that its work has broadened the market and appeal of catfish, the institute nearly doubled the size of its heartland target area for advertising to eighteen states and expanded to Los Angeles and the Washington, D.C., area.

In the end there's one challenge that the salesman in Allen can't ignore. While annual per capita consumption of seafood averages about fifteen pounds in the United States, compared with about sixty pounds for both chicken and beef, consumption of catfish averages just six tenths of a pound. "If we could get people to eat just one more catfish fillet a year, we could double the industry," he says.

Absolut Magic

Ideas from Everywhere

I magine having to sell a beverage that is really no different from your competitors'. It looks, smells, and even tastes virtually the same. Imagine that this product has to be imported and command a premium price in a flat-to-declining marketplace.

That was the awesome challenge facing Michel Roux a decade ago when his company, Carillon Importers, Ltd., took on the U.S. marketing chores for Sweden's Absolut vodka.

Since then, Roux has worked Absolut magic. Over that ten-year span, he masterminded an ad campaign that has turned Absolut into the most successful new liquor product in history. It has zoomed past Russian-made Stolichnaya ("Stolie") to capture 62 percent of the American imported vodka market. Only two domestic vodkas, Smirnoff and Popov, sell more than Absolut. In ten years, Absolut's sales skyrocketed from 5,000 cases to 1.9 million cases.

In 1988, while liquor sales fell 3 percent and vodka sales dipped 1 percent, Absolut chalked up a staggering 34 percent sales gain. That year, Roux and his advertising firm, TWBA Advertising, Inc., were rewarded with the prestigious Kelly Award by the Magazine Publishers of America. The Kelly presents $100,000 to the most creative magazine ads of the year.

Roux is a native Frenchman. Known for his bold business ventures, he got his start in 1967 when he opened the first authentic French restaurant in Dallas. Certain that his real strength was in sales, Roux looked around for an importer selling high-quality, luxury products. He discovered Carillon, a tiny New York City firm that sold chic Grand Marnier liqueur. Roux signed on as a salesman and, by 1979, had risen to become Carillon's marketing chief. Then he heard that the Swedish makers of Absolut were looking for a U.S. partner. Other American importers were cautious but Roux leapt at the opportunity.

Roux realized that the quality of the product, including its taste, were important but that he had to sell an image, not a product. So he focused on packaging and marketing. The Absolut container, he decided, should "reflect purity and cleanliness, just like the people of Sweden."

The solution: the now unmistakable Absolut bottle. To emphasize purity, the label is painted right on the glass in a silver-capped, short-necked bottle. Then Roux experienced his first crisis of faith. He paid market researchers $60,000 to assess Absolut's appeal. They told him that Absolut was a "gimmicky" name for a product from a relatively "unknown" country. They concluded that he was headed for an Absolut disaster. Roux decided to ignore them and trust his gut. It had worked before, he thought, so why not now?

Then Roux began to shop for an ad agency. He looked at ninety-eight in all, but most were too big. Roux wanted a company with less than $20 million in annual billings, "so they'd pay real attention to us." His choice was TWBA, a creative and aggressive New York firm with a short track record.

When Roux sat down with TWBA, they weren't sure where to begin. Most liquor advertising at the time was boring and pompous. Roux and the agency wanted something radical, something witty and entertaining to strike a nerve with the hip, young crowd.

"The original idea was a shot in the dark," recalls Jeff Hayes, the TWBA art director for the Absolut campaign. "We were sitting

*Michel Roux,
president of
Carillon Importers,
Ltd., distributors
of Absolut vodka*

in front of the TV set one night and we started drawing the bottle. We kept thinking of purity and perfection, and there it was: 'Absolut Perfection.' "

Instead of ignoring Absolut's supposed weaknesses, the odd-shaped bottle and the product's Swedish origins, they decided to emphasize them. The bottle would be photographed and displayed in virtually every ad. It would be accompanied by puns — "Absolut Larceny," "Absolut Attraction," "Absolut Magic" — in an array of eye-catching ads.

To Roux's credit, no idea was ignored. One of his own ideas was the "artist series," featuring a painting of the bottle by Andy Warhol. "Absolut Attraction" showed a martini glass bending toward the bottle; "Larceny" showed a pile of broken chains and no bottle at all.

With Roux, no creative stone is left unturned. He's been known to search his artists' wastebaskets to see what they threw out. He also asked the readers of *Spy* magazine to draw their own Absolut ad. Says Hayes, "The campaign became bigger than the team. Now everyone I meet has an Absolut ad."

The ad team welcomed ideas from the strangest places. "Absolut Magic," showing the bottle in an ice bucket shaped like a magician's hat, was created by the eleven-year-old daughter of Dick McEvoy, Carillon's senior vice president for sales and marketing. Another ad, "Absolut Wonderland," was dreamed up by Richard Lewis, a TWBA account director, while he was playing with the round glass "snowflake" ball on his office desk. His idea was incorporated into a full-page, holiday-season ad showing the Absolut bottle encased in a layer of plastic with instructions to shake it and watch the snowflakes fall. An ad like that costs more than $1 million, but it's "probably worth five million in free PR," says Hayes.

Cost has never been a major concern. One day, McEvoy walked into Roux's office with a bizarre idea. He wanted to spend $1 million to put a microchip in every copy of *New York* magazine. When the

244

reader turned the page, the chip would play a Christmas carol. Mc-Evoy said he had to know immediately. Roux said, "Do it," and never flinched.

"I still take risks — all the time," says Roux, who spends some of his spare time skydiving. "Very often, my own marketing department is worried. But if you think too much about others, you doubt yourself. A lot of corporations fail because they don't want to take a chance. They're afraid their heads will be shot off. But being afraid is their big mistake."

Corona Beer

A Mexican Miracle

Carlos Alvarez grew up in Mexico with a beer in his hand and a dream in his heart. The beer was almost always a Corona. His father had operated a Corona distributorship for forty years.

Young Carlos's dream was to sell Corona in the United States. He spent a lot of time talking with American fishermen who'd ventured down the Baja Peninsula or U.S. businessmen who crisscrossed the Texas-Mexico border. A lot of them loved Corona Extra, a smooth, less-filling beer with little aftertaste that came in a clear, long-necked bottle. Little did they know that it would soon become — with virtually no advertising — the number-two imported beer (after Heineken) in the United States. In mid-1990, Corona was still the number-one import in California.

In 1978, Alvarez got the opportunity he was waiting for. He was named the brewery's export director and sent north to study the territory. "I saw four hundred different beers on the market and only twelve had decent sales," says Alvarez, who in 1990 was running Gambrinus Importing Company in San Antonio, Texas. The imported beers were sold primarily at stores, not bars. Almost all looked the same: European-made, stubby green bottles with cheap paper labels. The beers usually had a heavier, more robust flavor than American beers.

Alvarez was confident that Corona would succeed. But he decided to move very slowly. He spent months talking with bartenders and waitresses about where and how Corona should be sold. Then he selected a small Austin, Texas, outlet as Corona's first U.S. distributor.

Demand for Corona began to swell. Again, Alvarez took his time. Remembering his conversations in Baja, he traveled to San Diego to analyze the market there. He hired a salesperson to spend six months pitching Corona to owners of popular restaurants and bars — never stores.

Alvarez spent months talking with bartenders and waitresses about where and how Corona should be sold.

"We wanted the beer to be sold only 'on premises,' " Alvarez recalls. Otherwise, it might wind up in the $1.99 "special discount" pile next to other imports at grocery stores.

The early going wasn't easy. Corona's San Diego salesman would mark down an order, but the distributors would deliver Miller's Löwenbrau instead. In the first month in California, only 600 cases of Corona were sold. Alvarez had no way to spread the word: he had no money for advertising.

Alvarez was under a lot of pressure, too. He only wanted the brewery to produce 3,000 to 4,000 cases for export. Instead, the brewery made what was for them the smallest feasible production run: 15,000 cases. Alvarez could have packaged Corona into six-packs and unloaded the supply at stores. But he wanted to portray Corona as a premium-priced import that could be found only at exclusive bars — often establishments frequented by college students.

"We probably lost $400 million in business by not selling to stores," Alvarez estimates. Not until 1984, three and a half years after it was introduced, was Corona sold in stores.

In the early going, though, several things paid off for Corona — some real, others intangible.

Restaurant and bar owners know that young people today are

prone to try almost any "new and different" beer. The owners also liked the fact that Corona came in long-necked nonreturnable bottles. Up until that time, nobody but Corona sold long-necks that bartenders could toss in the trash — instead of wasting time (and space) filing bottles into empty cases in the back room.

On the intangible side, young beer drinkers latched on to the product almost immediately. They liked the look of the bottle and the quality of the painted-on label. (An early import, Corona Regular, had been around for five years and had gotten nowhere.) Already prone to drink imports, they found in Corona Extra a beer perfectly suited to their tastes. In this age of across-the-board specialization, Corona became the beer for them.

"By and large, the other imports didn't taste very good, especially to the sugar babies — young adults raised on Coca-Cola and Froot Loops," says Mike Mazzoni, a Corona distributor at Chicago's Barton Beers, Ltd. "They could drink Corona because it was lighter, sweeter. And they could drink a lot more than one or two."

Robert Weinberg, a leading beer industry consultant, says most people who drink beer in bars are "putting on the dog. They don't really like the taste of beer, but they drink it to socialize. Of all the imported beers, Corona tasted most like a domestic."

Image was part of it, too. It became the in thing to drink Corona with a lime wedge shoved into either your bottle or your glass. In a way that nobody seems to understand, Corona made its way almost in cult fashion across the country by word of mouth. "Those fifty thousand U.S. college students really helped us a lot," says Alvarez.

As best as can be determined, the habit of using a lime started in a Tucson college bar. And it definitely wasn't Corona's idea. "I looked at them doing it and thought, Isn't that strange?" Alvarez recalls. "Waiters started telling people, 'That's the way the locals drink it.' "

Keeping the price high reinforced the notion that consumers were getting a high-quality product. Says Mazzoni, "Baby boomers

want to believe they're buying tradition and quality, just like BMWs."
Whatever the reason, Corona sales exploded. In 1984, sales reached
115,000 barrels. In just three years, they jumped tenfold, to 1.8 million barrels in 1987. In 1988 and 1989, Corona sales slipped back to
about 1.5 million barrels. The decline reflected several factors, including lower alcohol consumption nationwide and the cultlike emergence
of new rivals, including Pennsylvania's Rolling Rock (another long-
neck with a painted-on label) and Australia's Foster's, plus the multi-
million-dollar marketing blitzes behind Michelob Dry and Miller Gen-
uine Draft. Still, you can't deny Corona's success.

"There has never been another Corona," says Mazzoni. "The
key thing is that the market made Corona happen. Consumers discovered it. Corona was simply the real thing. And people appreciated
that."

Kodak's Ektar Film

Pictures Worth 10,000 Words

A little over a century ago, a twenty-three-year-old bookkeeper named George Eastman set out to revolutionize popular photography. Eastman hated the fact that his subjects had to sit virtually motionless for 20 to 30 seconds while he crouched behind a bulky tripod with a black cloth over his head. Eastman's idea: Speed up the film's exposure process so you could "snap" a photo and freeze motion in midair.

Eastman came up with a hand-held camera that did just that. He concocted the meaningless word "Kodak," borrowing the letter *K* from his mother's maiden name, which was Kilbourn. He told his customers to take snapshots, then mail the entire camera back to Rochester, New York, and Kodak would do the rest — develop the film and mail the camera and the photographs back to the customer.

Eastman's "faster-film" philosophy guided Eastman Kodak's approach to product development for ninety-six years. Virtually every new type of film for amateurs was designed to make exposures faster than its predecessor. Kodacolor 25 was introduced in 1942. It was followed by Kodacolor CU (32 speed) in 1956, Kodacolor X (64 speed) in 1963, Kodacolor II (100 speed) in 1978, Kodacolor 400 in 1977, and Kodacolor VR 1000 in 1982.

In late 1984, a group of eight Kodak employees (chemists, engineers, and marketing experts) sat down to debate photography's giant next step. Kodak is a very conservative company. The next step — the logical step — would have been to focus on an even faster film or a technology to improve the quality of the existing line.

That cloudy afternoon, the spirit of George Eastman was reborn. Instead of talking about technology, they began to talk about avid picture takers like themselves.

Kodak precisely identified two target markets for Ektar films.

"We began by looking at our own experiences," says Dick Lorbach, head of Kodak's consumer film division at the time. They asked: What kind of film would they love to have? How would you describe the ideal color negative film? They hammered out the answers: A film with the finest grain. The greatest sharpness. The finest color. The fastest speed. The widest latitude in its ability to produce quality photos at varying speeds and f-stops.

Of course, no film could match all those requirements. This Kodak team decided to forget about the need for speed, to ignore the need for latitude. Instead, they set out to develop film that could produce the highest-quality photographs anyone had ever seen.

"At that meeting, we decided to push quality to a totally new level — to set a new standard," says Gerhard Bopp, Kodak's director of negative-film development. They would call this breakthrough film Ektar.

At first glance, Bopp's goal might seem like a "can't miss" proposition. But photography these days revolves around point-and-shoot cameras that do everything for the picture taker. The films Bopp envisioned would require the photographer to set f-stops properly, adjust to lighting conditions, and (sometimes) keep the camera totally motionless.

Kodak's marketing department wasn't worried. With help from

251

consultants at Young & Rubicam, they precisely identified two target markets for Ektar films. The first group, dubbed "enthusiasts," are passionate photographers, primarily men between the ages of eighteen and forty-five who love their craft. This group includes professionals that shoot for *National Geographic, Life,* and other publications.

The second group, dubbed "influentials," are sophisticated amateurs who have invested thousands of hours in picture taking. Family members go to them for tips about picture taking. Influentials tend to be well educated and successful. In fact, this target group caused some Kodakers to label Ektar the yuppie film.

Marketing studies determined that the two groups make up about 20 percent of the market for 35mm film. The potential annual market for Ektar could approach $1.5 billion worldwide.

Kodak decided to develop two Ektar films, one at each end of the speed scale, to serve the needs of the enthusiasts and influentials. One, Ektar 25, would be an extremely slow film that would offer the finest grain and richest color ever. The other, Ektar 1000, would offer better color and sharpness than any other 1000-speed film.

As in the past, the development effort was assigned to teams of six to eight people. But this time, Kodak added an important new spin to the project. On previous products, researchers did their job and then handed the product over to engineering. Engineers would step in, make changes, and pass the product on to manufacturing. Nobody worked together. Nobody followed the product the entire way through. The result was often chaos, confusion, and unnecessary delays. Kodachrome film took eighteen years to make its way through Kodak's archaic development system.

Ektar 25 was shepherded through the entire development process — from basic research to manufacturing — by Kodak's Gary Einhaus; Ektar 1000, by John Becher. As a result, there were no surprises or unexpected delays. The Ektar films were brought to market on October 4, 1988, less than four years after they were conceived.

The film delivered on Bopp's promise. Ektar 25 provided photographers with the most lifelike prints they'd ever seen. "It's spectacular," said Herbert Keppler of *Popular Photography* magazine. "You can blow it up to the size of a wall and not see the grain."

Because they serve a limited market, Ektar films weren't envisioned to be huge moneymakers. Analyst Charles Ryan of Merrill Lynch said they added only about $20 million, or five cents a share, to Kodak's 1989 net income. But Ektar offered a much needed boost to Kodak's reputation. It proved that the Old Yellow Father, as Kodak is known in Rochester, still has the wherewithal to best its Japanese rivals. As camera columnist Andy Grundber noted on November 13, 1988, in the *New York Times*, "Ektar 25 is my nominee for print film of the year — and perhaps the decade."

March at a Slow and Steady Pace

eight

When the tortoise beat the hare, he had one big advantage over the rest of us. He couldn't move any faster if he wanted to. In society today, the tendency is to go as far, as fast, as you can. The downside is that you either burn out or get burned so badly that you have neither the will nor the resources to get up and try again.

The people featured in the next three chapters restrained themselves from lurching ahead too quickly. Like the tortoise, they inched along slowly, pragmatically, constantly studying others in the field. They endured setback after setback but channeled their frustration into determination to finish their unique version of a multiyear marathon.

Hyundai, the Korean carmaker, seemed to come from nowhere, but it spent more than ten years preparing to invade the U.S. marketplace. The Pro-Choice March, the largest peacetime rally in history, was the result of two decades of work by the National Organization for Women. Young Scott Isaacs lost his first two tries at the National Spelling Bee championship. He studied vocabulary words three hours a day to reach his goal.

Their achievements, though spectacular, were not the result of breathtaking insights or unusual intellect. They emanated from attention to the fundamentals — the nitty-gritty grunt work that many refuse to concentrate on. You'll see how

255

NOW assembled huge lists of people and home phone numbers as a data base to organize a march, and how Hyundai and a U.S. consultant put together a 500-page study on everything they needed to do.

By moving slowly, each of them picked up tricks of the trade. As you'll see, Isaacs learned to ask questions repeatedly during bees, to stall for time. Hyundai threw in accessories with popular brand names (Panasonic, Goodyear, Champion) to make Americans feel more comfortable. But the secret to their success was rooted in their diligence. They developed a game plan and stuck with it, every minuscule step of the way.

Scott Isaacs

The Making of a Spelling Bee Champ

Scott Isaacs won the 1989 Scripps-Howard National Spelling Bee, but give his mother, Kaye, some credit, too. And maybe even Taco Bell.

In the months leading up to the finals, spelling became an obsession for Scott, who lives in Littleton, Colorado. He studied words three hours a day, sometimes longer. When his little brother was at gymnastics practice three times a week, Scott and his mother would sit in a nearby Taco Bell restaurant, order burritos and spell for an hour and a half.

"It was a fun, close time," Kaye Isaacs says.

"I really like words," says Scott, who turned fourteen just months before his June championship. "They can be so eccentric, so strange. It amazes me every time I run into a new one."

The making of a spelling bee champ is not unlike the making of any successful person, whether in business, sports, entertainment, or other disciplines. In Scott's case, some early spelling success and encouragement from teachers and parents was combined with his own initiative and the lessons only experience can teach. Scott competed in the National Bee three straight years, learning something in each of the first two eliminations that eventually helped him win.

"This is an example of how praising students, or employees,

257

works," says Diane Peiker, one of Scott's teachers who also helped him study spelling. "Scott received enough praise along the way so that it was rewarding. We all need praise, and not just in the paycheck."

The National Spelling Bee began in 1925 as a creation of the *Louisville Courier* and *Journal* newspapers. Scripps-Howard began sponsoring the event in 1941 and it has continued every year since, except in the war years of 1943 to 1945. An estimated 9 million kids, eighth grade and younger, participated in the local spelling bees in 1989 that eventually led to the National, where a record 222 finalists, each sponsored by a newspaper, competed for the championship. In the early rounds, if a contestant misses a word, he or she is out. In the final spell-off, with just two finalists remaining, the winner must spell correctly the word his or her opponent misses and then spell correctly a new word. The spelling order of the contestants is predetermined by pulling the names of the sponsoring papers out of a hat. Spellers keep that order through the entire bee. It's usually considered an advantage, especially in the final spell-off, to be last. The order of the contest words is also predetermined and known only to the National Bee's judges and pronouncer.

Scott, who his mother says could read by the age of three, began spelling in contests in the fourth grade at the encouragement of a teacher. The first contest was at a local shopping mall. He won. "I was doing something I liked and something I was good at," Scott says. In 1987, while in the sixth grade, he won the district and regional spelling bees and advanced to the National Spelling Bee for the first time. He was eliminated in the sixth round. The word was "psittacine" (pronounced *sit-a-seen*), which means resembling or pertaining to parrots. "As soon as I heard the word, I knew I was out," Scott says. "I learned that luck is a very integral part of the bee."

The next year, as a seventh grader, Scott again advanced to the finals, which are held every year in Washington, D.C. And again he

Champion speller Scott Isaacs with William Burleigh, Scripps-Howard senior vice president/newspapers

was eliminated in the sixth round. This time the word was "telencephalon," the most anterior part of the forebrain. He put an *a* where the *o* is. "I learned not to get frustrated and to stay with every word as long as I could," Scott says. "I asked a lot of questions about the word, but I got worried that the judges were thinking I was taking too long. The one question I didn't ask was if the root was 'enceph,' which means brain. If I had asked that question, I might have spelled the ending right."

During the competition, contestants can ask the pronouncer to repeat the word, define it, and use it in a sentence. A speller may also ask for the language origin of a word, and if a particular word is listed in the dictionary as the root of the word to be spelled. Once a speller begins to spell a word, he can stop and start over, but he can't change the order of the letters from those first said.

Peiker thinks the lesson about asking questions was invaluable for Scott. "It may make the audience and judges antsy, but he learned that the longer he can ask legitimate questions they will answer, the longer he can continue thinking about the word," she says. "Scott has a talent for that. He's very poised."

Scott, who represented the *Rocky Mountain News* in Denver, says he studied spelling an average of thirty to forty-five minutes a day as a sixth grader, and an average of an hour to an hour and a half a day as a seventh grader. "He'd come in before school and give up his lunchtime just for me to pronounce words for him," Peiker says. "He spent much of the year going through the dictionary. He's not a memorizer. He's interested in the roots of words." Each year after the National Bee, Scott took a break during the summer. "I wanted to get as far away from the spelling bee as possible," he says. As an eighth grader, determined to win the national championship, he averaged three hours of study at home. He would make lists of about a hundred words a night on his computer, right from the dictionary. If he missed a word, it would go on another list, which he reviewed about once every two weeks. He studied practice words in booklets supplied by Scripps-Howard. He studied unusual engineering terms that his father, Bud, an oil engineer, spotted in reports. He even studied words in medical books sent to him by a relative.

"He kept saying, 'I know I can win it,' " says Christine Power of the *Rocky Mountain News*, who is the director of the Colorado Spelling Bee and was Scott's escort to Washington for three years. "I tried to play down the winning because there is so much luck involved."

The first bit of luck was in Scott's favor. When the newspaper sponsors were drawn to determine the spelling order in the nationals, the *Rocky Mountain News* was number 218, meaning only four spellers would be behind Scott. If and when they dropped out, he would be last. In the National Bee, more kids fall out on the fifth round than any other. In the first four rounds the words are taken from the "Words of Champions" booklet, supplied by Scripps-Howard to schools as a study tool. In the fifth round, anything in the dictionary becomes fair game. The number of spellers typically drops from about three quarters of the original contestants to one quarter.

Scott admits he was feeling a little nervous during the finals. But he says he likes being on stage and he gets caught up in the situation, almost as if he were an observer rather than a participant. "I love to see what turns up in the spelling bee, the chance that goes with it," he says. "Will it be an easy word, or will it be hard?"

The endless hours of preparation paid off in the early rounds of the finals. Four or five of the dictionary words Scott drew were ones he had already studied. When it came down to the final two contestants, he was spelling last against Ojas Tejani, a sixth grader from Chattanooga, Tennessee. "There's a lot of pressure on the first person," Scott says. "If he spells right, he just survives. If he's wrong, he may wind up in second place."

In the final showdown, both spelled their first words correctly. Scott's was "ideaphoria," which means the capacity for creative imagination. "I knew when I got it I would have to think as much as I could about it," Scott says. "Spellers study many more words that begin with 'ideo.' I took me about five minutes to figure that difference out."

In the next round, both spellers failed on "pasigraphy," then Ojas also missed "senescing." Scott spelled it correctly and then had to spell one more word to win — "spoliator," meaning one who robs, plunders, or despoils. "I didn't ask too many questions because as soon as I got that word I pretty much knew the bee was in the bag," Scott says. "I stalled for about a minute and twice asked for the derivation of the word. I had studied 'spoliation,' it was just the ending I wasn't sure of. *E-r* didn't sound as well placed as *o-r*."

With the championship Scott, who is studying foreign languages in school and working to be an Eagle Scout, won $1,500 and some celebrity. He visited Vice President Dan Quayle, appeared on the "Tonight" show with Jay Leno, "Good Morning America," and "Inside Edition." "Before, in school, I was pretty much considered a recluse," Scott says. "But afterwards at eighth-grade graduation, kids asked me for my autograph. I'm not half as much a recluse as I used to be."

Grit, Guts, and Genius

The Pro-Choice March

Two If by Sea . . . 400,000 If by Land

They came to Washington, D.C., from all fifty states. Thirty flew in from Alaska, and Hawaii sent twenty-five. Five busloads drove all night from Minneosta, six from Florida. Huge throngs came from the Northeast. New York sent an estimated sixty thousand, and Massachusetts, forty thousand.

In the end, more than four hundred thousand trekked to Washington at their own expense to participate in the April 9, 1989, Pro-Choice March, the largest and most effective political march in the last twenty years. Most had never marched before. But the pro-choice movement had lit a fire that burned in everyone from grandmothers to college-age boys.

"It was the most exciting experience I've ever had," seventy-three-year-old Frances Rachel of East Orange, New Jersey, said afterward. She climbed on a bus, in pouring-down rain, to make the five-hour drive to the capital.

The march itself was an awesome display of unity. The participants — 40 percent of them men and nearly half from college campuses — joined hands and marched peacefully, beating drums and waving banners, from the Washington Monument up to the Capitol. Thousands carried coat hangers as a symbol of their fears that abortion would once again be ruled illegal by the U.S. Supreme Court.

The march didn't immediately reverse any legislation, but it had an immeasurable impact on the way many Americans think. "This was a climate-changing event," says Eleanor Smeal, president of the Fund for the Feminist Majority. "Before this, the pro-lifers would chip away at our confidence, saying that people really don't care. The march told everyone, 'You can't ignore us.' It made the politicians think, 'My god, what are we unleashing now?' "

On October 12, 1989, the U.S. House of Representatives voted 216–206 to permit federally funded abortions for victims of rape or incest. The House had narrowly reversed its prior position, having denied such funding for eight straight years. Analyzing the vote, Representative Barbara Boxer, a California Democrat, cited a palpable shift in the nation's attitude. Boxer told the *Washington Post*, "I think members are telling me the sentiment is changing in their districts."

In Florida that same day, state legislative committees killed Governor Bob Martinez's proposals to restrict and regulate abortions. Florida House Speaker Tom Gustafson attributed the decision to women who had suddenly become politically active. Activists on both sides of the abortion issue agree that the march was the event that stirred many into action.

Americans, by their nature, are a conservative, some say apathetic, lot. Not until moved to the point of crisis, or to the brink of losing loved ones in a war like Vietnam, do many Americans get politically involved. So what made all those people drop what they were doing and trek to Washington?

To some extent, it was a result of a political decision made by President George Bush in early 1989. Two days after he took office, the president began to urge that the landmark *Roe vs. Wade* decision be reversed by the Supreme Court. That 1973 decision obliged all fifty states to legalize abortion. To challenge *Roe*, the Justice Department asked the Supreme Court to hear arguments in a Missouri case, *William L. Webster vs. Reproductive Health Services*. The Webster case

264

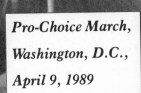

*Pro-Choice March,
Washington, D.C.,
April 9, 1989*

revolved around a state law that forbids abortions by doctors or hospitals that receive state funds.

The moment the Supreme Court agreed to hear *Webster*, a groundswell of support for the April 9 march turned into an instant avalanche. The National Organization for Women, which organized the event, was flooded with calls from volunteers. "We'd been trying to warn everyone about this case, but it wasn't real to them," says Sheri O'Dell, NOW's march coordinator. "They'd heard Reagan talk, but it was all just rhetoric. But then Bush did something very tangible. Bingo! That shook everyone out of their complacency. I've never seen anything like it."

O'Dell's theory is that Americans will put up with a lot, but they'll explode into action the moment the government tries to take something away from people. In this case, the right to abortion was something that more than four hundred thousand Americans weren't about to lose. But Bush's crusade and the Supreme Court's decision to hear *Webster* weren't the only reasons that plans for the April 9 march took off. Smeal and her NOW colleagues had been meticulously preparing for this event, or one like it, for over a decade.

In the late 1970s, Smeal began to study the logistics behind various marches and parades. She interviewed everyone she could, from the chief of Macy's holiday parades to those who organized antiwar marches in the sixties.

No one knew any magic formula. But she learned a few tips that helped NOW organize its pro-choice crusade: Get college students involved in the movement. Build your campaign from the grass roots. Make lists of everyone you can count on to organize local groups and spread the word. Bring in every organization you can to help you.

266

With that approach in mind, in the summer of 1985 Smeal began to organize NOW's first major march. That pro-choice march, held in April 1986, drew 126,000. It was not a spectacular success, but it laid the groundwork and helped to organize the lists for the march that lay three years down the road.

"We got to the people who did the old ERA [Equal Rights Amendment] marches," says Smeal. "At the last minute, Planned Parenthood and others pulled their march endorsements. But they got burned for doing that. In fact, they were so burned in '86 that they came in '89."

The 1986 march played a crucial role on another frontier: the college campus. After nearly two apathetic decades, women on campus began to get actively involved in the feminist movement.

"I had noticed the graying of the movement," says Susan Carroll, a political scientist at Rutgers University's Center for the American Woman in Politics. "Young women had begun to take so much for granted. But the pro-choice marches made them realize that the clock can be turned back. Abortion is an issue that deeply touches many people's lives."

NOW called for the 1989 march in the summer of 1988. Originally, it was conceived not as a pro-choice march, but a march for the ERA. The march's focus would ultimately change when Bush and the Supreme Court started to reexamine abortion rights.

Logistical planning began in mid-January 1989. O'Dell hired twelve people to organize the march, largely by phone, from an office in Washington. They spent about $500,000. Two people were hired to stay in constant contact with groups on four hundred college campuses. Their main focus was to help college organizations publicize the march by printing and distributing leaflets, writing newspaper articles, and scheduling radio interviews.

One person's full-time job was to contact about two thousand individuals and encourage them to convince at least one small club — such as a bridge club, a women's club, a church group — to participate. Another staffer worked with five hundred organizations such as labor unions, civil rights groups, and Planned Parenthood.

267

Two people worked primarily in the D.C. area. O'Dell figured that the majority of marchers would come from the metropolitan area and surrounding cities. The remaining staffers worked with NOW's seven hundred chapters nationwide to publicize the effort through leaflets, phone banks, posters, and newsletters.

Paid advertising was surprisingly limited. NOW hired consultants to create a series of radio ads that were supposed to air in five cities within driving distance: Washington, New York, Philadelphia, Boston, and Baltimore. But the ads were so controversial that several stations yanked them off the air.

One ad opened with sirens screaming and a news report about antiabortionists "blowing up another clinic." Then the voice of Vice President Dan Quayle told a young woman that she shouldn't be able to have an abortion even if she's a rape victim. When the radio stations pulled the ads, Smeal and her colleagues took the story to the print media. "That drew a lot of attention to us," Smeal says. "That was the turning point of the prepublicity."

Obviously, some people that were contacted, such as Frances Rachel, would have marched anytime, anyplace. When she was young, Rachel had an illegal abortion. She went to an alcoholic doctor in a dirty, back-alley office. When she hemorrhaged afterward, she called her regular doctor, but he refused to come because he didn't want to get involved.

Each year, about 1.6 million abortions are performed in the United States — comprising roughly 30 percent of all pregnancies, excluding miscarriages and stillbirths. One fifth of American women above the age of fifteen have had an abortion.

Before the 1989 march, the abortion rights movement had failed to tap into young women or men. What was most remarkable about O'Dell's premarch crusade was that it "mobilized a whole new generation," says Carroll. "I was amazed at how many young people came."

The pro-choice movement has suffered several setbacks. In the

Webster case, the Supreme Court ruled that states can prohibit public hospitals from performing abortions. (At the Truman Medical Center in Kansas City, the State of Missouri has done just that.)

At the national level, President Bush has been making good on his promise to veto any legislation that would provide federal funds for abortions, regardless of the situation. And a Supreme Court refashioned by President Ronald Reagan could tackle the *Roe vs. Wade* decision at any time. Smeal says, "One more Supreme Court justice and they'll reverse *Roe*."

But the Court won't do that without a fight. Thanks to the April 9 march, membership in NOW has soared from 165,000 to more than 205,000. A loud and clear message was delivered to Washington: If you try to reverse *Roe vs. Wade*, a wave of pro-choice sentiment will come crashing down upon you.

"Now people realize," says Smeal at her Washington office, "that if they reversed *Roe*, this city would just close down."

March at a Slow and Steady Pace

Hyundai

The Little Car That Could

Hyundai. The name doesn't really rhyme with "Sunday," but clever advertising said it did. It's not really a Japanese car, but many people were made to think it was. Even the exterior design of the subcompact was altered to make it appear longer and roomier than it actually is.

Those ingredients were part of a magical formula that enabled this plain-looking Korean import with the funny name to make automotive history. In 1986, Hyundai sold more than 168,000 of the Excel model in the United States, making it the number-one first-year import in U.S. history. The previous number one, the 1958 Renault from France, sold only 48,000. Even the fastest-growing Japanese automakers can't compare with Hyundai's feat: it took Mazda five years and Subaru four years to sell 100,000 cars. For three years, Hyundai kept right on rolling. In 1987 and 1988, Hyundai (actually pronounced *High-unn-day*) sold 253,000 and 264,000 Excels, respectively. In 1989, the company's sales nosedived, part of a slump that struck the entire industry, but particularly makers of subcompact cars. Yugo, a rival of Hyundai that sold cars for under $4,000, filed for protection from creditors under federal bankruptcy laws.

Whether Hyundai can stay in the hunt remains to be seen. But nobody can take away what the company has accomplished.

Hyundai set the record because a group of South Koreans, many of whom had never been to the United States before, learned to understand American car-buying needs and habits better than most Americans do. They knew exactly who they were targeting: highly educated, usually married women aged twenty-five to thirty, with up to $30,000 in annual income, who prefer the color red. The Koreans learned how to tantalize, and then sign up, the slickest brigade of car dealers in the United States. Then, with help from some top-notch U.S. marketing and advertising experts, they attacked the United States like it had never been attacked before.

"I've been in this business twenty years and worked for both Ford and Chevrolet, but I've never seen anything like this," says Don Reilly, a Hyundai dealer in Fairfax, Virginia.

The Hyundai seemed to come from nowhere. But the South Koreans actually had a ten-year master plan. Long before setting foot in the United States, they took painful steps to establish Hyundai — a huge steel and shipbuilding conglomerate — as a legitimate contender in cars. Ford provided some early technical help. But the Hyundai-Ford partnership fell apart. South Korea's Daewoo teamed with General Motors; Kia Motors with Ford. Hyundai chose to go it alone.

"Even back then, we knew what we wanted," recalls Son Wong Chon, the newly appointed president of Hyundai Motor Company. Speaking in his plush office in downtown Seoul, Chon recalled: "The oil crisis had just begun and we wanted a small, good-looking, European-style car. Nobody thought we would ever make it. But we thought, In seven to ten years, we will attack the United States with such a car."

In the early 1970s, Hyundai executives toured the world looking for help in designing a small, economical car. They hired Giorgetto Giugiaro of Italy's ItalDesign, the designer of the Fiat and Alfa Romeo, to design the car's body. Then they arranged to get the engine and transmission from Japan's Mitsubishi Corporation.

In 1976, Hyundai exported its first crudely built car, a predecessor of the Excel called the Pony, to tiny Ecuador. It was slow going. Over the next two years, the fledgling automaker sold just six thousand vehicles. Says Chon, "We didn't make a profit for several years."

Hyundai spent the late 1970s and early 1980s trying to crack the European market, primarily by selling through independent importers. The effort failed miserably. A joint venture in Holland collapsed. Then a young Hyundai executive, H. S. Park, suggested what turned out to be a brilliant strategy: set up a wholly owned subsidiary and attack Canada.

"Park pushed this idea through, and he went to Canada with a very young team," says John Schnapp of the Temple, Barker and Sloan management consulting firm in Lexington, Massachusetts. "They traveled around, made a plan, and essentially improvised it. They were lucky, though. The Canadian market was small enough to forgive their mistakes."

The first Hyundai Ponys rolled into Canada in early 1984 and, under Park's command, sales began to take off. Unlike their U.S. neighbors to the south, Canadians are more adventuresome and price-conscious when it comes to car buying. (As Schnapp points out, even the Russians exported a fair number of cars to Canada at one time.) And Canada levied no import duties on Korean-made cars. Over the next two years, the Pony became a knockout success. By late 1985, it was the number-one import in Canada, with 10 percent of total market share. U.S. dealers started hearing about Hyundai's Canadian coup. "We began to hear about it through the 'Toyota Twenty' [an informal group of North American dealers that meets regularly]," Reilly recalled. "These two Canadian dealers kept raving about how absolutely great this Korean franchise was."

So great, in fact, that Reilly hastily arranged to borrow a car for his showroom from a Canadian dealership. He drove nonstop from Virginia to Niagara Falls. The Canadian dealer drove the Pony across the border and Reilly drove it back to Virginia immediately.

The Hyundai Excel

"I got it back here on a Saturday afternoon, and we had people lined up outside the showroom waiting to see it. We instantly took fifty deposits."

As Hyundai's Canadian business erupted, Park turned his attention southward. He and two young staff members, John Kim and Hank Lee, began traveling down to the States.

As they started to study the U.S. market, the South Koreans walked into a popular San Francisco dealership run by Martin Zweig. They began to question him about the U.S. marketplace: "How do we set up dealerships? What kind of car would Americans buy?" Zweig knew they needed some sophisticated marketing help and suggested Temple, Barker and Sloan. He knew Schnapp had introduced Mitsubishi to the American market just a few years earlier. Park visited Schnapp, and Schnapp showed him what he had done for Mitsubishi. He figured out what a similar study would cost Hyundai. The estimate: $200,000 for expenses, fees, and services.

"I knew the numbers would be a tremendous shock, and I could see in Park's eyes that my expectation was true," Schnapp says. "But he's a brave tiger. He said, 'I'll have an answer for you in two or three days,' and he pushed it through."

Schnapp and his team spent three months amassing a 500-page study that told the Koreans everything they needed to know about the U.S. import car business: number of players, import history, product lines, competitors' strengths and weaknesses, future demand, and so on. Said Schnapp, "It was pretty much a cavalry charge."

Back in Seoul, Chon was busy testing a new model named Excel. The Koreans knew the rear-wheel-drive Pony, although inexpensive, would never cut it in the United States. They weren't worried about GM or Ford, but they were terrified of Honda, Toyota, and the other Japanese.

Excel was altogether different from Pony. It was front-wheel

274

drive. It was better built, sporty looking, and more powerful. Hyundai had closely watched an emerging American preference for European styling. So the Excel's design, says Chon, "was driven by European tastes."

The engine's specs came from Mitsubishi, but it was manufactured by Hyundai. This time, 98 percent of the parts came from Korean sources. To boost quality, Hyundai sent teams to study Japanese quality control methods. Says Chon, "We studied at Mitsubishi, electronics companies, even some textile companies."

Hyundai's success, though, had relatively little to do with the car's design or the way it was built. In fact, compared to today's highly automated Toyota and Nissan plants, the Excel factory in the city of Ulsan, South Korea, is primitive. It is dirty, poorly organized, and inadequately ventilated. But the advance publicity, marketing, and advertising for this inexpensive new subcompact would overcome the carmaker's drawbacks.

With Schnapp's help, the Koreans ran a series of carefully orchestrated focus groups with American car buyers and car dealers. First they brought in small groups of consumers who had recently purchased a low-priced Japanese car. Schnapp's team usually ran two sessions per evening, each session lasting about two hours. While the Koreans hid behind a one-way mirror, the team asked the consumers why they bought the car they did. What else did you consider? Was price your biggest concern? They showed them charts with the dimensions and features of the Excel compared to the cars they had just bought. Then they brought out enlarged photographs of the Excel.

"We played a little trick on them," says Schnapp. "The photos had a driver who was obviously Oriental. We knew most Americans can't tell a Korean from a Japanese. So we really let them believe it was a Japanese car. Ultimately, that would be advantageous, since people wouldn't think it was from some suspect location."

To the surprise of the Koreans, the car buyers' reaction to their car was, "Yeah, so what?" The Hyundai people were "just shattered by this, really upset, because they'd worked so hard," Schnapp says. "Their assumption was that Americans would just stand up and cheer."

Later in the evening, over some beers, Schnapp carefully explained that the car buyers' ho-hum reaction was nothing to be concerned about. "What that means is they accept it. They consider it a viable alternative to the cars they bought," he told them. "And you really can't expect much more than that."

Hyundai learned a lot from these focus groups. For example, people repeatedly said that the Excel looked small. Schnapp suggested that they add a dark "rub strip" the length of the car and add two inches to the front and rear bumpers to make the Excel look longer than it really is.

In some focus groups, Schnapp's team zeroed in on the car's nationality. They asked, What if this car came from Poland? Or Norway? Or Korea? In every group the reaction was, "Korea doesn't make cars. And if it is Korean, I'm uneasy because I don't want to be a guinea pig." Ultimately, though, one person in each group would say they'd heard about Koreans being very hard workers, like the Japanese. Then the group would pick up on that, Schnapp says. "That told us something very important: that the car was acceptable and that Korea could be acceptable, too."

To prepare for the advertising rollout, they asked, Would you feel more comfortable if the carmaker was a big, diversified company? The Americans said no. What if it was a construction firm that builds dams? No good. Sophisticated railroad equipment? So-so. The one description that boosted everyone's confidence was a company involved in high technology. So every effort would be made to trumpet Hyundai's high-tech skills, including sales of the IBM-compatible Hyundai personal computer.

During the dealer interviews, which also lasted two hours each,

Schnapp's team examined the marketing strategy. They showed the dealers photos of Excel and asked them to price the car. They asked how the cars should be equipped. And they talked about the engine. Hyundai's original plan was to equip Excel with a relatively weak, 1.3-liter engine. Schnapp knew that wouldn't work: U.S. highways can be hilly, and a lot of the cars would be automatics, often sold with air conditioning. He warned Hyundai that if the cars weren't test-driven on American roads, the carmaker was running a tremendous risk.

After lengthy deliberating, Hyundai's Park agreed to alter the exterior design and to test the cars in the United States. Eventually, they were sold with more powerful 1.5-liter engines.

To really make the U.S. effort fly, though, the Koreans knew they needed a top-notch U.S. manager to set up a dealership network.

They hired a Newport, California, headhunter named David Wess, of Mitchell, Larsen and Zilliacus. Wess showed them twelve potential candidates. He knew there was a management shakeup going on at Toyota's U.S. arm. So he took a chance and called Max Jamiesson, one of the industry's best-known executives. Jamiesson agreed to meet Wess for breakfast, out of curiosity more than anything else. The meeting lasted nearly six hours. The next day, Jamiesson had dinner with four Hyundai executives (Chon, Park, Roy Kim, and John Kim). When Jamiesson left, the Koreans voted and Jamiesson was in. The next afternoon, they invited him to visit Korea. Jamiesson knew why: he had to be approved by Hyundai's upper management back in Seoul. So he spent Christmas, 1984, in Seoul and on January 1, 1985, became Hyundai's first American employee.

Hiring Jamiesson turned out to be one of Hyundai's smartest moves. Because of Toyota's shakeup, executives were leaving in droves. "I didn't have to recruit anybody," Jamiesson recalls. "They called me." He quickly brought on board thirty of Toyota USA's top

277

employees, including most of its best marketing strategists. With their help, Hyundai came up with a unique strategy to attack the continental United States in a totally new way. In the past, carmakers had taken on the entire country at once. Hyundai had neither the money nor the cars to do that. Mitsubishi had followed what Schnapp calls a "Fort Apache strategy," in which the carmaker goes after only the major cities. That, too, would be expensive, and Hyundai would have a tough time setting up dealerships in so many cities at once. "The impact on the market would be too dispersed and diluted," Schnapp said. "The advertising would be inefficient, too."

So the Hyundai leaders came up with what Park nicknamed the "smile strategy." Basically, he took a pencil and drew a smile on a map of the United States: down the East Coast through New York and Washington, curving west across the South and up along the West Coast, through California, to Oregon. This way, Hyundai could hit what Chon called the "hot places": begin with the heavily populated West and East coasts, plus the Sun Belt, and then squeeze to the center of the continent.

"No one had ever done this before, though others have copied it since," says Schnapp. "It worked like a charm, an unblemished success."

Jamiesson's team had relatively little to do with the car itself. He did, however, warn Hyundai about things that American buyers really fret about, especially the car's appearance. Jamiesson told Hyundai the Excel's upholstery looked "like a dirty sweatshirt" and the interior colors didn't match. So Hyundai went outside Korea and bought higher-quality fabrics and trim. Jamiesson said the car should come equipped with a Panasonic radio, Goodyear tires, and Champion spark plugs. "That way, we could introduce a car with names Americans are comfortable with," Jamiesson says.

The feedback also convinced the Koreans to stock dealerships with more red cars than any other color — new American car buyers, especially women, prefer red. Says John Petersen, Jr., of Cormier Hyundai in Los Angeles, "Less than 20 percent of Hyundai buyers have ever bought a new car before. So what's the color that's really going to catch your eye? Some young kid doesn't want his first car to be doeskin tan."

Jamiesson's most important role was selecting dealers. Because the word had spread from Canada, dealers were champing at the bit to sell Excels. "I never saw the car, never even saw a picture of it," says John Petersen, "but I couldn't wait to get my hands on one."

When Hyundai announced it was looking for dealers, nearly four thousand applied. Among dealers like Don Reilly in Virginia, there was a growing sense that these Koreans, despite their inexperience, might repeat what Japan had done a decade before.

As Don Hankey, a Los Angeles Ford dealer, told the *Wall Street Journal* at the time, "I missed out on the gold mine when the Japanese first came here . . . I'm not going to miss again."

One reason for this determination was Hyundai's success in Canada. Another was the press. Stories about the Hyundai had begun to pop up in trade magazines, such as *Automotive News*, as early as 1982. "We couldn't have bought better publicity for hundreds of millions of dollars," Jamiesson says.

The Japanese were moving upscale, to higher-price ($7,000 to $10,000) and, of course, higher-profit subcompacts. The cheapest cars made in the United States — the Chevy Chevette, Dodge Omni, and Plymouth Horizon, sold for about $1,000 more. That left a huge void at the low end of the market. U.S. dealers were desperate for a reliable, cheap car that would fill this gaping hole. (In early tests, *Road and Track* magazine rated the Excel considerably better than the Yugo, about equal to the Ford Escort, somewhat below the Plymouth Horizon, and substantially below most Japanese models.) Says Petersen, "We needed a Volkswagen for the 1980s. We heard that the Excel was like the Beetle coming out all over again."

This left Hyundai in the enviable position of being able to hand-

279

pick dealers and coerce them to do exactly what Hyundai wanted them to do. "We looked for the best dealer in every single town," Jamiesson says. "It didn't matter if they were a Ford dealer, a GM dealer, Honda, or anything else. Then we'd ask that dealer to set Hyundai up in the location we wanted and to spend three times what they'd normally spend to open a dealership. In most cases, they agreed."

Dealers were required to build facilities with at least two acres of land, 1,200 square feet of floor space and twelve service bays. Not only did they agree, but Hyundai's 161 dealers committed an average of $1.9 million each — up to $4 million in some cases — to set up a sales facility exclusively for Hyundai. These dealerships occupied prime properties, often near major highways. Says John Petersen, "Of the seventeen dealers in California, fifteen were on a freeway. That's how you really get exposure."

In fact, the presence of specially designed Hyundai signs towering above major roads made it appear that tiny Hyundai was everywhere. Says Jamiesson, "People perceived that we had as many dealers as any other importer, when actually we had only 10 percent of theirs."

Following a strategy used by Honda, the dealerships were spaced at least ten miles apart. The slogan was "Fewer is better," Jamiesson says. "We wanted to make each dealer as profitable as possible. So we went with dealers large enough to get twice the sales volume with half as many dealers." (In 1986, Hyundai dealers averaged 677 sales a month, well ahead of the previous leader, Honda, which averaged 443 per month.)

The dealers Hyundai picked were well known and trusted in their local areas. Most of them had four or five locations where they sold cars. But their Hyundai sales took off faster than anyone could believe. Los Angeles Ford dealer Don Hankey accepted two hundred orders from customers who bought the car sight unseen.

"We had as many as several hundred orders just waiting for

shipments to arrive," says Reilly. "And that was with only one car on the showroom floor." In 1986, his dealership sold 1,673 Excels; in 1987, 2,039 Excels.

Helping to draw customers in was a masterly advertising campaign by Backer Spielvogel Bates, Inc., a New York–based firm that is the third largest ad agency in the world.

Hyundai knew that many of the Americans they wanted to sell cars to would be buying their first new car. But it didn't want to tout Excel on price alone. The cheap, shoddy-quality image killed cars like Yugo. So Backer Spielvogel Bates, which had never handled a car campaign, looked for a way to pitch Excel's quality and value. They came up with two themes: "Built like a Hyundai" and "Cars That Make Sense." The former would focus on Hyundai's experience making trains, ships, and other products. That would introduce Americans to the company. (William M. Backer, the agency's president, wrestled with the name, which he thought sounded too much like a karate chop. So he suggested using the pronunciation *Hun-day* in the ads.)

"We spent a lot of time debating how much, or how little, we should talk about Korea," says Backer. "People's image of Korea came more from "M*A*S*H" than anything else. We decided to tell them about the company, not the country."

That had another benefit as well. Since the country wasn't mentioned, many people were led to believe — and still do believe — that Hyundai is really a Japanese car. "I think a lot of people still think it's a Japanese product," admits John Petersen of Cormier, Hyundai's first U.S. dealership.

In ads for the car itself, Backer Spielvogel Bates focused on giving buyers value for their hard-earned money. Says Backer, "We worked very hard not to make the person buying a Hyundai feel poor, even though we know that's a major reason why they're buying."

Research showed that 70 percent of Hyundais would be bought

281

by those who couldn't afford anything else but a used car. Backer divided the buyers into three groups: (1) young people buying their first car; (2) people who could afford a bigger car but wanted to spend money on something else; and (3) people tired of big cars who wanted basic, reliable transportation.

All the early ads were targeted at group 2. They showed people who bought Hyundais and saved enough money to buy designer clothes, pay for a college education, even a backyard pool.

"We knew the last thing this car should do is shout," says Backer. "It should show common sense and a little twinkle, a little smile, a theme that said happy, cheerful, little chirpy motoring, and put it all together with quality."

One ad showed a Hyundai driver pulling up to a red light and scowling at the Mercedes driver next to him. The unspoken message, Backer says, was, "Boy, were you stupid to pay $50,000 for that hunk of junk. I can use my money to do something else." Another showed a husband taking his pregnant wife to the hospital. The voice-over said, "Hyundai, the new kid on the block, will help you afford the new kid on the block."

Those ads, Backer says, "didn't say Hyundai cars were better than these other cars. They said our drivers were better than the other drivers."

Oddly enough, he says the introductory campaign — estimated to cost $25 million, 80 percent of it spent on television ads — was "really underfunded." The dealers themselves picked up some of the slack. Petersen targeted his local Los Angeles campaign at minorities and ethnic groups. He would pick out a handful of zip codes, draw a ten-mile circle, and then attack the area with a print campaign. Reilly got a quick boost from an estimated one hundred thousand South Koreans living in the Washington-Baltimore area.

Perhaps the best selling point, though, was individuals like Backer who understood how to tap into a uniquely American attitude.

"I bought my wife an Excel and we kept it in a very fancy garage, just off Lexington near Central Park," he says. "Cadillacs and Mercedeses would pull out and then out of the elevator comes this little Hyundai. It was kind of fun just to get in and feel we weren't worried about image like those repulsive, overweight people in furs getting into the other cars. There's this American desire for personality in products. That's where we did our best job. We gave the car a personality all its own."

Acknowledgments

We'd like to thank *USA Today*, the *Dallas Morning News*, and our editor, Henry Ferris, for having the grit, guts, and genius to help us complete this book.